A Representative Bibliography

of American Labor History

A Representative Bibliography of

AMERICAN
LABOR HISTORY

MAURICE F. NEUFELD

Professor of Industrial and Labor Relations

CORNELL UNIVERSITY

Ithaca, New York, 1964

PUBLISHED BY

THE NEW YORK STATE SCHOOL OF
INDUSTRIAL AND LABOR RELATIONS

A Contract College of the State University
at Cornell University

Cloth: $1.50
Paper: $1.00

PRINTED IN THE UNITED STATES OF AMERICA BY
W. F. HUMPHREY PRESS INC., GENEVA, NEW YORK

Preface

THIS representative bibliography of American labor history has been arranged according to classifications which have proved useful to different kinds of individuals and groups: undergraduate and graduate students, university colleagues, librarians, labor unions, management officials, governmental agencies, extension classes, and public school teachers. These classifications are fully listed in the Contents.

Within each classification, items are arranged alphabetically by author whenever the author is indicated. Items without given authors are listed under their title when they appear in periodicals. In all other instances, they appear under the name of the organization, institution, or agency of origin, except that publications of the Congress and federal agencies generally appear under "U.S.," while publications of state and local units and agencies are found under the name of the state or political subdivision concerned. As an added convenience, an over-all index is provided at the end of this bibliography covering the authors, agencies, organizations, and institutions cited under each classification.

This bibliography is not comprehensive and excludes many titles which would merit attention in a bibliography aimed at full coverage of American labor history. In recompense, the items selected represent a wide variety of *types* of useful materials: books ranging in nature from popular to technical, scholarly monographs, theses, novels, plays, biographies, autobiographies, state and federal legislative investigations, governmental reports, union documents, management publications, and articles from both learned journals and magazines of mass circulation. Thus, by calling attention to examples of these diverse types of publications, the bibliography offers clues to additional possible sources of information and enlightenment.

Within its limitations, this bibliography also attempts to present different *points of view,* ranging from those representative of extreme left-wing attitudes to those which are clearly opposed to labor unions and to the entire process of collective bargaining.

Although the files upon which this bibliography is based contain citations about most of the international unions in this country, references have been included for only those international unions which operate in important sectors of the American economy or which represent the more significant types of American unionism.

A few notations of a housekeeping nature should be made at this point. When legislative committees are cited, the date in parenthesis after the name of the committee indicates the year of appointment. Titles have sometimes been repeated when such items cover more than one period or more than one union or industry. In the classification, Periods of Development, references dealing with a period earlier than that under survey are sometimes listed with those devoted to a subsequent era in order that all references to a given subject, which achieved importance during the later period under consideration, might be listed in one place. Finally, it should be noted that some items are not readily available in most libraries, but have been listed because of their historical importance.

The cultivation of bibliographical files is a gentle, patient, exacting, and thankless art. Every effort has been made to record all items with accuracy. Nonetheless, given the human condition, errors have undoubtedly survived. The identification of such errors would be most welcome.

I am much indebted to Mrs. Joyce Wright, my secretary, for her invaluable assistance. She not only prepared the manuscript with exemplary attention to detail, but also patiently checked and rechecked bibliographical items in all available sources of reference to improve their accuracy.

M.F.N.

Ithaca, New York
May 1964

Contents

A Representative Bibliography

of American Labor History

Bibliographies, Guides, and Archival Sources

BARNETT, GEORGE E. *A Trial Bibliography of American Trade-Union Publications.* Baltimore: The Johns Hopkins Press, 1907.

BLACK, J. WILLIAM. "References on the History of Labor and Some Contemporary Labor Problems." *Oberlin College Library Bulletin,* Vol. 1, No. 2, 1893.

BLUM, ALBERT A. "Local Union Archives in Michigan." *Labor History,* Vol. 3, No. 3, Fall 1962, pp. 335–340.

————. "Research in Progress in American Labor History." *Labor History,* Vol. 3, No. 2, Spring 1962, pp. 218–225.

BRICKETT, MARGARETT F. "Labor History Resources in the U.S. Department of Labor Library." *Labor History,* Vol. 2, No. 2, Spring 1961, pp. 236–240.

BROWNE, HENRY J. "Raiding Labor Records." *American Archivist,* Vol. XVII, July 1954, pp. 262–264.

COMMITTEE OF UNIVERSITY INDUSTRIAL RELATIONS LIBRARIANS. *Exchange Bibliographies.* (Approximately 1300 bibliographies on subjects in the field of industrial and labor relations are available (1962) in most University Industrial Relations Libraries. A specific subject approach to these bibliographies is provided. Irregular publication, mimeo.).

CONOVER, HELEN F., comp. *A Bibliography of Bibliographies of Trade Unions.* Washington: Library of Congress, 1937. (Mimeo.).

DI ROMA, EDWARD. "Notes on Resources for Research in Labor History in the Reference Department of the New York Public Library." *Labor History,* Vol. 4, No. 1, Winter 1963, pp. 93–99.

ECKERT, LEONE W., comp. *Guide to the Records [of the] Labor Management Documentation Center.* Ithaca: Library, New York State School of Industrial and Labor Relations, Cornell University, 1960.

————. *A Preliminary Bibliography of American Labor Leader Biographies.* Ithaca: Library, New York State School of Industrial and Labor Relations, Cornell University, 1961.

Employment Relations Abstracts, 1950– . Detroit: Information Service, 1950– . (A loose-leaf service which includes about 30 labor periodicals and bridges, in limited fashion, *Trade Union Publications* by Reynolds and Killingsworth and the *Index to Labor Union Periodicals* published at the University of Michigan).

GATES, FRANCIS. "Labor Resources in the University of California (Berkeley) Libraries." *Labor History,* Vol. 1, No. 2, Spring 1960, pp. 196–205.

————. *Reference Guides for Labor Research.* Berkeley: Labor Collection, Social Sciences Reference Service, General Library, University of California, 1957.

HARVEY, O. L. "Inventory of Department of Labor Archives." *Labor History,* Vol. 4, No. 2, Spring 1963, pp. 196–198.

Index to Labor Union Periodicals: A Subject Index to Materials from a Selected List of Newspapers and Journals Published by Major Labor Unions January–June 1960– . Ann Arbor: Bureau of Industrial Relations, University of Michigan, 1960– . (Monthly and cumulates annually).

Industrial Relations Theses and Dissertations Accepted at Universities, 1949–1950– . Berkeley: Institute of Industrial Relations, University of California, 1951– . (Annual).

LEWINSON, PAUL. "The Archives of Labor." *American Archivist,* Vol. XVII, January 1954, pp. 19–24.

————. "State Labor Agencies: Where Are Their Records?" *American Archivist,* Vol. XIX, January 1956, pp. 45–50.

————, and MORRIS RIEGER. "Labor Union Records in the United States." *The American Archivist,* Vol. 25, No. 1, January 1962, pp. 39–57.

McCOY, RALPH E., and DONALD GSELL. *History of Labor and Unionism in the United States: A Selected Bibliography.* Bibliographic Contributions No. 2. Champaign: Institute of Labor and Industrial Relations, University of Illinois, 1953.

————, and NED ROSEN, comps. *Doctoral Dissertations in Labor and Industrial Relations, 1933–1953.* Bibliographic Contributions No. 5. Champaign: Institute of Labor and Industrial Relations, University of Illinois, 1955.

NAAS, BERNARD G., and CARMELITA SAKR, comps. *American Labor Union Periodicals: A Guide to Their Location.* Ithaca: New York State School of Industrial and Labor Relations, Cornell University, 1956.

O'DONNELL, L. A., comp. *American Unionism and the Catholic Church, with Special Emphasis on the Association of Catholic Trade Unionists: Bibliography.* San Francisco: Labor-Management School, University of San Francisco, 1959.

PRESTRIDGE, VIRGINIA, comp. *The Worker in American Fiction: An Annotated Bibliography.* Bibliographic Contributions No. 4. Champaign: Institute of Labor and Industrial Relations, University of Illinois, 1954.

REYNOLDS, LLOYD G., and CHARLES C. KILLINGSWORTH. *Trade Union Publications: The Official Journals, Convention Proceedings and Constitutions of International Unions and Federations, 1850–1941.* 3 vols. Baltimore: Johns Hopkins Press, 1944–1945.

ROSE, FRED DUANE, comp. *American Labor in Journals of History: A Bibliography.* Bibliographic Contributions No. 7. Champaign: Institute of Labor and Industrial Relations, University of Illinois, 1962.

SHAUGHNESSY, D. F. "Labor in the Oral History Collection of Columbia University." *Labor History,* Vol. 1, No. 2, Spring 1960, pp. 177–195.

STATE UNIVERSITY OF IOWA, BUREAU OF LABOR AND MANAGEMENT. *A Guide to the Reference Collection.* Iowa City: The University, 1961.

STEWART, R. C. "The Labadie Labor Collection." *Michigan Alumnus Quarterly Review*, Vol. LIII, No. 20, May 10, 1947, pp. 247–253.

STROUD, GENE S., and GILBERT E. DONAHUE, comps. *Labor History in the United States: A General Bibliography.* Bibliographic Contributions No. 6. Urbana: Institute of Labor and Industrial Relations, University of Illinois, 1961.

U.S. BUREAU OF LABOR STATISTICS. *Subject Index of Bulletins Published by the Bureau of Labor Statistics, 1915–1959, with Annotated Listing of Bulletins, 1895–1959.* Bulletin No. 1281. Washington: G.P.O., 1960.

U.S. LIBRARY OF CONGRESS. *The National Union Catalog of Manuscript Collections, 1959–1961.* Ann Arbor: J. W. Edwards, 1962. This book catalog of archival collections contains more than 30,000 names, more than 3,000 main subject headings, and 400 repositories whose collections are reported in the volume.

U.S. NATIONAL ARCHIVES. *Guide to the Records in the National Archives.* Washington: G.P.O., 1948.

————. *National Archives Accessions. A Supplement to the Guide.* No. 31– . Washington: G.P.O., July 1947– . (Issued irregularly).

————. *Preliminary Inventory.* No. 1– . Washington: G.P.O., 1941– .

U.S. NATIONAL HISTORICAL PUBLICATIONS COMMISSION. *A Guide to Archives and Manuscripts in the United States.* Philip M. Hamer, ed. New Haven: Yale University Press, 1961.

U.S. WORKS PROGRESS ADMINISTRATION, FEDERAL WRITERS' PROJECT, NEW YORK CITY. *A Trial Bibliography of Bibliographies Relating to Labor.* New York: The Administration, 1937. (Mimeo.).

General Histories

BEARD, MARY. *The American Labor Movement: A Short History*. New York: Macmillan, 1939.

BIMBA, ANTHONY. *The History of the American Working Class*. New York: International Publishers, 1933.

CARLETON, FRANK TRACY. *Organized Labor in American History*. New York and London: Appleton, 1920.

CLARK, MARJORIE R., and S. FANNY SIMON. *The Labor Movement in America*. New York: W. W. Norton, 1938.

COMMONS, JOHN R., and ASSOCIATES. *History of Labour in the United States* (the beginnings to 1896). 2 vols. New York: Macmillan, 1918.

——————, and OTHERS, eds. *A Documentary History of American Industrial Society* (the beginnings to 1896). 11 vols. in 10. Cleveland: A. H. Clark, 1910–1911. (Reprinted, 10 vols. New York: Russell and Russell, 1958.)

DULLES, FOSTER RHEA. *Labor in America*. New York: Thomas Y. Crowell, 1960.

FAULKNER, HAROLD U., and MARK STARR. *Labor in America*. New York: Oxford Book Co., 1957.

FONER, PHILIP S. *History of the Labor Movement in the United States*. Vol. 1 (the beginnings to the formation of the AFL). Vol. 2 (1881 to the close of the nineteenth century). New York: International Publishers, 1947, 1955.

MILLIS, HARRY A., and ROYAL E. MONTGOMERY. *Organized Labor*. New York: McGraw-Hill, 1945.

ORTH, SAMUEL P. *The Armies of Labor*. New Haven: Yale University Press, 1921.

PELLING, HENRY. *American Labor*. Chicago: University of Chicago Press, 1960.

PERLMAN, SELIG. *A History of Trade Unionism in the United States*. New York: Macmillan, 1922. (Reprinted, New York: Augustus M. Kelley, 1949.)

——————, and PHILIP TAFT. *History of Labor in the United States, 1896–1932*. New York: Macmillan, 1935.

RAYBACK, JOSEPH G. *A History of American Labor*. New York: Macmillan, 1959.

TAFT, PHILIP. *Organized Labor in American History*. New York: Harper and Row, 1964.

WARE, NORMAN J. *Labor in Modern Industrial Society*. Boston and New York: D.C. Heath, 1935.

Periods of Development

The American Labor Movement
before the Knights of Labor

Аввотт, Едітн. "Harriet Martineau and the Employment of Women in 1836." *Journal of Political Economy*, Vol. 14, 1906, pp. 614–626.

Andrews, John B., and W. D. P. Bliss. "History of Women in Trade Unions." *Report on Condition of Woman and Child Wage-Earners in the United States*, Vol. X (1911), U.S. Bureau of Labor. Washington: G.P.O., 1910–1913. (U.S. Senate Document 645, 61st Congress, 2nd Session, 19 volumes.)

Arky, Louis H. "The Mechanics' Union of Trade Associations and the Formation of the Philadelphia Workingmen's Movement." *Pennsylvania Magazine of History and Biography*, Vol. LXXVI, April 1952, pp. 142–176.

Burn, James Dawson. *Three Years among the Working-Classes in the United States during the War.* London: Smith, Elder, 1865.

Cale, Edgar B. *The Organization of Labor in Philadelphia, 1850–1870.* Philadelphia: the Author, 1940.

Chamberlain, Edwin Martin. *The Sovereigns of Industry.* Boston: Lee & Shepard, 1875.

Cole, Margaret. *Robert Owen of New Lanark, 1771–1858.* New York: Oxford University Press, 1953.

Colton, Calvin. *The Rights of Labor.* New York: A. S. Barnes, 1847.

Commons, John R. "The American Shoemakers, 1648–1895," chap. 14, *Labor and Administration.* New York: Macmillan, 1913.

————, and Associates. *History of Labour in the United States.* 2 vols. New York: Macmillan, 1918.

————, and Others, eds. *A Documentary History of American Industrial Society.* 11 vols. in 10. Cleveland: A. H. Clark, 1910–1911.

————. "Ira Steward and the Hours of Labor," chap. III, *A Documentary History of American Industrial Society*, Vol. IX, pp. 277–330. Cleveland: A. H. Clark, 1910–1911.

Darling, Arthur B. "The Workingmen's Party in Massachusetts, 1833–1834." *American Historical Review*, Vol. XXIX, October 1923, pp. 81–86.

Dorfman, Joseph. "The Jackson Wage-Earner Thesis." *American Historical Review*, Vol. LIV, January 1949, pp. 296–306. [See also communication of Arthur M. Schlesinger, Jr. (April 1949), pp. 785–786.]

Douglas, Dorothy W. "Ira Steward on Consumption and Unemployment." *Journal of Political Economy*, Vol. 40, No. 4, August 1932, pp. 532–543.

Dyer, Walter A. *Early American Craftsmen.* New York: Century, 1915.

5

EVERETT, EDWARD. *A Lecture on the Working Men's Party.* Boston: Gray and Bowen, 1830.

FINE, NATHAN. *Labor and Farmer Parties in the United States, 1828–1928.* New York: Rand School of Social Science, 1928.

FITE, EMERSON D. *Social and Industrial Conditions in the North during the Civil War.* New York: Macmillan, 1910. (Reprinted, New York: Peter Smith, 1930.)

FONER, PHILIP S. *History of the Labor Movement in the United States,* Vol. 1. New York: International Publishers, 1947.

GROB, GERALD N. "Reform Unionism: The National Labor Union." *Journal of Economic History,* Vol. XIV, Spring 1954, pp. 126–142.

GROSSMAN, JONATHAN. *William Sylvis, Pioneer of American Labor.* New York: Columbia University Press, 1945.

HERRICK, CHEESMAN A. *White Servitude in Pennsylvania: Indentured and Redemption Labor in Colony and Commonwealth.* Philadelphia: McVey, 1926.

HICKS, OBADIAH. *The Life of Richard Trevellick, the Labor Orator, or the Harbinger of the Eight-Hour System.* Joliet, Ill.: J. F. Williams, 1896.

HUGINS, WALTER E. *Jacksonian Democracy and the Working Class, A Study of the New York Workingmen's Movement, 1829–1837.* Stanford: Stanford University Press, 1960.

JACKSON, SIDNEY L. "Labor, Education, and Politics in the 1830's." *Pennsylvania Magazine of History and Biography,* Vol. LXVI, July 1942, pp. 279–293.

JEFFREY, NEWMAN. *The Social Origins of George Henry Evans, Workingman's Advocate.* M.A. Thesis, Wayne State University, 1960.

JERNEGAN, MARCUS W. *Laboring and Dependent Classes in Colonial America, 1607–1783.* New York: Ungar, 1960.

KUGLER, ISRAEL. "The Trade Union Career of Susan B. Anthony." *Labor History,* Vol. 2, No. 1, Winter 1961, pp. 90–100.

LESCOHIER, DON D. *The Knights of St. Crispen, 1867–1874.* Bulletin 355. Madison: University of Wisconsin, 1910.

McKEE, SAMUEL, JR. *Labor in Colonial New York, 1664–1776.* New York: Columbia University Press, 1935.

McMASTER, JOHN B. *The Acquisition of Political, Social, and Industrial Rights of Man in America.* New York: Ungar, 1961.

MORRIS, RICHARD B. "Andrew Jackson, Strikebreaker." *American Historical Review,* Vol. LV, October 1949, pp. 54–68.

——————. *Government and Labor in Early America.* New York: Columbia University Press, 1946.

PERLMAN, SELIG. *History of Trade Unionism in the United States,* chaps. 1 and 2. New York: Macmillan, 1922.

PESSEN, EDWARD. "The Ideology of Stephen Simpson, Upperclass Champion of the Early Philadelphia Workingmen's Movement." *Pennsylvania History,* Vol. XXII, October 1955, pp. 328–340.

——————. "The Workingmen's Movement of the Jacksonian Era." *Mississippi Valley Historical Review,* Vol. XLIII, December 1956, pp. 428–443.

RANDALL, EDWIN T. "Imprisonment for Debt in America: Fact and Fiction." *Mississippi Valley Historical Review,* Vol. XXXIX, June 1952, pp. 89–102.

RAYBACK, JOSEPH G. "The American Workingman and the Antislavery Crusade." *Journal of Economic History,* Vol. III, November 1943, pp. 152–163.

REZNECK, SAMUEL. "The Social History of an American Depression, 1837–1843." *American Historical Review,* Vol. XL, July 1935, pp. 662–687.

SARTORIUS VON WALTERSHAUSEN, AUGUST JOHANN GEORG. *Die Arbeits-Verfassung der Englischen Kolonien in Nordamerika.* Strassburg: K. J. Trübner, 1894.

SCHLESINGER, ARTHUR M., JR. *The Age of Jackson.* Boston: Little, Brown, 1945.

SMITH, ABBOTT E. *Colonists in Bondage: White Servitude and Convict Labor in America, 1607–1776.* Chapel Hill: University of North Carolina Press, 1947.

STEDMAN, MURRAY S., and SUSAN W. STEDMAN. *Discontent at the Polls: A Study of Farmer and Labor Parties, 1827–1948.* New York: Columbia University Press, 1950.

STEVENS, HARRY R. "Did Industrial Labor Influence Jacksonian Land Policy?" *Indiana Magazine of History,* Vol. XLIII, June 1947, pp. 159–167.

SULLIVAN, WILLIAM A. *The Industrial Worker in Pennsylvania 1800–1840.* Harrisburg: Pennsylvania Historical and Museum Commission, 1955.

————. "Philadelphia Labor During the Jackson Era." *Pennsylvania History,* Vol. XV, October 1948, pp. 305–320.

SUMNER, HELEN L. "History of Women in Industry in the United States." *Report on Condition of Woman and Child Wage-Earners in the United States,* Vol. IX (1910), U.S. Bureau of Labor. Washington: G.P.O., 1910–1913. (U.S. Senate Document 645, 61st Congress, 2nd Session, 19 volumes.)

SYLVIS, JAMES C. *The Life, Speeches, Labors and Essays of William H. Sylvis, Late President of the Iron-moulders' International Union; and also of the National Labor Union.* Philadelphia: Claxton, Remsen, and Haffelfinger, 1872.

SYMES, LILLIAN, and TRAVERS CLEMENT. *Rebel America.* New York: Harper, 1934.

TAFT, PHILIP. "On the Origins of Business Unionism." *Industrial and Labor Relations Review,* Vol. 17, No. 1, October 1963, pp. 20–38.

TODES, CHARLOTTE. *William H. Sylvis and the National Labor Union.* New York: International Publishers, 1942.

WARE, NORMAN. *The Industrial Worker, 1840–1860.* Boston and New York: Houghton Mifflin, 1924. (Reprinted, Gloucester: Peter Smith, 1959.)

WHITMAN, ALDEN. *Labor Parties, 1827–1834.* New York: International Publishers, 1943.

WOLFSON, THERESA, and ALICE J. G. PERKINS. *Frances Wright: Free Enquirer; the Study of a Temperament.* New York: Harper, 1939.

WOOLEN, EVANS. "Labor Troubles between 1834 and 1837." *The Yale Review,* Vol. 1, No. 1, May 1892, pp. 87–100.

YEARLEY, CLIFTON K., JR. *Britons in American Labor: A History of the Influence of the United Kingdom Immigrants on American Labor, 1820–1914.* Baltimore: Johns Hopkins University Press, 1957.

————. "Richard Trevellick: Labor Agitator." *Michigan History,* Vol. 39, No. 4, December 1955, pp. 423–444.

ZAHLER, HELENE S. *Eastern Workingmen and National Land Policy, 1829–1862.* New York: Columbia University Press, 1941.

The Era of Upheaval and the Growth of the Knights of Labor

ADAMIC, LOUIS. *Dynamite* (an account of leading American strikes beginning in this period). New York: Viking Press, 1931.

————. *Grandsons* (a novel concerning the Haymarket Riot and the subsequent generation). New York: Harper, 1935.

BARNARD, HARRY. *Eagle Forgotten: The Life of John Peter Altgeld.* Indianapolis: Bobbs-Merrill, 1938.

BIMBA, ANTHONY. *The Molly Maguires.* New York: International Publishers, 1932.

BOUCHER, ARLINE, and JOHN TEHAN. *Prince of Democracy: James Cardinal Gibbons.* Garden City: Doubleday, 1962.

BROWNE, HENRY J. *The Catholic Church and the Knights of Labor.* Washington: Catholic University of America Press, 1949.

BUCHANAN, JOSEPH R. *The Story of a Labor Agitator.* New York: The Outlook Co., 1903.

CALMER, ALAN. *Labor Agitator: The Story of Albert R. Parsons.* New York: International Publishers, 1937.

CHRISTMAN, HENRY M., ed. *The Mind and Spirit of John Peter Altgeld: Selected Writings and Addresses.* Urbana: University of Illinois Press, 1960.

COLEMAN, J. WALTER. *Labor Disturbances in Pennsylvania, 1850–1880.* Washington: Catholic University of America, 1936. Ph.D. Thesis. (Published also as: *The Molly Maguire Riots: Industrial Conflict in the Pennsylvania Coal Region.* Richmond: Garrett, 1936.)

COMMONS, JOHN R., and OTHERS, eds. *A Documentary History of American Industrial Society.* 11 vols. in 10. Cleveland: A. H. Clark, 1910–1911.

DAVID, HENRY. *The History of the Haymarket Affair.* New York: Farrar & Rinehart, 1936. (Reprinted, New York: Russell and Russell, 1958.)

DE LEON, SOLON. "Daniel De Leon Bibliography." *The Tamiment Institute Library Bulletin,* No. 23, September–October 1959.

DESTLER, CHESTER McARTHUR. *American Radicalism, 1865–1901.* New London: Connecticut College, 1946.

ELY, RICHARD T. *The Labor Movement in America.* New York: Crowell Publishing, 1886.

ERICKSON, CHARLOTTE. *American Industry and the European Immigrant, 1860–1885.* Cambridge: Harvard University Press, 1957.

FAST, HOWARD. *The American* (a novel about John Peter Altgeld). New York: Duell, Sloan & Pearce, 1946.

FINE, SIDNEY, ed. "The Ely-Labadie Letters." *Michigan History*, Vol. 36, No. 1, March 1952, pp. 1–33.

GINGER, RAY. *Altgeld's America*. New York: Funk & Wagnalls, 1958.

GOMPERS, SAMUEL. *Seventy Years of Life and Labor*. 2 vols. New York: Dutton, 1925. See also, Philip Taft and John A. Sessions' one-volume edition. New York: Dutton, 1957.

GRANT, ROBERT (anonymously published). *Face to Face* (a novel set in New England, 1880's, showing the early problems of labor and capital and the changes wrought by labor unrest). New York: Scribner, 1886.

GROB, GERALD N. "The Knights of Labor, Politics, and Populism." *Mid-America*, Vol. 40 (New Series, Vol. 29), No. 1, January 1958, pp. 3–21.

——————. "The Knights of Labor and the Trade Unions, 1878–1886." *Journal of Economic History*, Vol. XVIII, June 1958, pp. 176–192.

——————. "Terence V. Powderly and the Knights of Labor." *Mid-America*, Vol. 39 (New Series, Vol. 28), No. 1, January 1957, pp. 39–55.

GUNTON, GEORGE. *Wealth and Progress: A Critical Examination of the Labor Problem*. New York: Appleton, 1887.

HARRIS, FRANK. *The Bomb* (a novel about the Haymarket Riot). New York: Mitchell Kennerley, 1909.

JAMES, EDWARD T. *American Labor and Political Action, 1865–1896: The Knights of Labor and Its Predecessors*. Ph.D. Thesis, Harvard University, 1954.

KEMMERER, DONALD L., and EDWARD D. WICKERSHAM. "Reasons for the Growth of the Knights of Labor in 1885–1886." *Industrial and Labor Relations Review*, Vol. 3, No. 2, January 1950, pp. 213–220.

KENNEDY, DOUGLAS R. *The Knights of Labor in Canada*. London, Ontario: University of Western Ontario, 1956.

KIRKLAND, EDWARD C. *Industry Comes of Age: Business, Labor, and Public Policy, 1860–1897*. New York: Holt, Rinehart and Winston, 1961.

KOGAN, BERNARD R., ed. *The Chicago Haymarket Riot: Anarchy on Trial*. Boston: Heath, 1959.

LABOR PUBLISHING COMPANY. *Labor: Its Rights and Wrongs. Statements and comments by the leading men of our nation on the labor question of to-day. With platforms of the various labor organizations, Knights of Labor, Federation of Trades, Agricultural Wheels of the South, Farmers' Alliance and full proceedings of the General Assembly of the Knights of Labor, at Cleveland, May 25 to June 3, 1886*. Washington: The Company, 1886.

LEIBY, JAMES. *Carroll Wright and Labor Reform: The Origin of Labor Statistics*. Cambridge: Harvard University Press, 1960.

MCCABE, JAMES D. (E. W. Martin, pseud.). *History of the Great Riots*. Philadelphia: National Publishing, 1877.

MCKEE, DON K. "Daniel De Leon: A Reappraisal." *Labor History*, Vol. 1, No. 3, Fall 1960, pp. 264–297.

MCNEILL, GEORGE E., ed. *The Labor Movement: The Problem of Today*. Boston: A. M. Bridgman, 1887. (Reprinted, New York: M. W. Hazen, 1892.)

MAROT, HELEN, comp. *A Handbook of Labor Literature*. Philadelphia: Free Library of Economics and Political Science, 1899.

MORRIS, JANE K. *Julie* (a novel set in New York and Chicago, late 19th century, about a labor organizer and leader). New York: McGraw-Hill, 1952.

PELLING, HENRY M. "The Knights of Labor in Great Britain, 1880–1901." *Economic History Review,* Vol. 9, December 1956, pp. 313–331.

PINKERTON, ALLAN. *The Molly Maguires and the Detectives.* New York: G. W. Carleton, 1878.

POLLARD, JOHN A. "Whittier on Labor Unions." *New England Quarterly,* Vol. XII, March 1939, pp. 99–102.

POWDERLY, TERENCE V. *The Path I Trod.* New York: Columbia University Press, 1940.

——————. *Thirty Years of Labor.* Columbus, Ohio: Excelsior Publishing House, 1889.

REUTER, FRANK T. "John Swinton's Paper." *Labor History,* Vol. 1, No. 3, Fall 1960, pp. 298–307.

RHODES, JAMES FORD. "The Molly Maguires in the Anthracite Region of Pennsylvania." *American Historical Review,* Vol. XV, April 1910, pp. 547–561.

ROBINSON, HARRY P. *Men Born Equal* (a novel set in the 1890's about a radical labor leader and the intrigue by which a strike is promoted to gain political advantage). New York: Harper, 1895.

SARTORIUS VON WALTERSHAUSEN, AUGUST JOHANN GEORG. *Die Nordamerikanischen Gewerkschaften unter dem Einfluss der Fortschreitenden Productionstechnik.* Berlin: H. Bahr, 1886.

U.S. CONGRESS. HOUSE. Select Committee on Depression in Labor and Business (1878). *The Causes of the General Depression in Labor and Business, Etc.* Washington: G.P.O., 1879.

——————. ——————. Select Committee on Existing Labor Troubles. *Investigation of Labor Troubles in Missouri, Arkansas, Kansas, Texas, and Illinois.* 1 vol., 2 parts. Washington: G.P.O., 1887.

U.S. CONGRESS. SENATE. Committee on Education and Labor (1883). *Report of the Committee of the Senate upon the Relations between Labor and Capital, and Testimony Taken by the Committee.* 5 vols. Washington: G.P.O., 1885.

WARE, NORMAN. *The Labor Movement in the United States, 1860–1895* (especially for the treatment of the Knights of Labor). New York: Appleton, 1929.

WATILLON, LÉON. *The Knights of Labor in Belgium* (translation and introduction by Frederic Meyers). Los Angeles: Institute of Industrial Relations, University of California, 1959.

WILLIAMS, BEN AMES. *Owen Glenn* (a novel about the Knights of Labor). Boston: Houghton Mifflin, 1950.

WRIGHT, CARROLL D. *The Battles of Labor.* Philadelphia: Jacobs, 1906.

——————. *The Industrial Evolution of the United States.* Meadville, Pa.: Flood & Vincent, 1895.

YELLEN, SAMUEL. *American Labor Struggles* (an account of leading American strikes, beginning in this period). New York: Harcourt, Brace, 1936.

The Era of the Triumph of the American Federation of Labor to World War I

GENERAL

AMERICAN FEDERATION OF LABOR AND CONGRESS OF INDUSTRIAL ORGANIZATIONS. *American Federation of Labor: History, Encyclopedia and Reference Book,* Vols. 1 and 2 (1881–1923). Washington: The AFL-CIO, 1960.

BABSON, ROGER. *W. B. Wilson and the Department of Labor.* New York: Brentano's, 1919.

BAKER, RAY STANNARD. *American Chronicle.* New York: Scribner, 1945.

CARTER, PAUL J., JR. "Mark Twain and the American Labor Movement." *New England Quarterly,* Vol. XXX, September 1957, pp. 382–388.

DARROW, CLARENCE. *The Story of My Life: An Autobiography.* New York: Scribner, 1932.

FITCH, JOHN A. *The Causes of Industrial Unrest.* New York: Harper, 1924.

FONER, PHILIP S. *History of the Labor Movement in the United States,* Vol. 2. New York: International Publishers, 1955.

GEORGE, HENRY. *The Condition of Labor: An Open Letter to Pope Leo XIII.* New York: United States Book Co., 1891.

GHENT, W. J. *Our Benevolent Feudalism.* New York: Macmillan, 1902.

GLADDEN, WASHINGTON. *The Labor Question.* Boston and New York: Pilgrim Press, 1911.

GOMPERS, SAMUEL. *Seventy Years of Life and Labor.* 2 vols. New York: Dutton, 1925. See also, Philip Taft and John A. Sessions' one-volume edition. New York: Dutton, 1957.

HAPGOOD, HUTCHINS. *The Spirit of Labor.* New York: Duffield, 1907.

HELBING, ALBERT T. *The Departments of the American Federation of Labor.* Baltimore: Johns Hopkins Press, 1931.

HOXIE, R. F. "The Trade Union Point of View." *Journal of Political Economy,* Vol. XV, June 1907, pp. 345–363.

—————. "Trade Unionism in the United States." *Journal of Political Economy,* Vol. XXII, March and May 1914, pp. 201–217, 464–481.

—————. *Trade Unionism in the United States.* New York: Appleton, 1917.

HUGHES, RUPERT. *The Giant Wakes: A Novel about Samuel Gompers.* Los Angeles: Borden, 1950.

JAMES, ALFRED P. "The First Convention of the American Federation of Labor, Pittsburgh, Pennsylvania, November 15th–18th, 1881: A Study in Contemporary Local Newspapers as a Source." *Western Pennsylvania Historical Magazine,* Vol. 6, No. 4, October 1923, pp. 201–233; Vol. 7, No. 1, January 1924, pp. 29–56; Vol. 7, No. 2, April 1924, pp. 106–120.

LANG, LUCY ROBINS. *Tomorrow Is Beautiful.* New York: Macmillan, 1948.

LEGIEN, CARL RUDOLPH. *Aus Amerikas Arbeiterbewegung.* Berlin: Verlag der Generalkommission der Gewerkschaften Deutschlands, 1914.

LEIBY, JAMES. *Carroll Wright and Labor Reform: The Origin of Labor Statistics.* Cambridge: Harvard University Press, 1960.

LORWIN, LEWIS L. *The American Federation of Labor: History, Policies, and Prospects.* Washington: Brookings Institution, 1933.

MCMURRY, DONALD L. *Coxey's Army: A Study of the Industrial Army Movement of 1894.* Boston: Little, Brown, 1929.

MILLIS, HARRY A., and ROYAL E. MONTGOMERY. *Organized Labor,* pp. 95–102. New York: McGraw-Hill, 1945.

MORRIS, JAMES O. *Conflict Within the AFL: A Study of Craft Versus Industrial Unionism, 1901–1938.* Cornell Studies in Industrial and Labor Relations, Vol. 10. Ithaca: New York State School of Industrial and Labor Relations at Cornell University, 1958.

ROLLINS, ALFRED B., JR. "Franklin Roosevelt's Introduction to Labor." *Labor History,* Vol. 3, No. 1, Winter 1962, pp. 3–18.

SMITH, JOHN S. "Organized Labor and Government in the Wilson Era; 1913–1921: Some Conclusions." *Labor History,* Vol. 3, No. 3, Fall 1962, pp. 265–286.

STEFFENS, LINCOLN. *The Autobiography of Lincoln Steffens.* 2 vols. New York and Chicago: Harcourt, Brace, 1937.

TAFT, PHILIP. *The A. F. of L. in the Time of Gompers.* New York: Harper, 1957.

TOBENKIN, ELIAS. *House of Conrad* (a novel, set in the eastern U.S. and California, 1868–1916, about a conservative labor leader). Philadelphia: Stokes, 1918.

U.S. COMMISSION ON INDUSTRIAL RELATIONS (1912). *Final Report and Testimony.* 11 vols. Washington: G.P.O., 1916.

U.S. INDUSTRIAL COMMISSION (1898). *Reports.* 19 vols. Washington: G.P.O., 1900–1902. See especially vols. VII and XIV, *Report on the Relations and Conditions of Capital and Labor Employed in Manufactures and General Business,* 1901.

WALLING, WILLIAM E. *American Labor and American Democracy.* New York: Harper, 1926.

CONDITIONS OF LABOR

AMERICAN ACADEMY OF POLITICAL AND SOCIAL SCIENCE. *The Improvements of Labor Conditions in the United States.* Philadelphia: The Academy, 1906.

GOLDMARK, JOSEPHINE. *Impatient Crusader: Florence Kelley's Life Story.* Urbana: University of Illinois Press, 1953.

NEW YORK STATE. Factory Investigating Commission (Robert Wagner, chairman). *Preliminary Report Transmitted to Legislature, March 1, 1912.* Albany: The Argus Co., 1912.

————. ————. *Second Report Transmitted to Legislature, January 15, 1913.* Senate Document 36. Albany: J. B. Lyon Co., 1913.

————. ————. *Third Report Transmitted to Legislature, February 14, 1914.* Assembly Document 28. Albany: J. B. Lyon Co., 1914.

————. ————. *Fourth Report Transmitted to Legislature, February 15, 1915.* Senate Document 43. Albany: J. B. Lyon Co., 1915.

STEIN, LEON. *The Triangle Fire.* Philadelphia and New York: J. B. Lippincott Company, 1962.

EMPLOYERS ASSOCIATIONS AND OFFENSIVES, THE OPEN AND CLOSED SHOP CONTROVERSY, LABOR SPIES, LABOR INJUNCTIONS, AND LEGISLATION

BERMAN, EDWARD. *Labor and the Sherman Act.* New York: Harper, 1930.

BONNETT, C. E. *Employers' Associations in the United States.* New York: Macmillan, 1922.

BURNS, WILLIAM J. *The Masked War.* New York: Doran, 1913.

COMMONS, J. R. "Causes of the Union-Shop Policy." *Publications of the American Economic Association, Third Series, Vol. VI, No. 1, Papers and Proceedings of the Seventeenth Annual Meeting, Part I,* February 1905, pp. 140–159.

ELIOT, C. E. "Employers' Policies in the Industrial Strife." *Harper's,* March 1905.

FRANKFURTER, FELIX, and NATHAN GREENE. *The Labor Injunction.* New York: Macmillan, 1930.

FRIEDMAN, MORRIS. *The Pinkerton Labor Spy.* New York: Wilshire Book Co., 1907.

GREEN, MARGUERITE. *The National Civic Federation and the American Labor Movement, 1900–1925.* Washington: Catholic University of America Press, 1956.

HOGG, J. BERNARD. "Public Reaction to Pinkertonism and the Labor Question." *Pennsylvania History,* Vol. XI, July 1944, pp. 171–199.

HUEBNER, GROVER G. *Blacklisting.* Madison: Wisconsin Free Library Commission, Legislative Reference Department, 1906.

KUTLER, STANLEY I. "Labor, the Clayton Act, and the Supreme Court." *Labor History,* Vol. 3, No. 1, Winter 1962, pp. 19–38.

MARCOSSON, ISAAC F. "The Fight for the Open Shop." *World's Work,* December 1905.

MASON, A. T. *Organized Labor and the Law, with Especial Reference to the Sherman and Clayton Acts.* Durham, N.C.: Duke University Press, 1925.

MERRITT, WALTER G. *History of the League for Industrial Rights* (in this period known as the American Anti-Boycott Association). New York: League for Industrial Rights, 1925.

STOCKTON, F. T. "The Closed Shop in American Unions." *Johns Hopkins University Studies in Historical and Political Science,* Series 29, 1911, pp. 431–611.

TAYLOR, A. G. *Labor Policies of the National Association of Manufacturers.* Urbana: University of Illinois, 1928.

U.S. CONGRESS. HOUSE. Committee on the Judiciary. *Investigation of the Employment of Pinkerton Detectives in Connection with the Labor Troubles at Homestead, Pennsylvania.* Washington: G.P.O., 1892.

WARNE, COLSTON, ed. *The Pullman Boycott of 1894: The Problem of Federal Intervention.* Boston: Heath, 1955.

IMMIGRATION AND MINORITY GROUPS

CHEN, TA. *Chinese Migrations, with Special Reference to Labor Conditions.* Bureau of Labor Statistics Bulletin 340. Washington: G.P.O., 1923.

DUBOFSKY, MELVYN. "Organized Labor and the Immigrant in New York City, 1900–1918." *Labor History*, Vol. 2, No. 2, Spring 1961, pp. 182–201.

EPSTEIN, MELECH. *Jewish Labor in the U.S.A., 1914–1952.* 2 vols. New York: Trade Union Sponsoring Committee, 1953.

FENTON, EDWIN. "Italians in the Labor Movement." *Pennsylvania History*, Vol. XXVI, No. 2, April 1959, pp. 133–148.

HERTZ, JACOB S., comp. *The Jewish Labor Bund: A Pictorial History, 1897–1957.* New York: Farlag Unser Tsait, 1958.

LEISERSON, WILLIAM M. *Adjusting Immigrant and Industry.* New York: Harper, 1924.

PATKIN, A. L. *The Origin of the Russian-Jewish Labour Movement.* Melbourne & London: F. W. Cheshire, 1947.

ROGOFF, ABRAHAM M. *Formative Years of the Jewish Labor Movement in the United States (1890–1900).* Ph.D. Thesis, Columbia University, 1945.

ROGOFF, HILLEL. *An East Side Epic: The Life and Work of Meyer London.* New York: Vanguard, 1930.

RUDOLPH, FREDERICK. "Chinamen in Yankeedom: Anti-Unionism in Massachusetts in 1870." *American Historical Review*, Vol. LIII, October 1947, pp. 1–29.

SHERIDAN, FRANK J. *Italian, Slavic, and Hungarian Unskilled Immigrant Laborers in the U.S.* Washington: G.P.O., 1907.

TCHERIKOWER, ELIAS, ed. *History of the Jewish Labor Movement in the United States* (in Yiddish). 2 vols. New York: Yiddish Scientific Institute, 1943, 1945. (Translated into English and revised by Aaron Antonovsky under the title, *The Early Jewish Labor Movement in the United States,* New York: Yivo Institute for Jewish Research, 1961.)

WARNE, FRANK J. *The Immigrant Invasion.* New York: Dodd, Mead, 1913.

THE I.W.W.

BRISSENDEN, PAUL F. *The I.W.W., A Study of American Syndicalism.* New York: Columbia University Press, 1920. (Reprinted, New York: Russell & Russell, 1957.)

——————. *The Launching of the Industrial Workers of the World.* Berkeley: University of California Press, 1913.

CHAPLIN, RALPH. *Wobbly: The Rough-and-Tumble Story of an American Radical.* Chicago: University of Chicago Press, 1948.

CHURCHILL, WINSTON. *The Dwelling Place of Light* (a novel). New York: Macmillan, 1917.

EBERT, JUSTUS. *The Trial of a New Society* (the Ettor, Giovannitti, and Caruso case). Cleveland: I.W.W. Publishing Bureau, 1913.

GAMBS, JOHN. *The Decline of the I.W.W.* New York: Columbia University Press, 1932.

HAYWOOD, WILLIAM D. *Bill Haywood's Book*. New York: International Publishers, 1929.

HOXIE, ROBERT. "The Truth about the I.W.W." *Journal of Political Economy*, Vol. XXI, November 1913, pp. 785–797.

STAVIS, BARRIE. *The Man Who Never Died: A Play about Joe Hill, with Notes on Joe Hill and His Times*. New York: Haven Press, 1954.

STEGNER, WALLACE. *The Preacher and the Slave* (a novel about Joe Hill). Boston: Houghton Mifflin, 1950.

TAFT, PHILIP. "The Federal Trials of the I.W.W." *Labor History*, Vol. 3, No. 1, Winter 1962, pp. 57–91.

——————. "The I.W.W. in the Grain Belt." *Labor History*, Vol. 1, No. 1, Winter 1960, pp. 53–67.

TYLER, ROBERT L. "The I.W.W. and the West." *American Quarterly*, Vol. XII, Summer 1960, pp. 175–187.

POLITICAL ACTION, SOCIALISM, AND IDEOLOGICAL UNIONISM

BEAN, WALTON. *Boss Ruef's San Francisco: The Story of the Union Labor Party, Big Business, and the Graft Prosecution*. Berkeley: University of California Press, 1952.

BELL, DANIEL. "The Background and Development of Marxian Socialism in the United States," chap. 6, *Socialism and American Life*, Vol. 1, Donald Drew Egbert and Stow Persons, eds. Princeton: Princeton University Press, 1952.

BERNSTEIN, IRVING, ed. "Samuel Gompers and Free Silver, 1896." *Mississippi Valley Historical Review*, Vol. XXIX, December 1942, pp. 394–400.

CARROLL, MOLLIE RAY. *Labor and Politics: The Attitude of the American Federation of Labor Toward Legislation and Politics*. Boston and New York: Houghton Mifflin, 1923.

FINE, NATHAN. *Labor and Farmer Parties in the United States, 1828–1928*. New York: Rand School of Social Science, 1928.

FOX, MARY HARRITA. *Peter E. Dietz, Labor Priest*. Notre Dame: University of Notre Dame Press, 1953.

GINGER, RAY. *The Bending Cross: A Biography of Eugene Victor Debs*. New Brunswick, N.J.: Rutgers University Press, 1949.

HESSELTINE, WILLIAM BEST. *The Rise and Fall of Third Parties*. Washington: Public Affairs Press, 1948.

HILLQUIT, MORRIS. *History of Socialism in the United States*. New York: Funk and Wagnalls, 1910.

HUNTER, ROBERT. *Labor in Politics*. Chicago: Socialist Party, 1915.

KARSON, MARC. *American Labor Unions and Politics*, Vol. 1 (1900–1918). Carbondale: Southern Illinois University Press, 1958.

LAIDLER, HARRY W. *Social-Economic Movements*, chap. 37, pp. 577–589. New York: Thomas Y. Crowell, 1945.

LOMBARDI, JOHN. *Labor's Voice in the Cabinet: A History of the Department of Labor from Its Origin to 1921*. New York: Columbia University Press, 1942.

MURRAY, ROBERT K. "Public Opinion, Labor, and the Clayton Act." *The Historian,* Vol. XXI, May 1959, pp. 255–270.

ROGIN, MICHAEL. "Voluntarism: The Political Functions of an Antipolitical Doctrine." *Industrial and Labor Relations Review,* Vol. 15, No. 4, July 1962, pp. 521–535.

SAPOSS, DAVID J. *Left-Wing Unionism.* New York: International Publishers, 1926.

SCHEINBERG, STEPHEN J. "Theodore Roosevelt and the A.F. of L.'s Entry into Politics, 1906–1908." *Labor History,* Vol. 3, No. 2, Spring 1962, pp. 131–148.

SCIENTIFIC MANAGEMENT

AITKEN, HUGH G. J. *Taylorism at Watertown Arsenal: Scientific Management in Action, 1908–1915.* Cambridge: Harvard University Press, 1960.

BRANDEIS, LOUIS D. "Organized Labor and Efficiency." *Survey,* April 22, 1911, pp. 148–151.

HOXIE, ROBERT F. *Scientific Management and Labor.* New York: Appleton, 1915.

KRAINES, OSCAR. "Brandeis and Scientific Management." *Publication of the American Jewish Historical Society,* Vol. XLI, September, 1951, pp. 41–60.

McKELVEY, JEAN T. *AFL Attitudes Toward Production, 1900–1932.* Cornell Studies in Industrial and Labor Relations, Vol. 2. Ithaca: New York State School of Industrial and Labor Relations at Cornell University, 1952.

NADWORNY, MILTON J. *Scientific Management and the Unions, 1900–1932.* Cambridge: Harvard University Press, 1955.

WOMEN

ANDERSON, MARY. *Woman at Work: The Autobiography of Mary Anderson as Told to Mary N. Winslow.* Minneapolis: University of Minnesota Press, 1951.

ANDREWS, JOHN B., and W. D. P. BLISS. "History of Women in Trade Unions." *Report on Condition of Woman and Child Wage-Earners in the United States,* Vol. X (1911), U.S. Bureau of Labor. Washington: G.P.O., 1910–1913. (U.S. Senate Document 645, 61st Congress, 2nd Session, 19 volumes.)

BOONE, GLADYS. *The Women's Trade Union Leagues in Great Britain and the United States of America.* New York: Columbia University Press, 1942.

CLARK, SUE AINSLIE, and EDITH WYATT. *Making Both Ends Meet: The Income and Outlay of New York Working Girls.* New York: Macmillan, 1911.

DREIER, MARY. *Margaret Dreier Robins: Her Life, Letters and Work.* New York: Island Press Cooperative, 1950.

HENRY, ALICE. *The Trade Union Woman.* New York: Appleton, 1915.

——————. *Women and the Labor Movement.* New York: Doran, 1923. (Reprinted, New York: Macmillan, 1927.)

HERRON, BELVA M. *Labor Organization Among Women.* Urbana: University of Illinois Press, 1905.

ILLINOIS BUREAU OF LABOR STATISTICS. "Working Women in Chicago." *Seventh Biennial Report, 1892,* Part I. Springfield: The Bureau, 1893.

MATTHEWS, LILLIAN RUTH. *Women in Trade Unions in San Francisco.* Berkeley: University of California Press, 1913.

NESTOR, AGNES. *Woman's Labor Leader: An Autobiography.* Rockford, Illinois: Bellevue Books Publishing Co., 1954.

SCHREINER, OLIVE. *Woman and Labor.* New York: Frederick A. Stokes Co., 1911.

SUMNER, HELEN L. "History of Women in Industry in the United States." *Report on Condition of Woman and Child Wage-Earners in the United States,* Vol. IX (1910), U.S. Bureau of Labor. Washington: G.P.O., 1910–1913. (U.S. Senate Document 645, 61st Congress, 2nd Session, 19 volumes.)

U.S. BUREAU OF LABOR. *Report on Condition of Woman and Child Wage-Earners in the United States.* 19 vols. Washington: G.P.O., 1910–1913. (U.S. Senate Document 645, 61st Congress, 2nd Session.)

U.S. DEPARTMENT OF LABOR. Women's Bureau. *Toward Better Working Conditions for Women: Methods and Policies of the National Women's Trade Union League.* Bulletin 252. Washington: G.P.O., 1953.

WOMEN'S TRADE UNION LEAGUE OF MASSACHUSETTS. *The History of Trade Unionism among Women in Boston.* Boston: The League, 1915.

World War I, the Golden Aftermath, and the Depression of the 1930's

AMERICAN FEDERATION OF LABOR AND CONGRESS OF INDUSTRIAL ORGANIZATIONS. *American Federation of Labor: History, Encyclopedia and Reference Book,* Vol. 3, Parts I and II (1924–1955). Washington: The AFL–CIO, 1960.

BAKER, R. S. *The New Industrial Unrest.* New York: Doubleday, Page, 1920.

BERNSTEIN, IRVING. *The Lean Years: A History of the American Worker, 1920–1933.* Boston: Houghton Mifflin, 1960.

BING, A. *War-Time Strikes and Their Adjustment.* New York: Dutton, 1921.

BORNET, VAUGHN D. *Labor and Politics in 1928.* Ph.D. Thesis, Stanford University, 1951.

CHILDS, HARWOOD LAWRENCE. *Labor and Capital in National Politics.* Columbus: Ohio State University Press, 1930.

DANISH, MAX. *William Green.* New York: Inter-Allied Publications, 1952.

DAUGHERTY, CARROLL R. *Labor under the N.R.A.* Boston: Houghton Mifflin, 1934.

DEARING, C. L., P. T. HOMAN, L. L. LORWIN, and L. S. LYON. *The ABC of the NRA.* Washington: Brookings Institution, 1934.

DUNN, ROBERT W. *The Americanization of Labor: The Employers' Offensive Against the Trade Unions.* New York: International Publishers, 1927.

——————. *Company Unions, Employers' "Industrial Democracy."* New York: Vanguard, 1927.

————. "The Industrial Welfare Offensive," chap. 19, *American Labor Dynamics*, J. B. S. Hardman, ed. New York: Harcourt, Brace, 1928.

DYCHE, JOHN A. *Bolshevism in American Labor Unions: A Plea for Constructive Unionism.* New York: Boni and Liveright, 1926.

ELDRIDGE, SEBA. "Labor and Independent Politics" (1920's), chap. 22, *American Labor Dynamics*, J. B. S. Hardman, ed. New York: Harcourt, Brace, 1928.

FOSTER, WILLIAM Z. *Misleaders of Labor.* Chicago: Trade Union Educational League, 1927.

Four Years in the Underbrush: Adventures of a Working Woman in New York. New York: Scribner, 1921.

GAGLIARDO, DOMENICO. *The Kansas Industrial Court.* Lawrence: University of Kansas Press, 1941.

GOMPERS, SAMUEL. *American Labor and the War.* New York: Doran, 1919.

HERBST, JOSEPHINE. *The Executioner Waits* (a novel of general labor unrest and the I.W.W., 1918–1929). New York: Harcourt, Brace, 1934.

HEWES, AMY, and HENRIETTE R. WALTER. *Women as Munition-Makers: A Study of Conditions in Bridgeport, Connecticut.* New York: Russell Sage Foundation, 1917.

HOURWICH, ANDRIA T., and GLADYS L. PALMER, eds. *I Am a Woman Worker: A Scrapbook of Autobiographies.* New York: Affiliated Schools for Workers, 1936.

HOWARD, SIDNEY. *The Labor Spy.* New York: Republic Publishing, 1924.

JESSUP, MARY F. *Women in the Railroad Industry during and after World War I.* Historical Studies of Wartime Problems No. 70. Washington: U.S. Bureau of Labor Statistics (Division of Historical Studies of Wartime Problems, 1941–1945), 1944. (Mimeo.).

JOHNSON, JOSEPHINE W. *Jordanstown* (a novel about workers during the depression). New York: Simon and Schuster, 1937.

JONES, MARY. *Autobiography of Mother Jones.* Chicago: C. H. Kerr, 1925.

LABOR RESEARCH ASSOCIATION. *The Palmer Raids.* New York: International Publishers, 1948.

LAIDLER, HARRY W. *Social-Economic Movements*, pp. 589–596. New York: Thomas Y. Crowell, 1945.

LANFEAR, VINCENT W. *Business Fluctuations and the American Labor Movement, 1915–1922.* New York: Columbia University, 1924.

LAUCK, WILLIAM J. *Political and Industrial Democracy, 1776–1926.* New York: Funk and Wagnalls, 1926.

————, and EDGAR SYDENSTRICKER. *Conditions of Labor in American Industries: A Summarization of the Results of Recent Investigations.* New York: Funk and Wagnalls, 1917.

————, and CLAUDE S. WATTS. *The Industrial Code.* New York: Funk and Wagnalls, 1922.

MERRITT, WALTER G. *Destination Unknown: Fifty Years of Labor Relations.* New York: Prentice-Hall, 1951.

————. *History of the League for Industrial Rights.* New York: League for Industrial Rights, 1925.

MILLER, ROBERT MOATS. *American Protestantism and Social Issues, 1919–1939*, Part III. Chapel Hill: University of North Carolina Press, 1958.

MILLIS, HARRY A., and ROYAL E. MONTGOMERY. "Employee Representation Plans and Independent Unions," chap. 15, *Organized Labor*. New York: McGraw-Hill, 1945.

MITCHELL, BROADUS. *Depression Decade: From New Era through New Deal, 1929–1941*. New York: Rinehart, 1947.

The Mooney-Billings Report: Suppressed by the Wickersham Commission. New York: Gotham House, 1932.

MURRAY, ROBERT K. *Red Scare: A Study in National Hysteria, 1919–1920*. Minneapolis: University of Minnesota Press, 1955.

MUSTE, ABRAHAM J. *The A.F. of L. in 1931*. New York: National Executive Commission of the Conference for Progressive Labor Action, 1932.

NASH, GERALD D. "Franklin D. Roosevelt and Labor: The World War I Origins of Early New Deal Policy." *Labor History*, Vol. 1, No. 1, Winter 1960, pp. 39–52.

NATIONAL INDUSTRIAL CONFERENCE BOARD. *Collective Bargaining through Employee Representation*. New York: The Board, 1933.

—————. *Experience with Works Councils in the United States*. Research Report 50. New York: Century, 1922.

ODEGARD, PETER H., and E. ALLEN HELMS. *American Politics: A Study in Political Dynamics*. New York: Harper, 1938.

ODENCRANTZ, LOUISE C. *Italian Women in Industry: A Study of Conditions in New York City*. New York: Russell Sage Foundation, 1919.

PERLMAN, SELIG, and PHILIP TAFT. *History of Labor in the United States, 1896–1932*, pp. 525–537, 580–602. New York: Macmillan, 1935.

RICE, STUART ARTHUR. *Farmers and Workers in American Politics*. New York: Columbia University, 1924.

SAPOSS, DAVID J. *Left Wing Unionism*. New York: International Publishers, 1926.

SAVAGE, MARION DUTTON. *Industrial Unionism in America*. New York: Ronald Press, 1922.

SCHNEIDER, D. M. *The Workers' (Communist) Party and American Trade Unions*. Baltimore: Johns Hopkins Press, 1928.

SEATTLE UNION RECORD PUBLISHING CO., INC. *The Seattle General Strike: An Account of What Happened in Seattle and Especially in the Seattle Labor Movement during the General Strike, February 6 to 11, 1919*. Seattle: The Company, 1919.

SELEKMAN, SYLVIA K. *Rebellion in Labor Unions*. New York: Boni and Liveright, 1924.

SHIELDS, E. L. *Negro Women in Industry*. Womens Bureau Bulletin No. 20. Washington: G.P.O., 1922.

SLICHTER, S. H. *Union Policies and Industrial Management*, chaps. 15 and 16. Washington: Brookings Institution, 1941.

SOROKIN, PITIRIM A. "Leaders of Labor and Radical Movements in the United States and Foreign Countries." *American Journal of Sociology*, Vol. XXXIII, November 1927, pp. 382–411.

TAFT, PHILIP. *The A.F. of L. From the Death of Gompers to the Merger.* New York: Harper, 1959.

TAYLOR, ALBION G. *Labor Policies of the National Association of Manufacturers.* Urbana: University of Illinois, 1928.

TEAD, ORDWAY, and H. C. METCALF. *Labor Relations under the Recovery Act.* New York: McGraw-Hill, 1933.

TIPPETT, THOMAS. *When Southern Labor Stirs.* New York: J. Cape & H. Smith, 1931.

U.S. DEPARTMENT OF LABOR. Bureau of Labor Statistics. *Characteristics of Company Unions.* Bulletin 634. Washington: G.P.O., 1938.

—————. —————. *National War Labor Board.* Bulletin 287. Washington: G.P.O., 1921.

VAN DER SLICE, AUSTIN. *International Labor, Diplomacy and Peace, 1914–1919* (labor movements of France, Great Britain, and the U.S. during the period of the war and the peace). Philadelphia: University of Pennsylvania Press, 1941.

WANDER, PAUL. "The Challenge of Company-Made Unionism," chap. 20, *American Labor Dynamics,* J. B. S. Hardman, ed. New York: Harcourt, Brace, 1928.

WARNE, FRANK J. *The Workers at War.* New York: Century, 1920.

WATKINS, GORDON S. *Labor Problems and Labor Administration in the United States during the World War.* Urbana: University of Illinois Press, 1920.

WOLFSON, THERESA. *The Woman Worker and the Trade Unions.* New York: International Publishers, 1926.

WOOD, LOUIS AUBREY. *Union-Management Cooperation on the Railroads.* New Haven: Yale University Press, 1931.

ZIMAND, SAVEL. *The Open Shop Drive.* New York: Bureau of Industrial Research, 1921.

The New Deal and the Rise of the CIO

BERNSTEIN, IRVING. *The New Deal Collective Bargaining Policy.* Berkeley: University of California Press, 1950.

BROOKS, R. R. R. *Unions of Their Own Choosing: An Account of the National Labor Relations Board and Its Work.* New Haven: Yale University Press, 1939.

—————. *When Labor Organizes.* New Haven: Yale University Press, 1937.

CALKINS, CLINCH. *Spy Overhead.* New York: Harcourt, Brace, 1937.

DERBER, MILTON, and EDWIN YOUNG, eds. *Labor and the New Deal.* Madison: University of Wisconsin Press, 1957.

DUNNE, WILLIAM F. *The Great San Francisco General Strike.* New York: Workers Library Publishers, 1934.

GALENSON, WALTER. *The CIO Challenge to the AFL: A History of the American Labor Movement, 1935–1941.* Cambridge: Harvard University Press, 1960.

————. *Rival Unionism in the United States*. New York: American Council on Public Affairs, 1940.

HARRIS, HERBERT. *American Labor*. New Haven: Yale University Press, 1939.

————. *Labor's Civil War*. New York: Knopf, 1940.

HIGGINS, GEORGE G. *Voluntarism in Organized Labor in the United States, 1930–1940*. Washington: Catholic University of America Press, 1944.

HORAN, J. D., and HOWARD SWIGGETT. *The Pinkerton Story*. New York: Putnam, 1951.

HUBERMAN, LEO. *The Labor Spy Racket*. New York: Modern Age Books, 1937.

KAMPELMAN, MAX M. *The Communist Party vs. the C.I.O.: A Study in Power Politics*. New York: F. A. Praeger, 1957.

LEVINSON, EDWARD. *I Break Strikes! The Technique of Pearl L. Bergoff*. New York: McBride & Co., 1935.

————. *Labor on the March*. New York: Harper, 1938.

MASON, LUCY R. *To Win These Rights: A Personal Story of the CIO in the South*. New York: Harper, 1952.

MILLIS, HARRY A., and ROYAL MONTGOMERY. "Employee Representation Plans and Independent Unions," chap. 15, *Organized Labor*. New York: McGraw-Hill, 1945.

NEWELL, BARBARA W. *Chicago and the Labor Movement: Metropolitan Unionism in the 1930's*. Urbana: University of Illinois Press, 1961.

PAUL, ELLIOT H. *The Stars and Stripes Forever* (a novel set in a New England town about workers who organize and strike under the impetus of the Wagner Act). New York: Random House, 1939.

PERKINS, FRANCES. *The Roosevelt I Knew*. New York: Viking Press, 1946.

PESOTTA, ROSE. *Bread Upon the Waters*. New York: Dodd, Mead, 1945.

PIDGEON, MARY E. *Employed Women under NRA Codes*. Women's Bureau Bulletin 130. Washington: G.P.O., 1935.

SAPOSS, DAVID J. *Communism in American Unions*. New York: McGraw-Hill, 1959.

STOLBERG, BENJAMIN. *The Story of the CIO*. New York: Viking Press, 1938.

U. S. CONGRESS. SENATE. Committee on Education and Labor (Robert M. LaFollette, Jr., chairman). *Violations of Free Speech and the Rights of Labor*. Parts 1–75. 75th to 78th Congress. Washington: G.P.O., 1937–1941.

U. S. DEPARTMENT OF LABOR. Bureau of Labor Statistics. *Characteristics of Company Unions*. Bulletin 634. Washington: G.P.O., 1938.

VORSE, MARY HEATON. *Labor's New Millions*. New York: Modern Age Books, 1938.

WALSH, J. R. *C.I.O.—Industrial Unionism in Action*. New York: W. W. Norton, 1937.

ZUGSMITH, LEANE. *Summer Soldier* (a novel of organizing in the South). New York: Random House, 1938.

Problems of Labor in the 1930's and 1940's

ARNOLD, DELBERT D. *The CIO's Role in American Politics, 1936–1948.* Ph.D. Thesis, University of Maryland, 1953.

BERNSTEIN, IRVING. "John L. Lewis and the Voting Behavior of the CIO." *Public Opinion Quarterly,* June 1941.

CALKINS, FAY. *The CIO and the Democratic Party.* Chicago: University of Chicago Press, 1952.

EPSTEIN, ALBERT, and NATHANIEL GOLDFINGER. "Communist Tactics in American Unions." *Labor and Nation,* Vol. VI, No. 4, Fall 1950, pp. 36–43.

GAER, JOSEPH. *The First Round: The Story of the CIO Political Action Committee.* New York: Duell, Sloan and Pearce, 1944.

KEEZER, DEXTER. "Observations on the Operations of the National War Labor Board." *American Economic Review,* June 1946.

KEMPTON, MURRAY. *Part of Our Time: Some Ruins and Monuments of the Thirties.* New York: Simon and Schuster, 1955.

KIRSHBAUM, LOUIS. *America's Labor Dictators.* New York: Industrial Forum Publications, 1940.

LENS, SIDNEY. *Left, Right and Center: Conflicting Forces in American Labor.* Hinsdale, Illinois: Henry Regnery, 1949.

MADISON, CHARLES A. *American Labor Leaders: Personalities and Forces in the Labor Movement.* New York: Harper, 1950.

MILLS, C. WRIGHT. *The New Men of Power: America's Labor Leaders.* New York: Harcourt, Brace, 1948.

MOTLEY, WILLARD. *We Fished All Night* (a novel about a Chicago labor leader, before and after World War II). New York: Appleton-Century-Crofts, 1951.

NATIONAL PLANNING ASSOCIATION. *Why I Am a Member of the Labor Movement, by 15 Labor Leaders.* Special Report No. 20. Washington: The Association, 1949. (Solomon Barkin, James B. Carey, Nelson H. Cruikshank, Katherine P. Ellickson, Frank P. Fenton, Sander Genis, Clinton Golden, Marion H. Hedges, Carl Holderman, Eric Peterson, Samuel E. Roper, Ted F. Silvey, William S. Townsend, Edward H. Weyler, Arnold S. Zander.)

OWEN, HOMER LEROY. *The Role of the CIO–PAC in the 1944 Elections.* M.S. Thesis, New York State School of Industrial and Labor Relations, Cornell University, 1952.

RIKER, WILLIAM H. *The CIO in Politics 1936–1946.* Ph.D. Thesis, Harvard University, 1948.

ROE, WELLINGTON. *Juggernaut: American Labor in Action.* Philadelphia: Lippincott, 1948.

SEIDMAN, JOEL. *American Labor from Defense to Reconversion.* Chicago: University of Chicago Press, 1953.

STEIN, BRUNO. "Labor's Role in Government Agencies During World War II." *Journal of Economic History,* Vol. XVII, September 1957, pp. 389–408.

"Ten Who Deliver." *Fortune Magazine,* Vol. XXXIV, No. 5, November 1946, pp. 146–151. (The Ten: William P. Nutter, James J. Matles, John

Owens, Norman Matthews, Gladys Dickason, Ralph Helstein, William S. Townsend, William L. McFetridge, Joseph A. Beirne, Harry Lundeberg.)

U. S. DEPARTMENT OF LABOR. *The National Wage Stabilization Board, January 1, 1946–February 24, 1947*. Washington: G.P.O., 1947.

U. S. DEPARTMENT OF LABOR. Bureau of Labor Statistics. *Problems and Policies of Dispute Settlement and Wage Stabilization during World War II*. Bulletin 1009. Washington: G.P.O., 1950.

————. ————. *Report on the Work of the National Defense Mediation Board, March 19, 1941–January 12, 1942*. Bulletin 714. Washington: G.P.O., 1942.

————. ————. Work Stoppages: 1941, Bulletin 711; 1942, Bulletin 741; 1943, Bulletin 782; 1944, Bulletin 833; 1945, Bulletin 878; 1946, Bulletin 918; 1947, Bulletin 935; 1948, Bulletin 963; 1949, Bulletin 1003. Washington: G.P.O.

U. S. LIBRARY OF CONGRESS. Legislative Reference Service. *Collective Bargaining and the Strike Limitation Issue 1933–1946*. Public Affairs Bulletin 39. Washington: The Library, 1946.

U. S. NATIONAL LABOR RELATIONS BOARD. *Legislative History of the Labor Management Relations Act, 1947*. 2 vols. Washington: G.P.O., 1948.

————. *Legislative History of the National Labor Relations Act, 1935*. 2 vols. Washington: G.P.O., 1949.

WARNE, COLSTON E., ed. *Labor in Postwar America*. Brooklyn: Remsen Press, 1949.

————, and Others, eds. *War Labor Policies*. New York: Philosophical Library, 1945.

Contemporary Problems of Organized Labor

CORRUPTION IN LABOR UNIONS

BEAN, WALTON E. "Boss Ruef, the Union Labor Party, and the Graft Prosecution in San Francisco, 1901–1911." *Pacific Historical Review*, Vol. XVII, November 1948, pp. 443–455.

HOSTETTER, GORDON L., and THOMAS Q. BEESLEY. *It's a Racket!* Chicago: Les Quin Books, 1929.

HUTCHINSON, JOHN. "Corruption in American Trade Unions." *The Political Quarterly*, Vol. 28, No. 3, July–September 1957.

JOHNSON, MALCOLM. *Crime on the Labor Front*. New York: McGraw-Hill, 1950.

KENNEDY, ROBERT F. *The Enemy Within*. New York: Harper, 1960.

"Labor Violence and Corruption." *Business Week*, August 31, 1957.

PERLMAN, SELIG, and PHILIP TAFT. *History of Labor in the United States, 1896–1932*, chap. 7, "The Labor Barony on the Pacific Coast." New York: Macmillan, 1935.

PETRO, SYLVESTER. *Power Unlimited: The Corruption of Union Leadership; A Report on the McClellan Committee Hearings.* New York: Ronald Press, 1959.

SEIDMAN, HAROLD. *Labor Czars: A History of Labor Racketeering.* New York: Liveright, 1938.

SHEFFERMAN, NATHAN. *The Man in the Middle.* Garden City: Doubleday, September 1961.

SULLIVAN, EDWARD D. *This Labor Union Racket.* New York: Hillman-Curl, 1936.

TAFT, PHILIP. *Corruption and Racketeering in the Labor Movement.* Bulletin 38. Ithaca: New York State School of Industrial and Labor Relations at Cornell University, February 1958.

———. "The Responses of the Bakers, Longshoremen and Teamsters to Public Exposure." *The Quarterly Journal of Economics,* Vol. LXXIV, August 1960, pp. 393–412.

U.S. CONGRESS. SENATE. See reports of the Select Committee on Improper Activities in the Labor or Management Field published beginning in 1957 (John L. McClellan, chairman).

VON RHAU, HENRY. *Fraternally Yours* (a novel on labor racketeering). Boston: Houghton Mifflin, 1949.

NATIONAL LABOR POLICY

BARBASH, JACK. *The Taft-Hartley Law in Action.* New York: League for Industrial Democracy, 1954.

BROWN, EMILY CLARK. *National Labor Policy: Taft-Hartley after Three Years and the Next Steps.* Washington: Public Affairs Institute, 1950.

METZ, HAROLD, and MEYER JACOBSTEIN. *A National Labor Policy.* Washington: Brookings Institution, 1947.

MILLIS, H. A., and E. C. BROWN. *From the Wagner Act to Taft-Hartley: A Study of National Labor Policy and Labor Relations.* Chicago: University of Chicago Press, 1950.

NATIONAL LABOR RELATIONS BOARD. *Legislative History of the Labor Management Relations Act, 1947.* 2 vols. Washington: G.P.O., 1948.

———. *Legislative History of the Labor-Management Reporting and Disclosure Act of 1959.* 2 vols. Washington: G.P.O., 1959.

POMPER, GERALD. "Labor and Congress: The Repeal of Taft-Hartley." *Labor History,* Vol. 2, No. 3, Fall 1961, pp. 323–343.

RASKIN, A. H. "The Outlook for Labor under Eisenhower." *Commentary,* April 1953, pp. 365–373.

NEGROES AND OTHER MINORITY GROUPS

ATTAWAY, WILLIAM. *Blood on the Forge* (a novel). New York: Doubleday, Doran, 1941.

BELL, DANIEL. "Reflections on the Negro and Labor." *The New Leader,* January 21, 1963, pp. 18–20.

BLOCH, HERMAN D. "Craft Unions and the Negro in Historical Perspective." *Journal of Negro History*, Vol. XLIII, January 1958, pp. 10–33.

BROOKS, TOM. "Negro Militants, Jewish Liberals, and the Unions." *Commentary*, Vol. 32, No. 3, September 1961, pp. 209–216.

CAYTON, HORACE R., and GEORGE S. MITCHELL. *Black Workers and the New Unions*. Chapel Hill: University of North Carolina Press, 1939.

COOK, FANNIE. *Mrs. Palmer's Honey* (a novel). New York: Doubleday, 1946.

FRANKLIN, CHARLES L. *The Negro Labor Unionist of New York: Problems and Conditions*. New York: Columbia University Press, 1936.

GINGER, RAY. "Were Negroes Strikebreakers?" *Negro History Bulletin*, Vol. XV, January 1952, pp. 73–74.

GREER, SCOTT A. *Last Man In: Racial Access to Union Power*. Glencoe: Free Press, 1959.

GROB, GERALD N. "Organized Labor and the Negro Worker, 1865–1900." *Labor History*, Vol. 1, No. 2, Spring 1960, pp. 164–176.

HANDLIN, OSCAR. *The Newcomers: Negroes and Puerto Ricans in a Changing Metropolis*. Cambridge: Harvard University Press, 1959.

HAYES, LAURENCE J. W. *The Negro Federal Government Worker*. Washington: Howard University, 1941.

HAYES, MARION. "A Century of Change: Negroes in the U. S. Economy, 1860–1960." *Monthly Labor Review*, Vol. 85, No. 12, December 1962, pp. 1359–1365.

HAYNES, GEORGE E. *The Negro at Work in New York City*. New York: Columbia University Press, 1912.

HILL, HERBERT. "Organized Labor and the Negro Wage Earner: Ritual and Reality." *New Politics*, Vol. 1, No. 2, Winter 1962, pp. 8–19.

HIMES, CHESTER B. *Lonely Crusade* (a novel). New York: Knopf, 1947.

HOLLEMAN, JERRY R. "The Job Ahead for the President's Committee on Equal Employment Opportunity." *Proceedings of the Spring Meeting of the Industrial Relations Research Association*, May 4–5, 1961, pp. 618–621. Reprinted from the *Labor Law Journal*, July 1961.

KARLIN, JULES ALEXANDER. "The Anti-Chinese Outbreak in Tacoma, 1885." *Pacific Historical Review*, Vol. XXIII, August 1954, pp. 271–283.

————. "The Anti-Chinese Outbreaks in Seattle, 1885–1886." *Pacific Northwest Quarterly*, Vol. XXXIX, April 1948, pp. 103–130.

KESSLER, SIDNEY H. "The Organization of Negroes in the Knights of Labor." *Journal of Negro History*, Vol. XXXVII, July 1952, pp. 248–276.

KORNHAUSER, WILLIAM A. "The Negro Union Official: A Study of Sponsorship and Control." *American Journal of Sociology*, Vol. 57, March 1952, pp. 443–452.

LADENSON, ALEX. "The Background of the Hawaiian-Japanese Labor Convention of 1886." *Pacific Historical Review*, Vol. IX, December 1940, pp. 389–400.

LOFTON, WILLISTON H. "Northern Labor and the Negro During the Civil War." *Journal of Negro History*, Vol. XXXIV, July 1949, pp. 251–273.

LUNDEN, LEON E. "Antidiscrimination Provisions in Major Contracts, 1961." *Monthly Labor Review*, Vol. 85, No. 6, June 1962, pp. 643–651.

MANDEL, BERNARD. "Anti-Slavery and the Southern Worker." *Negro History Bulletin,* Vol. XVII, February 1954, pp. 99–105.

——————. "Samuel Gompers and the Negro Workers, 1886–1914." *Journal of Negro History,* Vol. XL, January 1955, pp. 34–60.

——————. "Slavery and the Southern Workers." *Negro History Bulletin,* Vol. XVII, December 1953, pp. 57–62.

MARSHALL, RAY. "Some Factors Influencing Union Racial Practices." *Proceedings of the Fourteenth Annual Meeting of the Industrial Relations Research Association,* December 28–29, 1961, pp. 104–119. Madison: The Association, 1962.

——————. "Union Racial Problems in the South." *Industrial Relations,* Vol. 1, No. 3, May 1962, pp. 117–128.

MATISON, SUMNER ELIOT. "The Labor Movement and the Negro During Reconstruction." *Journal of Negro History,* Vol. XXXIII, October 1948, pp. 426–468.

MYRDAL, GUNNAR, and OTHERS. *An American Dilemma: The Negro Problem and Modern Democracy.* New York: Harper, 1962.

NATIONAL URBAN LEAGUE. *Negro Membership in American Labor Unions.* New York: Alexander Press, 1930.

NORGREN, PAUL H. "Governmental Fair Employment Agencies: An Appraisal of Federal and State and Municipal Efforts to End Job Discrimination." *Proceedings of the Fourteenth Annual Meeting of the Industrial Relations Research Association,* December 28–29, 1961, pp. 120–138. Madison: The Association, 1962.

——————, et al. *Employing the Negro in American Industry.* New York: Industrial Relations Counselors, 1959.

NORTHRUP, HERBERT R. *Organized Labor and the Negro.* New York: Harper, 1944.

RECORD, WILSON. *The Negro and the Communist Party.* Chapel Hill: University of North Carolina Press, 1951.

ROWLAND, DONALD. "The United States and the Contract Labor Question in Hawaii, 1862–1900." *Pacific Historical Review,* Vol. II, September 1933, pp. 249–269.

SANDMEYER, ELMER C. "California Anti-Chinese Legislation and the Federal Courts: A Study in Federal Relations." *Pacific Historical Review,* Vol. V, September 1936, pp. 189–211.

SAXTON, ALEXANDER P. *Bright Web in the Darkness* (a novel). New York: St. Martin's Press, 1958.

SIMON, HAL. "The Struggle for Jobs and for Negro Rights in the Trade Unions." *Political Affairs,* Vol. 29, No. 2, February 1950, pp. 33–48.

SPERO, STERLING D., and ABRAM L. HARRIS. *The Black Worker: The Negro and the Labor Movement.* New York: Columbia University Press, 1931.

"Union Program for Eliminating Discrimination." *Monthly Labor Review,* Vol. 86, No. 1, January 1963, pp. 58–59.

WARREN, SAMUEL E. "A Partial Background for the Study of the Development of Negro Labor: An Adventure in Teaching Certain Aspects of American

Labor History." *Journal of Negro History,* Vol. XXV, January 1940, pp. 45–59.

WEAVER, ROBERT C. *Negro Labor: A National Problem.* New York: Harcourt, Brace, 1946.

WILCOX, B. P. "Anti-Chinese Riots in Washington." *Washington Historical Quarterly,* Vol. XX, July 1929, pp. 204–212.

THE STATE OF THE LABOR MOVEMENT

ANNUAL REVIEW OF AMERICAN LABOR, *Monthly Labor Review:* 1950, Vol. 72, No. 2, February 1951, pp. 127–135; 1951, Vol. 74, No. 2, February 1952, pp. 130–139; 1952, Vol. 76, No. 2, February 1953, pp. 117–125; 1953, Vol. 77, No. 2, February 1954, pp. 121–127; 1954, Vol. 78, No. 7, February 1955, pp. 175–182; 1955, Vol. 79, No. 2, February 1956, pp. 150–155; 1956, Vol. 80, No. 2, February 1957, pp. 170–176; 1957, Vol. 81, No. 1, January 1958, pp. 6–13; 1958, Vol. 82, No. 1, January 1959, pp. 14–21; 1959, Vol. 83, No. 1, January 1960, pp. 10–17; 1960, Vol. 84, No. 1, January 1961, pp. 19–26; 1961, Vol. 85, No. 1, January 1962, pp. 1–8; 1962, Vol. 86, No. 1, January 1963, pp. 14–23.

BARKIN, SOLOMON. *The Decline of the Labor Movement and What Can Be Done About It.* Santa Barbara: Center for the Study of Democratic Institutions, 1961.

BELL, DANIEL. "The Next American Labor Movement." *Fortune,* April 1953, pp. 120–206.

BERNSTEIN, IRVING. "The Growth of American Unions." *The American Economic Review,* Vol. XLIV, No. 3, June 1954, pp. 301–318.

—————. "The Growth of American Unions, 1945–1960." *Labor History,* Vol. 2, No. 2, Spring 1961, pp. 131–157.

—————. "Union Growth and Structural Cycles." *Proceedings of the Seventh Annual Meeting of the Industrial Relations Research Association,* December 28–30, 1954, pp. 202–246. Madison: The Association, 1955.

BLOOMBERG, WARNER, JR., JOEL SEIDMAN, VICTOR HOFFMAN. *The State of the Unions.* Washington: National Publishing, 1960.

BOLINO, AUGUST C. "Sequential Growth and the Development of American Unionism." *Journal of Economic History,* Vol. XX, June 1960, pp. 314–317.

BROOKS, GEORGE W. "Reflections on the Changing Character of American Labor Unions." *Proceedings of the Ninth Annual Meeting of the Industrial Relations Research Association,* December 28–29, 1956, pp. 33–43. Madison: The Association, 1957.

—————. *The Sources of Vitality in the American Labor Movement.* Bulletin No. 41. Ithaca: New York State School of Industrial and Labor Relations, Cornell University, 1960.

CHAMBERLAIN, NEIL W. *Sourcebook on Labor,* chap. 24, "The Role of Unions in Society," pp. 1084–1101. New York: McGraw-Hill, 1958.

COCHRAN, BERT, ed. *American Labor in Midpassage.* New York: Monthly Review Press, 1959.

DUNLOP, JOHN. "The American Industrial Relations System in 1975," *U. S. Industrial Relations: The Next Twenty Years,* Jack Stieber, ed., pp. 27–54, 205–206. East Lansing: Michigan State University Press, 1958.

GALENSON, WALTER. "Why the American Labor Movement Is Not Socialist." *The American Review,* Vol. 1, No. 2, Winter 1961, pp. 1–19.

——————, and SEYMOUR MARTIN LIPSET. *Labor and Trade Unionism: An Interdisciplinary Reader.* New York: John Wiley, 1960.

HARRINGTON, MICHAEL, and PAUL JACOBS, eds. *Labor in a Free Society.* Berkeley: University of California Press, 1959.

INTERNATIONAL LABOR OFFICE. *The Trade Union Situation in the United States: Report of a Mission from the International Labour Office.* Geneva: ILO, 1960.

JACOBS, PAUL. *Old Before Its Time: Collective Bargaining at 28.* Santa Barbara: Center for the Study of Democratic Institutions, 1963.

KASSALOW, EVERETT M. "Occupational Frontiers of Trade Unionism in the United States." *Proceedings of the Thirteenth Annual Meeting of the Industrial Relations Research Association,* December 28–29, 1960, pp. 183–208. Madison: The Association, 1961.

KORNHAUSER, RUTH. "Some Social Determinants and Consequences of Union Membership." *Labor History,* Vol. 2, No. 1, Winter 1961, pp. 30–61.

KRISLOV, JOSEPH. "New Organizing by Unions During the 1950's." *Monthly Labor Review,* Vol. 83, No. 9, September 1960, pp. 922–924.

LENS, SIDNEY. *The Crisis of American Labor.* New York: Sagamore Press, 1959.

——————. *Left, Right and Center: Conflicting Forces in American Labor.* Hinsdale, Illinois: Henry Regnery, 1949.

MARSHALL, RAY. "Some Factors Influencing the Growth of Unions in the South." *Proceedings of the Thirteenth Annual Meeting of the Industrial Relations Research Association,* December 28–29, 1960, pp. 166–182. Madison: The Association, 1961.

MEANY, GEORGE. "What Labor Means by 'More'." *Fortune,* March 1955, pp. 1–12.

——————. *What Organized Labor Expects of Management,* pp. 4–11; and CHARLES R. SLIGH, JR. *What Management Expects of Organized Labor,* pp. 12–19. New York: National Association of Manufacturers, 1956.

MURPHY, GEORGE G. S., and ARNOLD ZELLNER. "Sequential Growth, the Labor—Safety-Valve Doctrine and the Development of American Unionism." *Journal of Economic History,* Vol. XIX, September 1959, pp. 402–421.

NEUFELD, MAURICE F. "The Historical Relationship of Liberals and Intellectuals to Organized Labor in the United States." *The Annals of the American Academy of Political and Social Science,* November 1963, pp. 115–128.

——————. "The Sense of History and the Annals of Labor." *Proceedings of the Fourteenth Annual Meeting of the Industrial Relations Research Association,* December 28–29, 1961, pp. 214–226. Madison: The Association, 1962.

POUND, ROSCOE. *Labor Unions and the Concept of Public Service.* Washington: American Enterprise Association, 1959.

REZLER, JULIUS. *Union Growth Reconsidered: A Critical Analysis of Recent Growth Theories.* New York: Kossuth Foundation, 1961.

ROBERTS, BENJAMIN C. *Trade Unions in a Free Society: Studies in the Organisation of Labour in Britain and the U.S.A.* London: Published for the Institute of Economic Affairs by Hutchinson, 1962.

—————. *Unions in America: A British View.* Princeton: Industrial Relations Section, Princeton University, 1959.

SHISTER, JOSEPH. "The Logic of Union Growth." *The Journal of Political Economy,* Vol. LXI, No. 5, October 1953, pp. 413–433.

SLICHTER, SUMNER H. "The Position of Trade Unions in the American Economy," *Labor in a Free Society,* Michael Harrington and Paul Jacobs, eds., pp. 17–44. Berkeley and Los Angeles: University of California Press, 1959.

SOLOMON, BENJAMIN. "Dimensions of Union Growth, 1900–1950." *Industrial and Labor Relations Review,* Vol. 9, No. 4, July 1956, pp. 544–561.

STIEBER, JACK, ed. *U. S. Industrial Relations: The Next Twenty Years.* East Lansing: Michigan State University Press, 1958.

TAFT, PHILIP. "Reflections on the Present State of the Labor Movement." *Proceedings of the Fourteenth Annual Meeting of the Industrial Relations Research Association,* December 28–29, 1961, pp. 3–14. Madison: The Association, 1962.

TROY, LEO. *Distribution of Union Membership Among the States, 1939 and 1953.* New York: National Bureau of Economic Research, 1957.

—————. "The Growth of Union Membership in the South, 1939–1953." *Southern Economic Journal,* Vol. 24, April 1958, pp. 407–420.

VELIE, LESTER. *Labor U.S.A.* New York: Harper, 1959.

WOLMAN, LEO. "Concentration of Union Membership." *Proceedings of the Fifth Annual Meeting of the Industrial Relations Research Association,* December 28–29, 1952, pp. 214–219. Madison: The Association, 1953.

—————. *Ebb and Flow in Trade Unionism.* New York: National Bureau of Economic Research, 1936.

—————. *The Growth of American Trade Unions, 1880–1923.* New York: National Bureau of Economic Research, 1924.

LEADERSHIP, DEMOCRACY, STRUCTURE, AND PRACTICES OF THE LABOR MOVEMENT

"The AFL–CIO Merger." *Industrial and Labor Relations Review,* Vol. 9, No. 3, April 1956 (entire issue).

GOLDBERG, ARTHUR J. *AFL–CIO: Labor United.* New York: McGraw-Hill, 1956.

KEMPTON, MURRAY. "Labor: The Alliance on the Plateau." *The Reporter,* June 30, 1955, pp. 26–30.

KERR, CLARK. *Unions and Union Leaders of Their Own Choosing.* New York: The Fund for the Republic, 1957.

LENS, SIDNEY. "Labor Unity Is No Panacea." *The Antioch Review,* Summer 1955, pp. 180–194.

—————. "Will Merged Labor Set New Goals?" *Harvard Business Review*, Vol. 34, No. 2, March-April 1956, pp. 57–63.

MADISON, CHARLES A. *American Labor Leaders: Personalities and Forces in the Labor Movement*. New York: Harper, 1950.

MILLS, C. WRIGHT. *The New Men of Power: America's Labor Leaders*. New York: Harcourt, Brace, 1948.

NATIONAL ASSOCIATION OF MANUFACTURERS. *Some Facts about the AFL-CIO Merger*. New York: The Association, 1956. (Processed).

ROE, WELLINGTON. *Juggernaut: American Labor in Action*. Philadelphia: Lippincott, 1948.

SEIDMAN, JOEL. *Democracy in the Labor Movement*. Bulletin 39. Ithaca: New York State School of Industrial and Labor Relations at Cornell University, February 1958.

U. S. CONGRESS. SENATE. Committee on Labor and Public Welfare. Subcommittee on Labor and Labor-Management Relations. *Communist Domination of Certain Unions*. Document 89. Washington: G.P.O., 1951.

U. S. DEPARTMENT OF LABOR. Bureau of Labor Statistics. Work Stoppages: 1950, Bulletin 1035; 1951, Bulletin 1090; 1952, Bulletin 1136; 1953, Bulletin 1163; 1954, Bulletin 1184; 1955, Bulletin 1196; 1956, Bulletin 1218; 1957, Bulletin 1234; 1958, Bulletin 1258; 1959, Bulletin 1278; 1960, Bulletin 1302; 1961, Bulletin 1339. Washington: G.P.O.

WEBER, ARNOLD R. "The Craft-Industrial Issue Revisited: A Study of Union Government." *Industrial and Labor Relations Review*, Vol. 16, No. 3, April 1963, pp. 381–404.

"What the AFL–CIO Merger Means." *U.S. News and World Report*, December 16, 1955, pp. 23–30.

POLITICAL ACTION

BIEMILLER, ANDREW J. "Labor Issues in the 1960 Political Campaign: A Labor View." *Proceedings of the Thirteenth Annual Meeting of the Industrial Relations Research Association*, December 28–29, 1960, pp. 218–229. Madison: The Association, 1961.

BLUM, ALBERT A. "The Political Alternatives of Labor." *Labor Law Journal*, September 1959, pp. 623–631.

BRAVERMAN, HARRY. "Labor and Politics." *Monthly Review*, July-August 1958, pp. 134–145.

BROWN, W. R. "State Regulation of Union Political Action." *Labor Law Journal*, November 1955, pp. 769–776.

CHAMBERLAIN, NEIL W. *Sourcebook on Labor*, chap. 6, "Political Activity," pp. 284–322. New York: McGraw-Hill, 1958.

DAVID, HENRY. "One Hundred Years of Labor in Politics," chap. 5, *The House of Labor*, J.B.S. Hardman and Maurice F. Neufeld, eds., pp. 90–112. New York: Prentice-Hall, 1951.

GAMBATESE, JOSEPH M. *Business and the Unions in Politics: A Post-Election Appraisal*. New York: Personnel Division, American Management Association, 1961.

LEISERSON, AVERY. "Organized Labor as a Pressure Group." *The Annals of the American Academy of Political and Social Science,* Vol. 274, March 1951, pp. 108–117.

PUBLIC OPINION INDEX FOR INDUSTRY. *Labor Union Power.* Princeton: The Index, May 1957.

SVIRIDOFF, MITCHELL. "Political Participation by Unions: The 1960 Situation." *Labor Law Journal,* July 1960, pp. 639–645.

City, Regional, and State Labor Movements and Conditions

City

BALTIMORE

GLOCKER, THEODORE W. *Trade Unionism in Baltimore Before the War of 1812*. Baltimore: Johns Hopkins University, 1907.

BUTTE

U. S. COMMISSION ON INDUSTRIAL RELATIONS (1912). *Final Report and Testimony*, Vol. IV, "Mining Conditions and Industrial Relations at Butte, Montana," pp. 3681–4095. Washington: G.P.O., 1916.

CHICAGO

BEHEN, DAVID M. *The Chicago Labor Movement, 1874–1896: Its Philosophical Bases*. Ph.D. Thesis, University of Chicago, 1954.

HALPER, ALBERT. *The Chute* (a novel about mail-order house workers during the 1930's; character study showing the discouragement of a routine job). New York: Viking, 1937.

MITTELMAN, EDWARD B. "Chicago Labor in Politics 1877–1896." *Journal of Political Economy*, Vol. XXVIII, No. 5, May 1920.

MORRIS, JANE K. *Julie* (a novel about a labor organizer and leader during the late 19th century). New York: McGraw-Hill, 1952.

MOTLEY, WILLARD. *We Fished All Night* (a novel about a labor leader before and after World War II). New York: Appleton-Century-Crofts, 1951.

NEWELL, BARBARA W. *Chicago and the Labor Movement: Metropolitan Unionism in the 1930's*. Urbana: University of Illinois Press, 1961.

O'BRIEN, HOWARD V. *New Men for Old* (a novel about preserving plant workers during the early 1900's). New York: M. Kennerley, 1914.

SINCLAIR, UPTON B. *The Jungle* (a novel about the horror and futility of a stockyard worker's life and failure in attempts to organize during the turn of the century). New York: Doubleday, Doran, 1906.

STEAD, WILLIAM THOMAS. *Chicago Today: Or, The Labour War in America*. London: "Review of Reviews" Office, 1894.

U. S. COMMISSION ON INDUSTRIAL RELATIONS (1912). *Final Report and Testimony*, Vol. IV, "Industrial Conditions in Chicago," pp. 3173–3457. Washington: G.P.O., 1916.

KANSAS CITY

U. S. CONGRESS. HOUSE. Committee on Education and Labor. *Strikes and Racketeering in the Kansas City Area*. Washington: G.P.O., 1953.

LOS ANGELES

BAISDEN, RICHARD N. *Labor Unions in Los Angeles Politics*. Ph.D. Thesis, University of Chicago, 1958–1959.

STIMSON, GRACE HEILMAN. *Rise of the Labor Movement in Los Angeles*. Berkeley: University of California Press, 1955.

TIPTON, GENE B. *The Labor Movement in the Los Angeles Area During the Nineteen-Forties*. Ph.D. Thesis, University of California, 1953.

U. S. COMMISSION ON INDUSTRIAL RELATIONS (1912). *Final Report and Testimony*, Vol. VI, "The Open and Closed Shop Controversy in Los Angeles," pp. 5485–5999. Washington: G.P.O., 1916.

MINNEAPOLIS

WALKER, CHARLES R. *American City: A Rank-and-File History*. New York: Farrar and Rinehart, 1937.

MUSCATINE

FEDERAL COUNCIL OF THE CHURCHES OF CHRIST IN AMERICA. Commission on the Church and Social Service. *Report on the Industrial Situation at Muscatine, Iowa, by a Special Committee* (Button Workers Strike, 1911). New York: The Council, 1912.

NEW ORLEANS

SHUGG, ROGER WALLACE. "The New Orleans General Strike of 1892." *Louisiana Historical Quarterly*, Vol. XXI, April 1938, pp. 547–560.

NEW YORK CITY

HAYES, ALFRED. *Shadow of Heaven* (a novel about a disenchanted labor leader during the mid-1940's). New York: Howell, Soskin, 1947.

HAYES, DORSHA. *Who Walk with the Earth* (a novel about a union education director showing intra-union conflict). New York: Harper, 1945.

VON RHAU, HENRY. *Fraternally Yours* (a novel on labor racketeering). Boston: Houghton Mifflin, 1949.

PADUCAH

Tripp, L. Reed, J. Keith Mann, and Frederick T. Downs. *Labor-Management Relations in the Paducah Area of Western Kentucky.* Bureau of Business Research Bulletin No. 28. Lexington: University of Kentucky, 1954.

PATERSON

U. S. Commission on Industrial Relations (1912). *Final Report and Testimony,* Vol. III, "Industrial Conditions and Relations in Paterson, N. J.," pp. 2411–2645. Washington: G.P.O., 1916.

PHILADELPHIA

Bernstein, Leonard. "The Working People of Philadelphia from Colonial Times to the General Strike of 1835." *Pennsylvania Magazine of History and Biography,* Vol. LXXIV, July 1950, pp. 322–339.

Sullivan, William A. "Philadelphia Labor During the Jackson Era." *Pennsylvania History,* Vol. XV, October 1948, pp. 305–320.

U. S. Commission on Industrial Relations (1912). *Final Report and Testimony,* Vol. III, "General Industrial Relations and Conditions in Philadelphia," pp. 2647–2730. Washington: G.P.O., 1916.

PITTSBURGH

Joseph, Myron L. *The Operation and Effects of the Taft-Hartley Law in the Pittsburgh District.* Ph.D. Thesis, University of Wisconsin, 1953.

Sullivan, William A. "The Pittsburgh Working Men's Party." *Western Pennsylvania Historical Magazine,* Vol. XXXIV, September 1951, pp. 151–161.

PORTLAND

U. S. Commission on Industrial Relations (1912). *Final Report and Testimony,* Vol. V, "General Industrial Conditions and Relations in Portland, Oregon," pp. 4573–4770. Washington: G.P.O., 1916.

ROCHESTER

McKelvey, Blake. *Rochester: An Emerging Metropolis, 1925–1961.* (Chapters on labor.) Rochester: Christopher Press, 1961.

——————. *Rochester, the Flower City, 1855–1890.* (Chapters on labor.) Cambridge: Harvard University Press, 1949.

——————. *Rochester: The Quest for Quality, 1890–1925.* (Chapters on labor.) Cambridge: Harvard University Press, 1956.

——————. *Rochester, the Water-Power City, 1812–1854.* (Chapters on labor.) Cambridge: Harvard University Press, 1945.

ST. LOUIS

BURBANK, DAVID T. *City of Little Bread: The St. Louis General Strike of 1877, the History of an American Strike.* St. Louis: David T. Burbank, 1957.

NOLEN, RUSSELL M. "The Labor Movement in St. Louis from 1860 to 1890." *Missouri Historical Review,* Vol. XXXIV, January 1940, pp. 157–181.

—————. "The Labor Movement in St. Louis Prior to the Civil War." *Missouri Historical Review,* Vol. XXXIV, October 1939, pp. 18–37.

SAN FRANCISCO

BEAN, WALTON. *Boss Ruef's San Francisco: The Story of the Union Labor Party, Big Business, and the Graft Prosecution.* Berkeley: University of California Press, 1952.

CRONIN, BERNARD C. *Father Yorke and the Labor Movement in San Francisco, 1900–1910.* Washington: Catholic University of America Press, 1943.

HICHBORN, FRANKLIN. *The System as Uncovered by the San Francisco Graft Prosecution.* San Francisco: Barry, 1915.

KNIGHT, ROBERT E. L. *Industrial Relations in the San Francisco Bay Area, 1900–1918.* Berkeley: University of California Press, 1960.

RYAN, FREDERICK LYNNE. *Industrial Relations in the San Francisco Building Trades.* Norman: University of Oklahoma Press, 1936.

U. S. COMMISSION ON INDUSTRIAL RELATIONS (1912). *Final Report and Testimony,* Vol. VI, "General Industrial Relations and Conditions in San Francisco," pp. 5421–5472. Washington: G.P.O., 1916.

SEATTLE

SEATTLE UNION RECORD PUBLISHING CO., INC. *The Seattle General Strike: An Account of What Happened in Seattle and Especially in the Seattle Labor Movement during the General Strike, February 6 to 11, 1919.* Seattle: The Company, 1919.

U. S. COMMISSION ON INDUSTRIAL RELATIONS (1912). *Final Report and Testimony,* Vol. V, "Industrial Relations and Remedies, Seattle, Washington," pp. 4097–4571. Washington: G.P.O., 1916.

SPRINGFIELD

HARDWICK, A. F., ed. and comp. *History of the Central Labor Union of Springfield, Massachusetts, with Some of the Pioneers: Brief Sketches of Affiliated Unions, 1887–1912.* Springfield: The Union, 1912.

STOCKTON

U. S. COMMISSION ON INDUSTRIAL RELATIONS (1912). *Final Report and Testimony,* Vol. V, "Open and Closed Shop Controversies in Stockton, California," pp. 4771–4909. Washington: G.P.O., 1916.

Regional

MIDWEST

KAPSTEIN, ISRAEL J. *Something of a Hero* (a novel about effects of industrialism on various people from 1907 to 1929). New York: Knopf, 1941.

NEW ENGLAND

FIELD, BEN. *Piper Tompkins* (a novel about a defense plant worker showing change of an individual from "lone wolf" to ardent unionist during World War II). New York: Doubleday, 1946.

FREEMAN, MARY E. WILKINS. *The Portion of Labor* (a novel about factory workers during late nineteenth century—one of the early capital vs. labor novels). New York: Harper, 1901.

ROBINSON, HARRIET H. *Early Factory Labor in New England.* Boston: Wright & Potter, 1889.

TURNER, GEORGE K. *The Taskmasters* (a novel about mill workers during 1890's—concern with industrial feudalism and political controls). New York: McClure, Phillips, 1902.

NORTHWEST

DAS, RAJANI K. *Hindustani Workers on the Pacific Coast.* Berlin: Walter de Gruyten, 1923.

STONE, HARRY W. "Beginnings of Labor Movement in the Pacific Northwest." *Oregon Historical Quarterly,* Vol. XLVII, June 1946, pp. 155–164.

THORSETH, MATTHEA. *Color of Ripening* (a novel about a Norwegian-American labor leader and his activities in the IWW movement around 1915). Seattle: Superior Publishers, 1949.

SOUTH

BERGLUND, ABRAHAM, GEORGE T. STARNES, and FRANK T. DeVYVER. *Labor in the Industrial South: A Survey of Wages and Living Conditions in Three Major Industries of the New Industrial South.* Institute for Research in the Social Sciences, Monograph No. 9. Charlottesville: University of Virginia, 1930.

DeVYVER, FRANK T. "The Present Status of Labor Unions in the South, 1948." *The Southern Economic Journal,* Vol. XVI, No. 1, July 1949.

"Labor Drives South." *Fortune Magazine,* Vol. XXXIV, No. 5, November 1946.

McCoy, A. D. *Thoughts on Labor in the South: Past, Present and Future.* New Orleans: Blelock, 1865.

MEIKLEJOHN, KENNETH, and PETER NEHEMKIS. *Southern Labor in Revolt.* New York: Intercollegiate Student Council of the League for Industrial Democracy, 1930.

"Southern Campaign, 1946." *Labor and Nation,* April-May 1946, pp. 32–46.
TIPPETT, THOMAS. *When Southern Labor Stirs.* New York: J. Cape and H. Smith, 1931.

State

ALASKA

U. S. BUREAU OF LABOR STATISTICS. *The Status of Labor in Puerto Rico, Alaska, Hawaii.* Bulletin No. 1191. Washington: G.P.O., 1956.

ARKANSAS

SIMON, CHARLIE M. *The Share-Cropper* (a novel during the 1930's about sharecroppers' attempts at organizing, with resultant blacklisting and other social evils). New York: Dutton, 1937.

CALIFORNIA

CHEVALIER, HAAKON M. *For Us the Living* (a novel about farm laborers and longshoremen from 1929–1941—a murder mystery serves as vehicle for telling this story of labor's struggle for organization). New York: Knopf, 1948.

CROSS, IRA BROWN. *History of the Labor Movement in California.* Berkeley: University of California Press, 1935.

EAVES, LUCILE. *A History of California Labor Legislation: With an Introductory Sketch of the San Francisco Labor Movement.* Berkeley: University of California, 1910.

KAUER, RALPH. "The Workingmen's Party of California." *Pacific Historical Review,* Vol. XIII, September 1944, pp. 278–291.

MCENTIRE, DAVIS. *The Labor Force in California: A Study of Characteristics and Trends in Labor Force, Employment, and Occupations in California, 1900–1950.* Berkeley: University of California Press, 1952.

MCWILLIAMS, CAREY. *Factories in the Field: The Story of Migratory Farm Labor in California.* Boston: Little, Brown, 1939.

MITCHELL, RUTH C. *Of Human Kindness* (a novel about farm workers and owners during the 1930's). New York: Appleton-Century, 1940.

OLDER, FREMONT. *My Own Story.* San Francisco: Call Publishers, 1919.

RONEY, FRANK. *Frank Roney, Irish Rebel and California Labor Leader.* Berkeley: University of California, 1931.

STEDMAN, J. C., and R. A. LEONARD. *The Workingmen's Party of California.* San Francisco: Bacon and Co., 1878.

STEINBECK, JOHN. *In Dubious Battle* (a novel about fruit pickers, social injustice, and a strike during early 1930's). New York: Covici-Friede, 1936.

TOBENKIN, ELIAS. *House of Conrad* (a novel about a conservative labor leader from 1868–1916). Philadelphia: Stokes, 1918.

COLORADO

BARDWELL, GEORGE E., and HARRY SELIGSON. *Organized Labor and Political Action in Colorado, 1900–1960.* Denver: College of Business Administration, University of Denver, 1959.

U. S. BUREAU OF LABOR. *A Report on Labor Disturbances in the State of Colorado, From 1880 to 1904, Inclusive, with Correspondence Relating Thereto.* Washington: G.P.O., 1905. (Printed as Senate Document No. 122, 58th Congress, 3rd Session.)

CONNECTICUT

PRESTON, JOHN H. *The Liberals* (a novel where the owner of the leading factory, a liberal, is opposed by strikers and the CIO). New York: John Day, 1938.

HAWAII

JOHANNESSEN, EDWARD. *The Hawaiian Labor Movement: A Brief History.* Boston: Bruce Humphries, 1956.

PERLMAN, MARK. "Organized Labor in Hawaii." *Labor Law Journal,* Vol. 3, No. 4, April 1952, pp. 263–275.

——————, and JOHN B. FERGUSON. *Labor, Trade Unionism and the Competitive Menace in Hawaii.* Honolulu: Industrial Relations Center, University of Hawaii, 1952.

ROBERTS, HAROLD SELIG, ed. *Labor-Management Relations in Hawaii,* 3 parts. Honolulu: University of Hawaii, 1955–1956.

U. S. BUREAU OF LABOR STATISTICS. *The Status of Labor in Puerto Rico, Alaska, Hawaii.* Bulletin No. 1191. Washington: G.P.O., 1956.

U. S. CONGRESS. HOUSE. Committee on Un-American Activities. *Hearings regarding Communist Activities in the Territory of Hawaii,* 4 vols. Washington: G.P.O., 1951.

U. S. CONGRESS. SENATE. Committee on Labor and Public Welfare. *Hawaiian Labor Situation.* Washington: G.P.O., 1949.

IDAHO

HARRIMAN, JOB. *The Class Struggle in Idaho.* New York: Labor Publishing Association, 1904.

ILLINOIS

DESTLER, CHESTER McA. "Consummation of a Labor-Populist Alliance in Illinois, 1894." *Mississippi Valley Historical Review,* Vol. XXVII, March 1941, pp. 589–602.

STALEY, EUGENE. *History of the Illinois State Federation of Labor.* Chicago: University of Chicago Press, 1930.

INDIANA

AYER, HUGH MASON. *Hoosier Labor in the Second World War.* Ph.D. Thesis, Indiana University, 1957.

VAN VALER, RALPH WALDEN. "The Indiana State Federation of Labor." *Indiana Magazine of History,* Vol. XI, March 1915, pp. 40–58.

IOWA

BISSELL, RICHARD P. *7½ Cents* (a contemporary novel about pajama factory workers who are about to strike for a 7½ cent increase). Boston: Little, Brown, 1953.

DOWNEY, EZEKIEL H. *History of Labor Legislation in Iowa.* Iowa City: The State Historical Society of Iowa, 1910.

STUCKEY, LORIN. *The Iowa State Federation of Labor.* Iowa City: University of Iowa, 1916.

KANSAS

WALKER, EDITH and DOROTHY LEIBENGOOD. "Labor Organizations in Kansas in the Early Eighties." *Kansas Historical Quarterly,* Vol. IV, August 1935, pp. 283–290.

MASSACHUSETTS

GARSIDE, EDWARD B. *Cranberry Red* (a novel about cranberry factory workers during the 1930's—proletarian novel about oppressed "hyphenated" American workers). New York: Little, Brown, 1938.

HEINTZ, ALBERT M., and JOHN R. WHITNEY. *History of the Massachusetts State Federaton of Labor, 1887–1935.* Worcester: The Federation, 1935.

MICHIGAN

GLAZER, SIDNEY. "The Michigan Labor Movement." *Michigan History Magazine,* Vol. XXIX, January–March 1945, pp. 73–82.

MINNESOTA

ENGBERG, GEORGE B. "The Knights of Labor in Minnesota." *Minnesota History,* Vol. XXII, December 1941, pp. 367–390.

——————. "The Rise of Organized Labor in Minnesota." *Minnesota History,* Vol. XXI, December 1940, pp. 372–394.

MITAU, G. THEODORE. "The Democratic-Farmer-Labor Party Schism of 1948." *Minnesota History,* Vol. XXXIV, Spring 1955, pp. 187–194.

MORLAN, ROBERT L. "The Nonpartisan League and the Minnesota Campaign of 1918." *Minnesota History,* Vol. XXXIV, Summer 1955, pp. 221–232.

NAFTALIN, ARTHUR. "The Tradition of Protest and the Roots of the Farmer-Labor Party." *Minnesota History,* Vol. XXXV, June 1956, pp. 53–63.

MISSOURI

FORSYTHE, EDWIN JAMES. *The St. Louis Central Trades and Labor Union, 1887–1945.* Ph.D. Thesis, University of Missouri, 1956.

MERIWETHER, LEE. "A Century of Labor in Missouri." *The Missouri Historical Review,* Vol. XV, No. 1, October 1920, pp. 163–175.

NEW JERSEY

NADWORNY, MILTON J. "New Jersey Workingmen and the Jacksonians." *New Jersey Historical Society Proceedings: A Magazine of New Jersey History,* Vol. LXVII, July 1949, pp. 185–198.

NEW YORK

GROAT, GEORGE C. *Trade Unions and the Law in New York.* New York: Columbia University Press, 1905.

HURWITZ, HOWARD L. *Theodore Roosevelt and Labor in New York State, 1880–1900.* New York: Columbia University Press, 1943.

MCKEE, SAMUEL, JR. *Labor in Colonial New York, 1664–1776.* New York: Columbia University Press, 1935.

MAHER, RICHARD A. *Gold Must Be Tried By Fire* (a novel about industrial conditions among paper mill workers in northern New York around 1915). New York: Macmillan, 1917.

NEWHOUSE, EDWARD. *This Is Your Day* (a novel about a young communist's attempts to organize farm workers during the 1930's). New York: Lee Furman, 1937.

NEW YORK STATE. FACTORY INVESTIGATING COMMISSION (Robert Wagner, chairman). *Preliminary Report Transmitted to Legislature, March 1, 1912.* Albany: The Argus Co., 1912.

—————. —————. *Second Report Transmitted to Legislature, January 15, 1913.* Senate Document 36. Albany: J. B. Lyon Co., 1913.

—————. —————. *Third Report Transmitted to Legislature, February 14, 1914.* Assembly Document 28. Albany: J. B. Lyon Co., 1914.

—————. —————. *Fourth Report Transmitted to Legislature, February 15, 1915.* Senate Document 43. Albany: J. B. Lyon Co., 1915.

WINDMULLER, JOHN P. *Union Organization and Collective Bargaining in Manufacturing and Public Utility Industries in Chemung County, New York.* M.S. Thesis, New York State School of Industrial and Labor Relations, Cornell University, 1949.

NORTH CAROLINA

JOLLEY, HARLEY E. "The Labor Movement in North Carolina, 1880–1922." *North Carolina Historical Review,* Vol. XXX, No. 3, July 1953, pp. 354–375.

OHIO

CLOPPER, EDWARD S. "The Ohio Mechanics Institute—Its 125th Anniversary." *Bulletin of the Historical and Philosophical Society of Ohio*, Vol. XI, No. 3, July 1953, pp. 179–191.

HATCHER, HARLAN H. *Central Standard Time* (a novel about manufacturing workers' industrial conflict during 1934). New York: Farrar & Rinehart, 1937.

OKLAHOMA

LANHAM, EDWIN M. *The Stricklands* (a novel about an organizer of tenant farmers during the 1930's). Boston: Little, Brown, 1939.

U. S. WORK PROJECTS ADMINISTRATION, FEDERAL WRITERS' PROJECT, OKLAHOMA WRITERS' PROGRAM. *Labor History of Oklahoma*. Oklahoma City: A. M. Van Horn, 1940.

OREGON

MORGAN, MURRAY C. (Cromwell Murray, pseud.). *Viewless Winds* (a novel about labor-capital conflict in a logging town). New York: Dutton, 1949.

TOBIE, HARVEY ELMER. "Oregon Labor Disputes, 1919–23: I, The Living Wage." *Oregon Historical Quarterly*, Vol. XLVIII, March 1947, pp. 7–24; "II, Government and Wages," September 1947, pp. 195–213; "III, Local Controversies," December 1947, pp. 309–321.

PENNSYLVANIA

COLEMAN, JAMES W. *Labor Disturbances in Pennsylvania, 1850–1880*. Washington: Catholic University of America, 1936.

HERRICK, CHEESMAN ABIAH. *White Servitude in Pennsylvania: Indentured and Redemption Labor in Colony and Commonwealth*. Philadelphia: McVey, 1926.

RICKER, RALPH R. *The Greenback-Labor Movement in Pennsylvania, 1865–1880*. Ph.D. Thesis, Pennsylvania State University, 1955.

SULLIVAN, WILLIAM A. *The Industrial Worker in Pennsylvania 1800–1840*. Harrisburg: Historical and Museum Commission, 1955.

SOUTH CAROLINA

SNOWDEN, YATES. *Notes on Labor Organizations in South Carolina, 1742–1861*. Bulletin 38, Part 4. Columbia: University of South Carolina, 1914.

SOUTH DAKOTA

U.S. COMMISSION ON INDUSTRIAL RELATIONS (1912). *Final Report and Testimony*, Vol. IV, "Industrial Conditions and Relations in the Gold-Mining Operations Lead and Black Hills, S. D.," pp. 3537–3679. Washington: G.P.O., 1916.

TENNESSEE

Givens, Charles G. *The Devil Takes a Hill Town* (a novel about factory workers, AFL and CIO, during 1930's—described as the hillbilly workers' "Green Pastures"). Indianapolis: Bobbs-Merrill, 1939.

TEXAS

Allen, Ruth A. *Chapters in the History of Organized Labor in Texas.* Austin: University of Texas, 1941.

Meyers, Frederic. "The Growth of Collective Bargaining in Texas—A Newly Industrialized Area." *Proceedings of the Seventh Annual Meeting of the Industrial Relations Research Association,* December 28–30, 1954, pp. 286–297. Madison: The Association, 1955.

WASHINGTON

Grey, Zane. *Desert of Wheat* (a novel, anti-IWW, during 1917–1920). New York: Grossett & Dunlap, 1918.

WEST VIRGINIA

Harris, Evelyn L. K., and Frank J. Krebs. *From Humble Beginnings: West Virginia State Federation of Labor, 1903–1957.* Charleston: West Virginia Labor History Publishing Fund, 1960.

Skidmore, Hubert. *Hawk's Nest* (a novel about tunnel-drillers during the early 1930's—a tragic story of the victims of silicosis). New York: Doubleday, Doran, 1941.

WISCONSIN

Altmeyer, Arthur J. *The Industrial Commission of Wisconsin: A Case Study in Labor Law Administration.* Madison: University of Wisconsin, 1932.

Taber, Gladys. *A Star To Steer By* (a novel about a mill town strike). Philadelphia: Macrae Smith, 1938.

Witte, Edwin E. "Labor in Wisconsin History." *Wisconsin Magazine of History,* Vol. XXXV, Winter 1951, pp. 83–86, 137–142.

American Labor and
International Affairs

ALEXANDER, ROBERT J. "International Labor Groups in the Americas." *Labor Law Journal*, Vol. 13, No. 7, July 1962, pp. 507–515.

—————. "Labor and Inter-American Relations." *American Academy of Political and Social Science Annals*, Vol. 334, March 1961, pp. 41–53.

AMERICAN FEDERATION OF LABOR. *Labor and the War: American Federation of Labor and the Labor Movements of Europe and Latin America. From the Proceedings of the Conventions of 1914–15–16–17–18 American Federation of Labor and from The American Federationist and Labor's Book of All Colors as Published in the American Federationist November and December, 1916, January, May, and November, 1917, and April, 1918.* Washington: American Federation of Labor, 1918.

AMERICAN FEDERATION OF LABOR. Free Trade Union Committee. *American Labor Looks at the World*, Vols. 1–9, 1947–1955. New York: Free Trade Union Committee, 1947–1955.

BRUCKNER, MOLLY ACREMAN. *The Role of Labor in the Conduct of United States Foreign Affairs.* Ph.D. Thesis, University of Chicago, 1950.

CARWELL, JOSEPH. *The International Role of American Labor.* Ph.D. Thesis, Columbia University, 1956.

CORNELL UNIVERSITY, NEW YORK STATE SCHOOL OF INDUSTRIAL AND LABOR RELATIONS. *American Labor's Role in Less Developed Countries: A Report on a Conference Held at Cornell University, October 12–17, 1958.* Ithaca: The School, 1959.

DALE, L. "La Participation du Mouvement Syndical Americain a l'establissement de l'Organisation internationale du travail." *Relations Industrielles,* Quebec, Vol. 17, No. 1, January 1962, pp. 34–42.

DAVIES, MARGARET M. *The Role of the American Trade Union Representatives in the Aid-to-Greece Program.* Ph.D. Thesis, University of Washington, 1960.

DUBINSKY, D. "Rift and Realignment in World Labor." *Foreign Affairs,* Vol. 27, January 1949, pp. 232–245.

EDELMAN, MURRAY. "Labor's Influence in Foreign Policy." *Labor Law Journal,* May 1954, pp. 323–329.

FINGER, ELEANOR. "Labor and European Recovery," chap. 12, *The House of Labor,* J.B.S. Hardman and Maurice F. Neufeld, eds., pp. 159–167. New York: Prentice-Hall, 1951.

GOMBERG, WILLIAM. "Labor's Participation in the European Productivity Program: A Study of Frustration." *Political Science Quarterly,* Vol. 74, No. 2, June 1959, pp. 240–255.

GOMPERS, SAMUEL. *Seventy Years of Life and Labor,* Vol. II, Chapters XVII, XXXVII–XLVI. New York: Dutton, 1925.

HANDLEY, WILLIAM J. "American Labor and World Affairs." *Annals of the American Academy of Political and Social Science,* Vol. 274, March 1951, pp. 131–138.

HARDY, MARGARET. *The Influence of Organized Labor on the Foreign Policy of the United States.* Liége, Belgium: H. Vaillant-Carmanne, 1936.

HEAPS, DAVID. "Union Participation in Foreign Aid Programs." *Industrial and Labor Relations Review,* Vol. 9, No. 1, October 1955, pp. 100–108.

JACOBSON, H. R. "Labor, the U.N. and the Cold War." *International Organization,* Vol. 11, No. 1, Winter 1957, pp. 55–67.

LASSER, DAVID. "Labor and World Affairs." *Foreign Policy Reports,* Vol. XXV, No. 13, November 15, 1949.

LEUCK, MIRIAM SIMONS. *The American Socialist and Labor Mission to Europe 1918; Background, Activities and Significance: An Experiment in Democratic Diplomacy.* Ph.D. Thesis, Northwestern University, 1941.

LODGE, GEORGE C. *Spearheads of Democracy: Labor in the Developing Countries.* New York: Harper and Row, 1962.

LORWIN, LEWIS L. *The International Labor Movement.* New York: Harper, 1953.

—————. *Labor and Internationalism.* New York: Macmillan, 1929.

LORWIN, VAL R. "Labor's International Relations," chap. 11, *The House of Labor,* J.B.S. Hardman and Maurice F. Neufeld, eds., pp. 145–158. New York: Prentice-Hall, 1951.

LOVESTONE, JAY. "American Labor and the World Crisis." *Proceedings of the Ninth Annual Meeting of the Industrial Relations Research Association,* December 28–29, 1956, pp. 50–66. Madison: The Association, 1957.

McKEE, DELBER L. *The American Federation of Labor and American Foreign Policy.* Ph.D. Thesis, Stanford University, 1953.

—————. "Samuel Gompers, the A. F. of L., and Imperialism, 1895–1900." *The Historian,* Vol. XXI, February 1959, pp. 187–199.

MADDOX, WILLIAM P. "Labor's Stake in American Foreign Policy." *Political Science Quarterly,* Vol. 50, No. 3, September 1935, pp. 405–418.

MORSE, DAVID A. "Labor and American Foreign Policy." *Industrial and Labor Relations Review,* Vol. 1, No. 1, October 1947, pp. 18–28.

ROSS, MICHAEL. "American Labor's World Responsibilities." *Foreign Affairs,* Vol. 30, October 1951, pp. 112–122.

—————. "American Unions and West European Recovery." *Proceedings of the Fourth Annual Meeting of the Industrial Relations Research Association,* December 28–29, 1951, pp. 94–99. Madison: The Association, 1952.

SNOW, SINCLAIR. *Samuel Gompers and the Pan-American Federation of Labor.* Ph.D. Thesis, University of Virginia, 1960.

STURMTHAL, ADOLF. "The Labor Movement Abroad," chap. VI, *A Decade of Industrial Relations Research 1945–1956,* Neil Chamberlain, Frank C. Pierson, and Theresa Wolfson, eds. New York: Harper, 1958.

Van der Slice, Austin. *International Labor, Diplomacy and Peace, 1914–1919.* Philadelphia: University of Pennsylvania, 1941.

Windmuller, John P. *American Labor and the International Labor Movement 1940 to 1953.* Ithaca: The Institute of International Industrial and Labor Relations, Cornell University, 1954.

————. "Foreign Affairs and the AFL–CIO." *Industrial and Labor Relations Review,* Vol. 9, No. 3, April 1956, pp. 419–432.

————. "ICFTU After Ten Years: Problems and Prospects." *Industrial and Labor Relations Review,* Vol. 14, No. 2, January 1961, pp. 257–272.

Theories of the American Labor Movement

"American Labor Theory, Philosophy: Reappraisal of General Motivations and Aims of American Trade Union Movement—9 Articles." *Labor and Nation*, Vol. VII, No. 1, Winter 1951, pp. 43–71.

BAUDER, RUSSELL. "Three Interpretations of the American Trade Union Movement." *Social Forces*, Vol. 22, No. 2, December 1943, pp. 215–224.

BILLINGTON, RAY ALLEN. *The American Frontier*. Washington, D.C.: Service Center for Teachers of History, A Service of the American Historical Association, Publication Number 8, 1958.

COMMONS, JOHN R. *Labor and Administration*, chap. 14, "The American Shoemakers, 1648–1895." New York: Macmillan, 1913.

DOLNICK, DAVID. "History and Theory of the Labor Movement," chap. 5, *Employment Relations Research: A Summary and Appraisal*, Heneman, Brown, Chandler, Kahn, Parnes, and Shultz, eds., pp. 172–189. New York: Harper, 1960.

DUNLOP, JOHN T. "The Development of Labor Organization: A Theoretical Frame-Work," *Insights into Labor Issues*, Richard A. Lester and Joseph Shister, eds., pp. 163–193. New York: Macmillan, 1948.

GULICK, CHARLES A., and MELVIN K. BERS. "Insight and Illusion in Perlman's Theory of the Labor Movement." *Industrial and Labor Relations Review*, Vol. 6, No. 4, July 1953, pp. 510–531.

HARDMAN, J. B. S. "From 'Job-Consciousness' to Power Accumulation." *Proceedings of the Third Annual Meeting of the Industrial Relations Research Association*, December 28–29, 1950, pp. 146–157. Madison, Wisconsin: The Association, 1951.

HOLT, W. STULL. "Hegel, the Turner Hypothesis, and the Safety-Valve Theory." *Agricultural History*, Vol. XXII, July 1948, pp. 175–176.

HOXIE, ROBERT F. "A Sociopsychological Interpretation," *Unions, Management and the Public*, E. Wight Bakke and Clark Kerr, eds., pp. 35–38. New York: Harcourt, Brace, 1948.

INDUSTRIAL RELATIONS RESEARCH ASSOCIATION. *Interpreting the Labor Movement*. Madison, Wisconsin: The Association, 1952.

KERR, CLARK, and ABRAHAM SIEGEL. "The Structuring of the Labor Force in Industrial Society: New Dimensions and New Questions." *Industrial and Labor Relations Review*, Vol. 8, No. 2, January 1955, pp. 151–168.

KONVITZ, MILTON R. "An Empirical Theory of the Labor Movement: W. Stanley Jevons." *Philosophical Review*, Vol. LVII, No. 1, January 1948, pp. 59–76.

LIPSET, SEYMOUR MARTIN. "Trade Unions and Social Structure." *Industrial Relations*. Part I: Vol. 1, No. 1, October 1961, pp. 75–89; Part II: Vol. 1, No. 2, February 1962, pp. 89–110.

MCKEE, DON K. "Daniel De Leon: A Reappraisal." *Labor History*, Vol. 1, No. 3, Fall 1960, pp. 264–297.

PARKER, CARLETON H. *The Casual Laborer and Other Essays*. New York: Harcourt, Brace & Howe, 1920.

PERLMAN, MARK. *Labor Union Theories in America: Background and Development*. Evanston: Row, Peterson, 1958.

PERLMAN, SELIG. *A Theory of the Labor Movement*. New York: Macmillan, 1928.

PHELPS, ORME W. "The Trade Unionism of Henry Simons." *Proceedings of the Seventh Annual Meeting of the Industrial Relations Research Association*, December 28–30, 1954, pp. 280–285. Madison, Wisconsin: The Association, 1955.

SHANNON, FRED A. "The Homestead Act and the Labor Surplus." *American Historical Review*, Vol. XLI, July 1936, pp. 637–651.

——————. "A Post Mortem on the Labor-Safety-Valve Theory." *Agricultural History*, Vol. XIX, January 1945, pp. 31–37.

SIMLER, NORMAN J. "The Safety-Valve Doctrine Re-evaluated." *Agricultural History*, Vol. XXXII, October 1958, pp. 250–257.

SIMONS, HENRY C. "Some Reflections on Syndicalism." *The Journal of Political Economy*, Vol. 52, No. 1, March 1944, pp. 1–25.

SOFFER, BENSON. "A Theory of Trade Union Development: The Role of the 'Autonomous' Workman." *Labor History*, Vol. 1, No. 2, Spring 1960, pp. 141–163.

STURMTHAL, ADOLF. "Comments on Selig Perlman's 'A Theory of the Labor Movement.'" *Industrial and Labor Relations Review*, Vol. 4, No. 4, July 1951, pp. 483–496.

TAFT, PHILIP. "Commons-Perlman Theory: A Summary." *Proceedings of the Third Annual Meeting of the Industrial Relations Research Association*, December 28–29, 1950, pp. 140–145. Madison, Wisconsin: The Association, 1951.

——————. "A Rereading of Selig Perlman's 'A Theory of the Labor Movement.'" *Industrial and Labor Relations Review*, Vol. 4, No. 1, October 1950, pp. 70–77.

TANNENBAUM, FRANK. *The Labor Movement: Its Conservative Functions and Social Consequences*. New York: Putnam, 1921.

——————. *A Philosophy of Labor*. New York: Knopf, 1951.

TURNER, F. J. *The Frontier in American History*. New York: Holt, 1920.

ULMAN, LLOYD. *The Rise of the National Trade Union*, chap. 18, "Some Theories of the Labor Movement." Cambridge: Harvard University Press, 1955.

WRIGHT, DAVID MCCORD, ed. *The Impact of the Labor Union*. New York: Harcourt, Brace, 1951.

Individual Occupations, Trades, and Industries

Agriculture

ANDERSON, NELS. *Men on the Move*. Chicago: University of Chicago Press, 1940.

BECKER, WILLIAM. "Conflict as a Source of Solidarity: Some Notes on the California Farm Labor Scene." *The Journal of Social Issues*, Vol. IX, No. 1, 1953. Special Issue: "Trade Unions and Minority Problems," Daniel Bell and Seymour Martin Lipset, eds.

CHEVALIER, HAAKON M. *For Us the Living* (a murder mystery novel dealing with California farm laborers and longshoremen, 1929–1941). New York: Knopf, 1948.

COX, LAWANDA F. "The American Agricultural Wage Earner, 1865–1900: The Emergence of a Modern Labor Problem." *Agricultural History*, Vol. XXII, April 1948, pp. 95–114.

DANIEL, FRANZ. "Problems of Union Organization for Migratory Workers." *Proceedings of the Spring Meeting of the Industrial Relations Research Association*, May 4–5, 1961, pp. 636–643. Reprinted from the *Labor Law Journal*, July 1961.

ENGLER, ROBERT, and ROSALIND ENGLER. *The Farmers' Union in Washington*. Denver: National Farmers Union, 1948.

FOLSOM, J. C., comp. *Agricultural Labor in the United States, 1943–1952*. Washington: U.S. Department of Agriculture, Library, 1954.

GREENE, JOSIAH E. *Not in Our Stars* (a novel about a large Eastern dairy farm, featuring the people on the farm, their personal problems, and labor difficulties). New York: Macmillan, 1945.

GREY, ZANE. *Desert of Wheat* (a novel set in the state of Washington, 1917–1920, about the IWW). New York: Grossett & Dunlap, 1918.

HERBST, JOSEPHINE. *The Rope of Gold* (a novel about a farm labor organizer, 1933–1937). New York: Harcourt, Brace, 1939.

JAMIESON, STUART M. *Labor Unionism in American Agriculture*. U.S. Bureau of Labor Statistics Bulletin 836. Washington: G.P.O., 1945.

KESTER, HOWARD. *Revolt Among the Sharecroppers*. New York: Covici-Friede, 1936.

"Labor Department Study Is First of Its Kind: Survey Reports on Earnings of Migrant Farm Workers." *Industrial Bulletin* (New York State), Vol. 40, No. 2, February 1961, pp. 8–11, 18.

LANHAM, EDWIN M. *The Stricklands* (a novel set in Oklahoma during the 1930's about an organizer of tenant farmers). Boston: Little, Brown, 1939.

LEAGUE FOR INDUSTRIAL DEMOCRACY AND NATIONAL SHARECROPPERS FUND. *Down on the Farm: The Plight of Agricultural Labor.* New York: The League, 1955.

LEVINE, LOUIS. "The Migratory Worker in the Farm Economy." *Proceedings of the Spring Meeting of the Industrial Relations Research Association,* May 4–5, 1961, pp. 622–630. Reprinted from the *Labor Law Journal,* July 1961.

LISS, SAMUEL. "Farm Wage Boards Under the Cooperative Extension Service During World War II." *Agricultural History,* Vol. XXVII, July 1953, pp. 103–108.

—————. "Farm Wage Boards Under the Wage Stabilization Program During World War II." *Agricultural History,* Vol. XXX, July 1956, pp. 128–137.

LUMPKIN, GRACE. *A Sign for Cain* (a novel about sharecroppers and other workers in a small town during the early 1930's). New York: Lee Furman, 1935.

McWILLIAMS, CAREY. *Factories in the Field: The Story of Migratory Farm Labor in California.* Boston: Little, Brown, 1939.

—————. *Ill Fares the Land: Migrants and Migratory Labor in the United States.* Boston: Little, Brown, 1942.

MARSHALL, F. RAY and LAMAR B. JONES. "Agricultural Unions in Louisiana." *Labor History,* Vol. 3, No. 3, Fall 1962, pp. 287–306.

MITCHELL, RUTH C. *Of Human Kindness* (a novel about farm workers in California during the 1930's). New York: Appleton-Century, 1940.

MORIN, ALEXANDER. *The Organizability of Farm Labor in the United States.* Cambridge: Harvard University Press, 1952.

NATIONAL CHILD LABOR COMMITTEE. *Migrant Farm Labor in Colorado: A Study of Migratory Families.* New York: The Committee, 1951.

NEWHOUSE, EDWARD. *This Is Your Day* (a novel set in upstate New York during the 1930's about a young communist's attempts to organize farm workers). New York: Lee Furman, 1937.

RAPER, ARTHUR M., and IRA DE A. REID. *Sharecroppers All.* Chapel Hill: University of North Carolina, 1940.

RASMUSSEN, WAYNE D. *A History of the Emergency Farm Labor Supply Program, 1943–1947.* U.S. Department of Agriculture Monograph No. 13. Washington: G.P.O., 1951.

ROBBINS, HAYES. *The Labor Movement and the Farmer.* New York: Harcourt, Brace, 1922.

SABGHIR, IRVING HOWARD. *Mexican Contract Labor in the United States, 1948–1953: A Political and Economic Analysis.* Ph.D. Thesis, Harvard University, 1956.

SCARBOROUGH, DOROTHY. *Can't Get a Red Bird* (a novel about economic conditions among the Texas cotton growers and their ultimate organization). New York: Harper, 1929.

SCHWARTZ, HARRY. *Seasonal Farm Labor in the United States.* New York: Columbia University Press, 1945.

SCRUGGS, OTEY M. "The Bracero Program under the Farm Security Administration, 1942–1943." *Labor History,* Vol. 3, No. 2, Spring 1962, pp. 149–168.

SHOTWELL, LOUISA R. *The Harvesters: The Story of the Migrant People.* New York: Doubleday, 1961.

SIMON, CHARLIE M. *The Share-Cropper* (a novel set in Arkansas during the early 1930's about attempts at organizing sharecroppers). New York: Dutton, 1937.

STEINBECK, JOHN. *The Grapes of Wrath* (a novel about migrant workers during the 1930's). New York: Viking Press, 1939.

——————. *In Dubious Battle* (a novel set in California during the early 1930's about fruit pickers). New York: Covici-Friede, 1936.

SYKES, HOPE W. *Second Hoeing* (a novel about immigrant life among sugar-beet growers in Colorado). New York: G. P. Putnam's Sons, 1935.

U.S. COMMISSION ON INDUSTRIAL RELATIONS (1912). *Final Report and Testimony,* Vol. V, "The Seasonal Labor Problem in Agriculture," pp. 4911–5027. Washington: G.P.O., 1916.

U.S. CONGRESS. SENATE. Committee on Labor and Public Welfare. Subcommittee on Labor and Labor-Management Relations. *Migratory Labor.* Parts 1 and 2 of Hearings before 82nd Congress, 2nd Session. Washington: G.P.O., 1952.

U.S. INDUSTRIAL COMMISSION (1898). *Reports of the Commission.* 19 vols. Vol. X (1901), "Report of the Industrial Commission on Agriculture and Agricultural Labor." Washington: G.P.O., 1901.

U.S. PRESIDENT'S COMMISSION ON MIGRATORY LABOR. *Migratory Labor in American Agriculture.* Washington: G.P.O., 1951.

VENKATARAMANI, M. S. "Norman Thomas, Arkansas Sharecroppers, and the Roosevelt Agricultural Policies, 1933–1937." *Mssissippi Valley Historical Review,* Vol. XLVII, September 1960, pp. 225–246.

WARING, P. ALSTON, and CLINTON S. GOLDEN. *Soil and Steel: Exploring the Common Interests of Farmers and Wage Earners.* New York: Harper, 1947.

WHITTEN, WOODROW C. "The Wheatland Episode." *Pacific Historical Review,* Vol. XVII, February 1948, pp. 37–42.

WILLIAMS, HARRISON A., JR. "Proposed Legislation for Migratory Workers." *Proceedings of the Spring Meeting of the Industrial Relations Research Association,* May 4–5, 1961, pp. 630–636. Reprinted from the *Labor Law Journal,* July 1961.

Automobile, Aircraft, Agricultural Implement, and Aerospace

ANDERSON, SHERWOOD. *Poor White* (a novel). New York: Huebsch, 1920.

BENNETT, HARRY (as told to Paul Marcus). *We Never Called Him Henry.* New York: Fawcett Publications, 1951.

BERNSTEIN, IRVING. *The Automobile Industry: Post War Developments, 1918–1921.* Historical Studies of Wartime Problems No. 52. Washington: U.S.

Bureau of Labor Statistics (Division of Historical Studies of Wartime Problems, 1941–1945), 1942. (Mimeo.).

BLACKWOOD, GEORGE D. *The United Automobile Workers of America, 1935–51.* Ph.D. Thesis, University of Chicago, 1952.

BONOSKY, PHILLIP. *Brother Bill McKie: Building the Union at Ford.* New York: International Publishers, 1953.

BORTZ, NELSON M. "Cost-of-Living Wage Clauses and UAW-GM Pact." *Monthly Labor Review,* Vol. 67, No. 1, July 1948, pp. 1–7.

CARLTON, FRANCIS. "The G M Strike." *Antioch Review,* Vol. 6, September 1946, pp. 426–441.

CHESTER, HARRY. "GM-UAW Wage Settlement." *Labor and Nation,* July-August 1948, p. 12.

CHINOY, ELY. *Automobile Workers and the American Dream.* Garden City: Doubleday, 1955.

CHRISTMAN, HENRY M., ed. *Walter P. Reuther, Selected Papers.* New York: Macmillan, 1961.

CONRAD, LAWRENCE H. *Temper* (a novel). New York: Dodd, Mead, 1924.

CORT, JOHN C. "Fight for the Ford 600." *Commonweal,* Vol. 43, March 22, 1946.

CUSHMAN, EDWARD L. "The American Motors—UAW Progress Sharing Agreement." *Proceedings of the Fourteenth Annual Meeting of the Industrial Relations Research Association,* December 28–29, 1961, pp. 315–324. Madison, Wisconsin: The Association, 1962.

DAHLHEIMER, HARRY. *A History of the Mechanics Educational Society of America in Detroit from Its Inception in 1933 through 1937.* Detroit: Wayne University Press, 1951.

DAYTON, ELDOROUS L. *Walter Reuther: The Autocrat at the Bargaining Table.* New York: Devin-Adair, 1958.

"Detroit Auto Worker." *Fortune,* Vol. 34, No. 2, August 1946, pp. 126–129.

DUNN, ROBERT W. *Labor and Automobiles.* New York: International Publishers, 1929.

FACT FINDING BOARD IN RE *General Motors Corporation and United Automobile Workers (CIO), January 10, 1946.* Washington: Bureau of National Affairs, Labor Arbitration Reports, 1 LA 125.

FAUNCE, WILLIAM A. "Automation and the Automobile Worker," *Labor and Trade Unionism: An Interdisciplinary Reader,* Walter Galenson and Seymour Lipset, eds., pp. 370–379. New York: John Wiley & Sons, 1960.

FINE, SIDNEY. "The Ford Motor Company and the N.R.A." *Business History Review,* Vol. 32, Winter 1958, pp. 353–385.

———. "The Origins of the United Automobile Workers, 1933–1935." *Journal of Economic History,* Vol. XVIII, September 1958, pp. 249–282.

———. "President Roosevelt and the Automobile Code." *Mississippi Valley Historical Review,* Vol. 45, June 1958, pp. 23–50.

———. "Proportional Representation of Workers in the Auto Industry, 1934–1935." *Industrial and Labor Relations Review,* Vol. 12, No. 2, January 1959, pp. 182–205.

——————. "The Toledo Chevrolet Strike of 1935." *Ohio Historical Quarterly,* Vol. LXVII, October 1958, pp. 326–356.

——————. "The Tool and Die Makers Strike of 1933." *Michigan History,* Vol. 42, September 1958, pp. 297–323.

FISHER, THOMAS R. *Industrial Disputes and Federal Legislation, with Special Reference to the Railroad, Coal, Steel, and Automobile Industries in the U.S. Since 1900.* New York: Columbia University Press, 1940.

FOUNTAIN, CLAYTON W. *Union Guy.* New York: Viking Press, 1949.

GALENSON, WALTER. *The CIO Challenge to the AFL,* chap. 3, "The Automobile Industry," pp. 123–192. Cambridge: Harvard University Press, 1960.

GUEST, ROBERT H. "Work Careers and Aspirations of Automobile Workers," *Labor and Trade Unionism: An Interdisciplinary Reader,* Walter Galenson and Seymour Lipset, eds., pp. 319–328. New York: John Wiley & Sons, 1960.

HARBISON, F. H., and ROBERT DUBIN. *Patterns of Union-Management Relations.* Chicago: Science Research Associates, 1947.

HARRIS, HERBERT. *American Labor,* pp. 267–304. New Haven: Yale University Press, 1939.

HART, C. W. M. "Industrial Relations Research and Social Theory." *Canadian Journal of Economics and Political Science,* February 1949.

HAWES, ELIZABETH. *Hurry Up, Please, It's Time.* New York: Reynal and Hitchcock, 1946.

HIMES, CHESTER B. *Lonely Crusade* (a novel). New York: Knopf, 1947.

HOWARD, J. WOODFORD, JR. "Frank Murphy and the Sit-Down Strikes of 1937." *Labor History,* Vol. 1, No. 2, Spring 1960, pp. 103–140.

HOWE, IRVING, and B. J. WIDICK. *The UAW and Walter Reuther.* New York: Random House, 1949.

KORNHAUSER, A. W., H. L. SHEPPARD, and A. J. MAYER. *When Labor Votes: A Study of Auto Workers.* New York: University Books, 1956.

KRAUS, HENRY. *The Many and the Few: A Chronicle of the Dynamic Auto Workers.* Los Angeles: Plantin, 1947.

LEE, HARRY. *Sir and Brother* (a novel). New York: Appleton-Century-Crofts, 1948.

LEVINSON, EDWARD. *Rise of the Auto Workers.* Detroit: UAW, 1946.

LEVINSON, HAROLD M. "Pattern Bargaining by the United Automobile Workers." *Proceedings of the Spring Meeting of the Industrial Relations Research Association,* May 2–3, 1958, pp. 669–674. Reprinted from the *Labor Law Journal,* September 1958.

McBRIDE, ROBERTA. *Labor Relations in the Automobile Industry* (a bibliography). Detroit: Detroit Public Library, Social Science Department, 1950.

McPHERSON, WILLIAM H. "Automobiles," chap. 11, *How Collective Bargaining Works,* Harry A. Millis, research director. New York: Twentieth Century Fund, 1945.

——————. *Labor Relations in the Automobile Industry.* Washington: Brookings Institution, 1940.

MALTZ, ALBERT. *The Underground Stream* (a novel). Boston: Little, Brown, 1940.

Morris, Bruce R. "Industrial Relations in the Automobile Industry," chap. 17, *Labor in Postwar America*, Colston E. Warne, ed. Brooklyn: Remsen Press, 1949.

Muste, Abraham J. *The Automobile Industry and Organized Labor.* Baltimore: Christian Social Justice Fund, 1936.

Neikind, Claire. "Beck and Reuther." *The Reporter,* July 5, 1949.

"No-Raid Agreement between UAW and IAM." *Monthly Labor Review,* Vol. 70, No. 3, March 1950, pp. 278–279.

Norwood, E. P. *Ford: Men and Methods.* Garden City: Doubleday, Doran, 1931.

Opinion Research Corporation. *The General Motors Strike.* Princeton: The Corporation, 1945.

Ozanne, Robert. "Union-Management Relations: McCormick Harvesting Machine Company, 1862–1886." *Labor History,* Vol. 4, No. 2, Spring 1963, pp. 132–160.

——————. "Union Wage Impact: A Nineteenth-Century Case." *Industrial and Labor Relations Review,* Vol. 15, No. 3, April 1962, pp. 350–375.

Pesotta, Rose. *Bread Upon the Waters* (description of Fisher Body sitdown strike). New York: Dodd, Mead, 1945.

Petro, Sylvester. *The Kohler Strike: Union Violence and Administrative Law.* Chicago: H. Regnery, 1961.

Pierson, Frank C. *Collective Bargaining Systems: A Study of Union-Employer Responsibilities and Problems,* pp. 109–132. Washington: American Council on Public Affairs, 1942.

Pollack, Jerome. "Kaiser-Frazer UAW-CIO Social Security Program." *Industrial and Labor Relations Review,* Vol. 6, No. 1, October 1952, pp. 94–109.

Pollard, Spencer D. *Some Problems of Democracy in the Government of Labor Unions, with Special Reference to the United Mine Workers of America and the United Automobile Workers of America.* Ph.D. Thesis, Harvard University, 1940.

Raushenbush, Carl. *Fordism: Ford and the Workers, Ford and the Community.* New York: League for Industrial Democracy, 1937.

Reuther, Walter P. *Purchasing Power for Prosperity: In the Matter of International Union, UAW, and General Motors Corporation, October 1945—The Case for Maintaining Take-Home Pay without Increasing Prices.* Detroit: The Union, G. M. Department, 1945.

Rice, Charles Owen. "Verdict at Kohler." *The Commonweal Magazine,* November 11, 1960.

Rowe, Evan Keith. "Health and Welfare Plans in the Automobile Industry." *Monthly Labor Review,* Vol. 73, No. 3, September 1951, pp. 277–282.

Saposs, David J. *Communism in American Unions,* pp. 119–270 *passim.* New York: McGraw-Hill, 1959.

Schwartz, Donald A. *The 1941 Strike at Allis-Chalmers.* Madison: University of Wisconsin, 1943. (Mimeo.).

Skeels, Jack. "The Background of UAW Factionalism." *Labor History,* Vol. 2, No. 2, Spring 1961, pp. 158–181.

Smitter, Wessel. *F.O.B., Detroit* (a novel). New York: Harper, 1938.

SOCIETY FOR THE PSYCHOLOGICAL STUDY OF SOCIAL ISSUES. *Industrial Conflict: A Psychological Interpretation* (a study of Detroit). New York: Cordon, 1939.

STANLEY, J. PERHAM. "Pension Plans Negotiated by the UAW-CIO." *Monthly Labor Review*, Vol. 77, No. 1, January 1954, pp. 13–15.

STANLEY, MARJORIE THINES. "The Amalgamation of Collective Bargaining and Political Activity by the UAW." *Industrial and Labor Relations Review*, Vol. 10, No. 1, October 1956, pp. 40–47.

STEELE, JAMES. *Conveyor* (a novel). New York: International Publishers, 1935.

STIEBER, JACK. *Governing the UAW*. New York: John Wiley & Sons, 1962.

SWADOS, HARVEY. *On the Line* (a novel). Boston: Atlantic, Little, Brown, 1957.

SWARD, KEITH. *The Legend of Henry Ford*. New York: Rinehart, 1948.

SWARTHOUT, GLENDON F. *Willow Run* (a novel). New York: Crowell, 1943.

THOMAS, R. J. *Automobile Unionism*. Reports of the President of the U.A.W. Submitted to the 1941 Convention of the U.A.W., Vol. 6. Detroit: The Union, 1941.

U.S. CONGRESS. Joint Committee on Labor-Management Relations. *Labor-Management Relations*. Senate Report 986, 80th Congress, 2nd Session, pp. 115–131, "UAW and the International Harvester Co.;" and pp. 154–177, "UAW Local 2 and the Murray Corporation of America." Washington: G.P.O., 1948.

U.S. CONGRESS. SENATE. Committee on Government Operations. Permanent Subcommittee on Investigations. *Work Stoppage at Missile Bases*. Report No. 1312. Washington: G.P.O., 1962.

U.S. NATIONAL RECOVERY ADMINISTRATION. *Preliminary Report on Study of Regularization of Employment and Improvement of Labor Conditions in the Automobile Industry*. Washington: G.P.O., 1935.

VAN DE WATER, JOHN R. "Applications of Labor Law to Construction and Equipping of United States Missile Bases." *Labor Law Journal*, November 1961, pp. 1003–1024.

WALKER, CHARLES R., and ROBERT H. GUEST. *The Man on the Assembly Line*. Cambridge: Harvard University Press, 1952.

WEBER, ARNOLD R. "Craft Representation in Industrial Unions." *Proceedings of the Fourteenth Annual Meeting of the Industrial Relations Research Association*, December 28–29, 1961, pp. 82–92. Madison: The Association, 1962.

WECHSLER, JAMES A. "Labor's Bright Young Man." *Harper's*, March 1948, p. 264.

Chemicals, Atomic Energy, Oil

CHASE, STUART. *A Generation of Industrial Peace: 30 Years of Labor Relations at Standard Oil Company (N.J.)*. New York: Standard Oil of New Jersey, 1946.

CRAWFORD, ROBERT C. "Government Intervention in Emergency Labor Disputes in Atomic Energy." *Labor Law Journal*, June 1959, Vol. 10, pp. 414–434.

FEIS, HERBERT. *Labor Relations: A Study Made in the Proctor and Gamble Company*. New York: Adelphi Company, 1928.

GALENSON, WALTER. *The CIO Challenge to the AFL*, chap. 12, "The Petroleum Industry," pp. 409–426. Cambridge: Harvard University Press, 1960.

HICKS, CLARENCE J. *My Life in Industrial Relations: Fifty Years in the Growth of a Profession*. New York and London: Harper, 1941.

JOHNSON, DAVID B. "Dispute Settlement in Atomic Energy Plants." *Industrial and Labor Relations Review*, Vol. 13, No. 1, October 1959, pp. 38–53.

————. "Labor Relations in the Atomic Program." *Vanderbilt Law Review*, Vol. 12, December 1958, pp. 161–178.

MCGREGOR, DOUGLAS, and JOSEPH N. SCANLON. *The Dewey and Almy Chemical Company and the International Chemical Workers Union*. Washington: National Planning Association, Committee on the Causes of Industrial Peace Under Collective Bargaining, December 1948.

MARSHALL, F. RAY. "Independent Unions in the Gulf Coast Petroleum Refining Industry—The Esso Experience." *Labor Law Journal*, Vol. 12, No. 9, September 1961, pp. 823–840.

NATIONAL INDUSTRIAL CONFERENCE BOARD. *Labor Relations in the Atomic Energy Field*. New York: The Board, 1957.

O'CONNOR, HARVEY. *History of the Oil Workers International Union-CIO*. Denver: Oil Workers International Union, CIO, 1950.

ROTHBAUM, MELVIN. *The Government of the Oil, Chemical, and Atomic Workers Union*. New York: Wiley, 1962.

SMITH, M. MEAD. "Labor and the Savannah River AEC Project: Part II, Unionization and Industrial Relations." *Monthly Labor Review*, Vol. 75, No. 1, July 1952, pp. 12–21.

SOMERS, GERALD G. "Small Establishments and Chemicals." *Proceedings of the Ninth Annual Meeting of the Industrial Relations Research Association*, December 28–29, 1956, pp. 248–254. Madison, Wisconsin: The Association, 1957.

STRAUS, DONALD B. *The Development of a Policy for Industrial Peace in Atomic Energy*. Washington: National Planning Association, Committee on the Causes of Industrial Peace Under Collective Bargaining, July 1950.

U.S. CONGRESS. Joint Committee on Atomic Energy. *Labor Policy in Atomic Energy Plants*. Washington: G.P.O., 1948.

WEBER, ARNOLD R. "Competitive Unionism in the Chemical Industry." *Industrial and Labor Relations Review*, Vol. 13, No. 1, October 1959, pp. 16–37.

————. "Union-Management Power Relations in the Chemical Industry: The Economic Setting." *Proceedings of the Spring Meeting of the Industrial Relations Research Association*, May 2–3, 1958, pp. 664–668. Reprinted from the *Labor Law Journal*, September 1958.

Clothing—Men's

ADAMS, SAMUEL HOPKINS. *Sunrise to Sunset* (a novel). New York: Random House, 1950.

ALEXANDER, JOSEPH. *Development of Labor Relations in the New York Garment Industry: A Study in Industry-Wide Collective Bargaining in the Local Area Level.* Ph.D. Thesis, New York University, 1955.

AMALGAMATED CLOTHING WORKERS OF AMERICA. *Documentary History.* 6 vols. New York: The Union, 1914–1916.

——————. *Ever Forward: Forty Years of Progress.* New York: The Union, 1954.

——————. New York Joint Board. *The Book of the Amalgamated in New York, 1914–1940.* New York: The Amalgamated Joint Boards and Local Unions in New York, 1940.

——————. Research Department. *The Clothing Workers of Chicago, 1910–1922* by Leo Wolman, *et al.* Chicago: The Chicago Joint Board, Amalgamated Clothing Workers of America, 1922.

BAUM, MORTON J. "Maturity in Industrial Relations: A Case Study." *Industrial and Labor Relations Review,* Vol. 4, No. 2, January 1951, pp. 257–264.

BISNO, BEATRICE. *Tomorrow's Bread* (a novel). New York: Liveright, 1938.

BISSELL, RICHARD P. *7½ Cents* (a novel). Boston: Little, Brown, 1953.

BOOKBINDER, HYMAN H., and ASSOCIATES. *To Promote the General Welfare: The Story of the Amalgamated.* New York: The Amalgamated Clothing Workers of America, 1950.

BRAUN, KURT. *Union-Management Cooperation: Experience in the Clothing Industry.* Washington: Brookings Institution, 1947.

BUDISH, J. M., and GEORGE SOULE. *The New Unionism in the Clothing Industry.* New York: Harcourt, Brace, and Howe, 1920.

CHANDLER, MARGARET K. "Case Study 3, Garment Manufacture," in *Labor-Management Relations in Illini City,* Vol. 1. Champaign: University of Illinois, 1953.

CHICAGO TRADE AND LABOR ASSEMBLY. *New Slavery: Investigation into the Sweating System as Applied to the Manufacturing of Wearing Apparel.* Chicago: Rights of Labor Office, 1891.

COLLINS, GEORGE L. *The Amalgamated Clothing Workers.* (Unpublished manuscript, University of Wisconsin.)

COOPER, LYLE W. "The Clothing Workers' Factory in Milwaukee." *Harvard Business Review,* Vol. 9, No. 1, October 1930, pp. 89–100.

CROWE, ROBERT. *The Reminiscences of Robert Crowe, the Octogenarian Tailor.* Publisher unknown, n.d. (Can be found at Library of Congress.)

FELDMAN, EGAL. *Fit for Men: A Study of New York's Clothing Trade.* Washington: Public Affairs Press, 1960.

GALENSON, WALTER. *The CIO Challenge to the AFL,* chap. 7, "The Men's Clothing Industry," pp. 283–299. Cambridge: Harvard University Press, 1960.

GALTON, FRANK W., ed. *The Tailoring Trade: Select Documents Illustrating the History of Trade Unionism.* New York: Longmans, Green, 1896.

GOULD, JEAN. *Sidney Hillman: Great American.* Boston: Houghton, Mifflin, 1952.

HAAS, FRANCIS J. *Shop Collective Bargaining: A Study of Wage Determination in the Men's Garment Industry*. Washington: Catholic University of America, 1922.

HARDMAN, J. B. S., ed. *The Amalgamated—Today and Tomorrow*. New York: The Amalgamated Clothing Workers of America, 1939.

—————. "The Needle-Trades Unions: A Labor Movement at Fifty." *Social Research*, Vol. 27, No. 3, Autumn 1960, pp. 321–358.

—————, and LEN GIOVANNITTI. *Sidney Hillman: Labor Statesman*. New York: The Amalgamated Clothing Workers of America, 1948.

HARDY, JACK. *The Clothing Workers*. New York: International Publishers, 1935.

HELFGOTT, ROY B. "Trade Unionism among the Jewish Garment Workers of Britain and the United States." *Labor History*, Vol. 2, No. 2, Spring 1961, pp. 202–214.

ILLINOIS BUREAU OF LABOR STATISTICS. *Seventh Biennial Report*, Part II, "The Sweating System in Chicago." Springfield, Ill.: The Bureau, 1893.

JOSEPHSON, MATTHEW. *Sidney Hillman, Statesman of American Labor*. Garden City: Doubleday, 1952.

KIRSHBAUM, LOUIS. *The Sewing Circle*. Los Angeles: De Vorss, 1952.

"Labor Violence and Corruption." *Business Week*, August 31, 1957, pp. 76–90. [The Amalgamated Clothing Workers and Louis (Buchalter) Lepke.]

LAMAR, ELDEN. *The Clothing Workers in Philadelphia: History of Their Struggles for Union and Security*. Philadelphia: The Amalgamated Clothing Workers of America, Philadelphia Joint Board, 1940.

MARCOVITZ, LAZARUS. "Out of Labor's Past—Way Back in Boston." *Labor and Nation*, January–February 1948, pp. 33–35.

MARIMPIETRI, A. D. *From These Beginnings—The Making of the Amalgamated*. Chicago: The Amalgamated Clothing Workers of America, The Chicago Joint Board, 1943.

MITCHELL, BROADUS. "Industrial Relations in the Men's and Women's Garment Industry," chap. 23, *Labor in Postwar America*, Colston Warne, ed. Brooklyn: Remsen Press, 1949.

MORGAN, RITA. *Arbitration in the Men's Clothing Industry in New York City: A Case Study of Industrial Arbitration and Conference Method with Particular Reference to Its Educational Implications*. New York: Teachers' College, Columbia University, 1940.

MYERS, ROBERT J., and JOSEPH W. BLOCH. "Men's Clothing," chap. 8, *How Collective Bargaining Works*, Harry A. Millis, research director. New York: Twentieth Century Fund, 1945.

NATIONAL INDUSTRIAL CONFERENCE BOARD. *Experience with Trade Union Agreements—Clothing Industries*. New York: Century, 1921.

NATIONAL LABOR RELATIONS BOARD. Division of Economic Research. *Written Trade Agreements in Collective Bargaining*, chap. 5, "The Clothing Industry," pp. 63–79. Washington: G.P.O., 1940.

NESTEL, LOUIS P. *Labor Relations in the Laundry Industry in Greater New York*. New York: Claridge, 1950.

NEW YORK CLOTHING MANUFACTURERS' EXCHANGE, INC. *The New York Story—A History of the New York Clothing Industry, 1924–1949*. New York: The Exchange, 1949.

"New York State Survey of Industry—Apparel." *Industrial Bulletin,* Vol. 26, No. 3, March 1947, pp. 5–9.

PERLMAN, SELIG, and PHILIP TAFT. *History of Labor in the United States, 1896–1932,* pp. 289–317, 435–439, 500–504, 546–555, 587–588. New York: Macmillan, 1935.

POPE, JESSE E. *The Clothing Industry in New York.* Columbia: University of Missouri, 1905.

POTOFSKY, J. S., ed. *John E. Williams, First Chairman of the Board of Arbitration under the Hart, Schaffner and Marx Labor Agreement, 1912–1919, in Tribute.* Chicago: The Amalgamated Clothing Workers of America, Chicago Joint Board, n.d.

RAYACK, ELTON. "The Impact of Unionism on Wages in the Men's Clothing Industry, 1911–1956." *Proceedings of the Spring Meeting of the Industrial Relations Research Association,* May 2–3, 1958, pp. 674–688. Reprinted from the *Labor Law Journal,* Vol. 9, No. 9, September 1958.

ROVERE, RICHARD H. "Sidney Hillman and the Housebroken Workers." *The Reporter,* Vol. 8, No. 4, February 17, 1953, pp. 36–40.

SAMUEL, HOWARD D., and LYNNE RHODES. *Profile of a Union.* New York: The Amalgamated Clothing Workers of America, 1958.

SCHLOSSBERG, JOSEPH. *The Rise of the Clothing Workers.* New York: The Amalgamated Clothing Workers of America, 1921.

SEIDMAN, JOEL. *The Needle Trades.* New York: Farrar and Rinehart, 1942.

SOULE, GEORGE. *Sidney Hillman, Labor Statesman.* New York: Macmillan, 1939.

STOWELL, CHARLES J. *The Journeymen Tailors' Union of North America: A Study in Trade Union Policy.* Urbana: University of Illinois, 1918.

—————. *Studies in Trade Unionism in the Custom Tailoring Trade.* Bloomington: Journeymen Tailors' Union of America, 1913.

STRAUS, DONALD B. *Hickey-Freeman Company and Amalgamated Clothing Workers of America.* Washington: National Planning Association, 1949.

STRONG, EARL D. *The Amalgamated Clothing Workers of America.* Grinnell: Herald Register, 1940.

U.S. COMMISSION ON INDUSTRIAL RELATIONS (1912). *Reports,* vol. 2, "Men's Garment Trades of New York City," pp. 1963–2050. Washington: G.P.O., 1916.

WILLETT, MABEL H. *The Employment of Women in the Clothing Trade, New York.* New York: Columbia University Press, 1902.

WOMEN'S TRADE UNION LEAGUE OF CHICAGO. *Official Report of the Strike Committee, Chicago Garment Workers' Strike, October 29, 1910–February 18, 1911.* Chicago: The League, 1911.

ZARETZ, CHARLES E. *The Amalgamated Clothing Workers of America: A Study in Progressive Trades Unionism.* New York: Ancon, 1934.

Clothing—Women's

ASCH, SHALOM. *East River* (a novel). New York: Putnam, 1946.

BERMAN, HYMAN. *The Era of the Protocol: A Chapter in the History of the International Ladies' Garment Workers' Union, 1910–16.* Ph.D. Thesis, Columbia University, 1956.

BISNO, BEATRICE. *Tomorrow's Bread* (a novel). New York: Liveright, 1938.

BRYNER, EDNA. *The Garment Trades.* Cleveland: Survey Committee of the Cleveland Foundation, 1916.

BULLARD, ARTHUR (Albert Edwards, pseud.). *Comrade Yetta* (a novel). New York: Macmillan, 1913.

CARSEL, WILFRED. *A History of the Chicago Ladies' Garment Workers' Union.* Chicago: Normandie House, 1940.

CHICAGO TRADE AND LABOR ASSEMBLY. *New Slavery: Investigation into the Sweating System as Applied to the Manufacturing of Wearing Apparel.* Chicago: Rights of Labor Office, 1891.

CLARK, SUE, and EDITH WYATT. *Making Both Ends Meet,* chap. 2, "The Shirtwaist Makers' Strike," chap. 5, "The Cloak Makers' Strike and the Preferential Shop." New York: Macmillan, 1911.

COHEN, HYMAN, and LESTER COHEN. *Aaron Traum* (a novel). New York: Liveright, 1930.

COHEN, JULIUS H. *Law and Order in Industry: Five Years' Experience.* New York: Macmillan, 1916.

————. *They Builded Better Than They Knew.* New York: Julian Messner, 1946.

CRAWFORD, JOHN S. *Luigi Antonini: His Influence on Italian-American Relations.* New York: International Ladies' Garment Workers' Union, Local 89, 1950.

DANISH, MAX D. *The World of David Dubinsky.* Cleveland: World, 1957.

————, and LEON STEIN, eds. *ILGWU News—History, 1900–1950.* New York: International Ladies' Garment Workers' Union, 1950.

DAVIS, PHILIP. *And Crown Thy Good.* New York: Philosophical Library, 1952.

DEWEY, JOHN. *David Dubinsky: A Pictorial Biography.* New York: Inter-allied, 1951.

GALENSON, WALTER. *The CIO Challenge to the AFL,* chap. 8, "The Women's Clothing Industry," pp. 300–324. Cambridge: Harvard University Press, 1960.

"The Garment Workers." *Fortune,* November 1946, pp. 173–179, 226–229.

HARRIS, HERBERT. *American Labor,* pp. 193–224. New Haven: Yale University Press, 1938.

HASKEL, HARRY. *A Leader of the Garment Workers: The Biography of Isidore Nagler.* New York: International Ladies' Garment Workers' Union, Local 10, 1950.

HERBERG, WILL. 'The Old-Timers and the Newcomers: Ethnic Group Relations in a Needle Trades Union.' "Trade Unions and Minority Problems." *The Journal of Social Issues,* Vol. IX, No. 1, 1953, pp. 12–19.

INTERNATIONAL LADIES' GARMENT WORKERS' UNION. *The Position of the International Ladies' Garment Workers' Union in Relation to CIO and AFL, 1934–1938.* New York: The Union, 1938.

—————. *Souvenir History of the Strike of the Ladies' Waist Makers' Union.* New York: The Union, 1910.

—————. General Executive Board. *The Hourwich Affair.* New York: The Union, 1914.

—————. Welfare and Health Benefits Department. *The Thread of Life.* Atlantic City: The Union, 1956.

JACOBS, PAUL. "David Dubinsky: Why His Throne Is Wobbling." *Harper's Magazine,* Vol. 225, No. 1351, December 1962, pp. 75–84.

KAZIN, ALFRED. "A Brooklyn Childhood—The Kitchen." *The New Yorker,* September 15, 1951, pp. 53–63.

LANG, HARRY. *"62": Biography of a Union* (Undergarment and Negligee Workers Union). New York: The International Ladies' Garment Workers' Union, Local 62, 1940.

LEAGUE FOR INDUSTRIAL DEMOCRACY NEWS BULLETIN. *Israel Feinberg (1887–1952).* Vol. XVI, No. 4, October 1952, p. 3.

LORWIN, LEWIS (Louis Levine). *The Women's Garment Workers: A History of the International Ladies' Garment Workers' Union.* New York: Huebsch, 1924.

LUBELL, SAMUEL. "Dictator in Sheep's Clothing" (David Dubinsky). *Saturday Evening Post,* November 19, 1949, pp. 19–21, 66–72.

LYONS, EUGENE. "A Remarkable Union—And Union Leader" (Julius Hochman). *Reader's Digest,* Vol. 48, April 1946. (Condensed from *The New Leader,* March 16, 1946.)

MALKIEL, T. *The Diary of a Shirtwaist Striker.* New York: Co-operative Press, 1910.

MEYERSBURG, DOROTHY. *Seventh Avenue* (a novel). New York: Dutton, 1940.

MITCHELL, BROADUS. "Industrial Relations in the Men's and Women's Garment Industries," chap. 23, *Labor in Postwar America,* Colston Warne, ed. Brooklyn: Remsen Press, 1949.

NATIONAL INDUSTRIAL CONFERENCE BOARD. *Experience with Trade Union Agreements—Clothing Industries.* New York: Century, 1921.

NATIONAL LABOR RELATIONS BOARD. Division of Economic Research. *Written Trade Agreements in Collective Bargaining,* chap. 5, "The Clothing Industry," pp. 63–79. Washington: G.P.O., 1940.

NEW YORK STATE. *Report of Governor's Advisory Commission, Cloak, Suit and Skirt Industry, New York City.* New York: Bureau of Research, Cloak, Suit and Skirt Industry, 1926.

ONEAL, JAMES. *A History of the Amalgamated Ladies' Garment Cutters' Union, Local 10, Affiliated with the International Ladies' Garment Workers' Union.* New York: International Ladies' Garment Workers' Union, Local 10, 1927.

PERLMAN, SELIG, and PHILIP TAFT. *History of Labor in the United States, 1896–1932,* pp. 289–317, 435–439, 500–504, 546–555, 587–588. New York: Macmillan, 1935.

PESOTTA, ROSE. *Bread upon the Waters.* New York: Dodd, Mead, 1945.

PIERSON, FRANK C. *Collective Bargaining Systems,* pp. 133–169. Washington: American Council on Public Affairs, 1942.

RICH, J. C. "How the Garment Unions Licked the Communists." *Saturday Evening Post,* Vol. 220, August 9, 1947.

ROBINSON, DWIGHT E. *Collective Bargaining and Market Control in the New York Coat and Suit Industry.* New York: Columbia University Press, 1949.

ROSENBERG, ABRAHAM. *The Cloakmakers and Their Unions: Memoirs of a Cloakmaker* (Yiddish). New York: Cloak Operators' Union, Local 1, 1920.

ROSS, IRWIN. "Labor's Needle Man" (David Dubinsky). *Reader's Digest,* November 1947. (Condensed from the *American Magazine,* August 1947.)

SEAMAN, BERNARD, and MAX D. DANISH. *The Story of the ILGWU.* New York: International Ladies' Garment Workers' Union, 1947.

STEIN, LEON. *The Triangle Fire.* Philadelphia and New York: Lippincott, 1962.

STOLBERG, BENJAMIN. *Tailor's Progress: The Story of a Famous Union and the Men Who Made It.* Garden City: Doubleday, 1944.

TEPER, LAZARE. *The Women's Garment Industry.* New York: International Ladies' Garment Workers' Union, 1937.

U.S. COMMISSION ON INDUSTRIAL RELATIONS (1912). *Reports,* vol. 2, "Cloak, Suit, and Waist Industry," pp. 1025–1161. Washington: G.P.O., 1916.

————. *Reports,* vol. 4, "The Women's Garment Industry of Philadelphia," pp. 3091–3171. Washington: G.P.O., 1916.

U.S. INDUSTRIAL COMMISSION (1898). *Reports,* vol. 7, "Report on the Relations and Conditions of Capital and Labor Employed in Manufactures and General Business." *Digest,* pp. 181–189. Washington: G.P.O., 1901.

VANDECARR, ANNIE B. *Frances Neureld* (a novel). New York: Warwick, 1950.

WILLETT, MABEL H. *The Employment of Women in the Clothing Trade, New York.* New York: Columbia University Press, 1902.

WOLFSON, THERESA. "Role of the ILGWU in Stabilizing the Women's Garment Industry." *Industrial and Labor Relations Review,* Vol. 4, No. 1, October 1950, pp. 33–43.

Coal

An Account of the Coal Bank Disaster at Blue Rock, Ohio. Malta, Ohio: No publisher indicated, 1856.

ALINSKY, SAUL. *John L. Lewis.* New York: Putnam's, 1949.

ANGLE, PAUL M. *Bloody Williamson: A Chapter in American Lawlessness.* New York: Knopf, 1952.

ANTHRACITE BUREAU OF INFORMATION. *The Anthracite Strike of 1922: A Chronological Statement.* Philadelphia: The Bureau, 1922.

————. *The Anthracite Strike of 1925–1926: A Chronological Statement.* Philadelphia: The Bureau, 1926.

"The Anthracite Coal Production Control Plan." *University of Pennsylvania Law Review,* Vol. 102, No. 3, January 1954, pp. 368–394.

ATHERTON, SARAH H. *Mark's Own* (a novel). Indianapolis: Bobbs-Merrill, 1941.

ATKINSON, HENRY. *The Church and Industrial Warfare: A Report on the Labor Troubles in Colorado and Michigan.* New York: Federal Council of the Churches of Christ in America, 1914.

BAKER, RALPH H. *The National Bituminous Coal Commission: Administration of the Bituminous Coal Act, 1937–1941.* Baltimore: Johns Hopkins Press, 1942.

BARATZ, MORTON S. *The Union and the Coal Industry.* New Haven: Yale University Press, 1955.

BEAME, EDMOND M. "The Jacksonville Agreement: Quest for Stability in Coal." *Industrial and Labor Relations Review,* Vol. 8, No. 2, January 1955, pp. 195–203.

BEARD, DANIEL C. *Moonblight and Six Feet of Romance* (a novel). New York: Charles Webster, 1892.

BERNSTEIN, IRVING, and HUGH G. LOVELL. "Are Coal Strikes National Emergencies?" *Industrial and Labor Relations Review,* Vol. 6, No. 3, April 1953, pp. 352–367.

BESHOAR, BARRON B. *Out of the Depths: The Story of John R. Lawson, a Labor Leader.* Denver: Colorado Labor Historical Committee of the Denver Trades and Labor Assembly, 1942.

BLANKENHORN, HEBER. *The Strike for Union: A Study of the Non-Union Question in Coal and the Problems of a Democratic Movement Based on the Record of the Somerset Strike, 1922–23.* New York: Wilson, 1924.

BLOCH, LOUIS. *The Coal Miners' Insecurity.* New York: Russell Sage Foundation, 1922.

BROPHY, JOHN. "Long Range Plans for the Coal Industry and Union." *Labor and Nation,* September-October 1947, pp. 32–35.

BROWN, ROLLO W. *Firemakers* (a novel). New York: Coward-McCann, 1931.

CARNES, CECIL. *John L. Lewis: Leader of Labor.* New York: Speller, 1936.

CARTER, JOHN F., JR. *The Destroyers* (a novel). Washington: Neale, 1907.

CHRISTENSON, C. L. "The Theory of the Offset Factor: The Impact of Labor Disputes upon Coal Production." *The American Economic Review,* Vol. XLIII, No. 4, September 1953, pp. 513–547.

"Coal I: The Industrial Darkness," *Fortune,* Vol. XXXV, No. 3, March 1947, pp. 86–95, 221–232; "Coal II: The Coal Miner Speaks," *Fortune,* Vol. XXXV, No. 3, March 1947, pp. 97–99, 202–206; "Coal III: The Fuel Revolution," *Fortune,* Vol. XXXV, No. 4, April 1947, pp. 99–105, 238–254.

COLEMAN, MCALISTER. *Men and Coal.* New York: Farrar and Rinehart, 1943.

————, and H. S. RAUSHENBUSH. *Red Neck* (a novel). New York: Random House, 1936.

CONROY, JACK. *The Disinherited* (a novel). New York: Covici-Friede, 1933.

COOKE, GRACE M. *The Grapple* (a novel). Boston: Page, 1905.

CORNELL, ROBERT J. *The Anthracite Coal Strike of 1902.* Washington: Catholic University of America Press, 1957.

CULIN, STEWART. *A Trooper's Narrative of Service in the Anthracite Coal Strike, 1902.* Philadelphia: Jacobs, 1903.

DANISH, MAX. "Lewis Takes Another Walk. What Next?" *New Leader*, December 20, 1947, pp. 1, 15.

DARGAN, OLIVE T. (Fielding Burke, pseud.). *Sons of the Stranger* (a novel). New York: Longmans, Green, 1947.

ELLIOTT, RUSSELL R. *Radical Labor in the Nevada Mining Booms, 1900–1920.* Carson City, Nevada: State Printing Office, 1961.

EVANGELA, SISTER MARY. "Bishop Spalding's Work on the Anthracite Coal Strike Commission." *Catholic Historical Review*, Vol. XXVIII, July 1942, pp. 184–205.

EVANS, CHRIS. *History of the United Mine Workers of America.* Indianapolis: The United Mine Workers of America, 1918.

FAST, HOWARD M. *Power* (a novel about John L. Lewis). Garden City: Doubleday, 1962.

FEDERAL COUNCIL OF THE CHURCHES OF CHRIST IN AMERICA. Commission on the Church and Social Service. *The Coal Controversy.* New York: The Council, 1922.

————. Department of Research and Education. *The Coal Strike in Western Pennsylvania.* New York: The Council, 1928.

FISHER, THOMAS R. *Industrial Disputes and Federal Legislation, with Special Reference to the Railroad, Coal, Steel, and Automobile Industries in the United States since 1900.* New York: Columbia University Press, 1940.

FISHER, WALDO E. "Anthracite," chap. 6, *How Collective Bargaining Works,* Harry A. Millis, research director. New York: Twentieth Century Fund, 1945.

————. "Bituminous Coal," chap. 5, *How Collective Bargaining Works,* Harry A. Millis, research director. New York: Twentieth Century Fund, 1945.

————. *Collective Bargaining in the Bituminous Coal Industry.* Philadelphia: University of Pennsylvania Press, 1948.

————. *Economic Consequences of the Seven-Hour Day and Wage Changes in the Bituminous Coal Industry.* Philadelphia: University of Pennsylvania Press, 1939.

————, and A. BEZANSON. *Wage Rates and Working Time in the Bituminous Coal Industry, 1912–1922.* Philadelphia: University of Pennsylvania Press, 1932.

————, and CHARLES M. JAMES. *Minimum Price Fixing in the Bituminous Coal Industry.* Princeton: Princeton University Press, 1955.

FOWLER, CHARLES B. *Collective Bargaining in the Bituminous Coal Industry.* New York: Prentice-Hall, 1927.

GALENSON, WALTER. *The CIO Challenge to the AFL,* chap. 4, "Coal Mining," pp. 193–238. Cambridge: Harvard University Press, 1960.

GIBBONS, WILLIAM F. *Those Black Diamond Men* (a novel). New York: Revell, 1902.

GILFILLAN, LAUREN. *I Went to Pit College.* New York: Viking Press, 1934.

GINGER, RAY. "Company-Sponsored Welfare Plans in the Anthracite Industry before 1900." *Bulletin of the Business Historical Society,* Vol. XXVII, No. 2, June 1953, pp. 112–120.

GLASSER, CARRIE. "Union Wage Policy in Bituminous Coal." *Industrial and Labor Relations Review*, Vol. 1, No. 4, July 1948, pp. 609–623.

GLÜCK, ELSIE. *John Mitchell, Miner: Labor's Bargain with the Gilded Age.* New York: John Day, 1929.

GOODRICH, CARTER L. *The Miner's Freedom.* Boston: Marshall Jones, 1925.

GRAHAM, MARGARET (Grace Lois McDonald, pseud.). *Swing Shift* (a novel). New York: Citadel Press, 1951.

GREEN, ARCHIE. "The Death of Mother Jones." *Labor History*, Vol. 1, No. 1, Winter 1960, pp. 68–80.

——————. "A Discography of American Coal Miners' Songs." *Labor History*, Vol. 2, No. 1, Winter 1961, pp. 101–115.

GREENE, HOMER. *Coal and the Coal Mines.* Boston: Houghton Mifflin, 1889.

GREENSLADE, RUSH V. *The Economic Effects of Collective Bargaining in Bituminous Coal Mining.* Ph.D. Thesis, University of Chicago, 1953.

GUTMAN, HERBERT G. "The Braidwood Lockout of 1874." *Journal of the Illinois State Historical Society*, Vol. LIII, No. 1, Spring 1960, pp. 5–28.

——————. "Reconstruction in Ohio: Negroes in the Hocking Valley Coal Mines in 1873 and 1874." *Labor History*, Vol. 3, No. 3, Fall 1962, pp. 243–264.

——————. "Two Lockouts in Pennsylvania 1873–1874." *The Pennsylvania Magazine of History and Biography*, Vol. LXXXIII, No. 3, July 1959, pp. 307–326.

HAMILTON, WALTON H., and HELEN R. WRIGHT. *The Case of Bituminous Coal.* New York: Macmillan, 1925.

——————. *A Way of Order for Bituminous Coal.* New York: Macmillan, 1928.

HARDMAN, J. B. S. "John L. Lewis, Labor Leader and Man: An Interpretation." *Labor History*, Vol. 2, No. 1, Winter 1961, pp. 3–29.

HARRIS, HERBERT. *American Labor*, pp. 97–148. New Haven: Yale University Press, 1938.

HASS, ERIC. *John L. Lewis Exposed.* New York: New York Labor News Co., 1938.

HAYWOOD, WILLIAM D. The trial of William Haywood and the Western Federation of Miners for the murder of the Governor of Idaho in 1906–1907. Archival Material, ILR Labor-Management Documentation Center, Cornell University. Six rolls of microfilm covering the Pinkerton Reports and the testimony of some of the witnesses. From the Idaho Historical Society.

HICKEN, VICTOR. "The Virden and Pana Mine Wars of 1898." *Journal of the Illinois State Historical Society*, Vol. LII, Summer 1959, pp. 263–278.

HINRICHS, A. F. *The United Mine Workers of America and the Non-Union Coal Fields.* New York: Columbia University Press, 1923.

HOWE, FREDERICK. *The Confessions of a Reformer.* New York: Scribner, 1925.

HUDSON, HARRIET D. *The Progressive Mine Workers of America: A Study in Rival Unionism.* Urbana: University of Illinois, 1952.

HUNT, EDWARD E., F. G. TRYON, and JOSEPH H. WILLITS, eds. *What the Coal Commission Found.* Baltimore: Williams & Wilkins, 1925.

IDELL, ALBERT. *Stephen Hayne* (a novel). New York: Sloane, 1951.

ITTER, WILLIAM A. "Early Labor Troubles in the Schuylkill Anthracite District." *Pennsylvania History*, Vol. I, January 1934, pp. 28–37.

"John Owens, President, District 6 (Ohio) United Mine Workers, AFL." *Fortune*, November 1946, p. 148.

KARSH, BERNARD, and JACK LONDON. "The Coal Miners: A Study of Union Control." *Quarterly Journal of Economics*, August 1954, pp. 415–436.

KORSON, GEORGE G. *Coal Dust on the Fiddle: Songs and Stories of the Bituminous Industry*. Philadelphia: University of Pennsylvania Press, 1943.

—————. *Minstrels of the Mine Patch: Songs and Stories of the Anthracite Industry*. Philadelphia: University of Pennsylvania Press, 1938.

—————, ed. *Songs and Ballads of the Anthracite Miner*. New York: Hitchcock, 1926.

LANE, WINTHROP D. *Civil War in West Virginia: A Story of the Industrial Conflict in Coal Mines*. New York: Huebsch, 1921.

LANGDON, EMMA F. *Labor's Greatest Conflict: The Formation of the Western Federation of Miners—A Brief Account of the Rise of the United Mine Workers of America*. Denver: Great Western, 1908.

LEWIS, JOHN L. *The Miners' Fight for American Standards*. Indianapolis: Bell, 1925.

LLOYD, HENRY D. *A Strike of Millionaires against Miners: Or the Story of Spring Valley*. Chicago: Belford-Clarke, 1890.

LUBIN, ISADORE. *Miners' Wages and the Cost of Coal*. New York: McGraw-Hill, 1924.

McCLURG, DONALD J. "The Colorado Coal Strike of 1927—Tactical Leadership of the IWW." *Labor History*, Vol. 4, No. 1, Winter 1963, pp. 68–92.

McDONALD, DAVID J., and EDWARD A. LYNCH. *Coal and Unionism: A History of the American Coal Miners' Unions*. Silver Springs, Md.: Cornelius Printing Co., 1939.

McGOVERN, GEORGE S. *The Colorado Coal Strike, 1913–1914*. Ph.D. Thesis, Northwestern University, 1953.

McKENNEY, RUTH. *Jake Home* (a novel). New York: Harcourt, Brace, 1943.

MALTZ, ALBERT. *The Black Pit* (a drama). New York: Putnam's, 1935.

MANFREDINI, DOLORES M. "The Italians Come to Herrin." *Journal of the Illinois State Historical Society*, Vol. XXXVII, December 1944, pp. 317–328.

MARTIN, JOHN BARTLOW. "The Blast in Centralia No. 5: A Mine Disaster No One Stopped." *Harper's*, Vol. 196, No. 1174, March 1948, pp. 193–220.

MERRICK, SISTER MARY A. *A Case in Practical Democracy: Settlement of the Anthracite Coal Strike of 1902*. Notre Dame: University of Notre Dame Library, 1942.

MILLER, STANLEY. *The United Mine Workers of America: A Study of How Trade Union Policy Relates to Technological Change*. Ph.D. Thesis, University of Wisconsin, 1957.

MINTON, BRUCE B. (Richard Bransten, pseud.), and JOHN STUART. *Men Who Lead Labor* (John L. Lewis). New York: Modern Age Books, 1937.

MITCHELL, JOHN. *Organized Labor.* Philadelphia: American Book and Bible House, 1903.

MORRIS, HOMER L. *The Plight of the Bituminous Coal Miner.* Philadelphia: University of Pennsylvania Press, 1934.

MORROW, ELSIE. "Portrait of a Union Boss" (George Titler). *Saturday Evening Post,* February 28, 1948, pp. 25, 110–114.

MYERS, ROBERT J. "Experience of the UMWA Welfare and Retirement Fund." *Industrial and Labor Relations Review,* Vol. 10, No. 1, October 1956, pp. 93–100.

NATIONAL COAL ASSOCIATION. *The Herrin Conspiracy.* Washington: The Association, 1922.

NATIONAL COMMITTEE FOR THE DEFENSE OF POLITICAL PRISONERS. *Harlan Miners Speak: Report on Terrorism in the Kentucky Coal Fields.* New York: Harcourt, Brace, 1932.

NATIONAL LABOR RELATIONS BOARD. Division of Economic Research. *The Effect of Labor Relations in the Bituminous Coal Industry upon Interstate Commerce.* Washington: G.P.O., 1938.

——————. ——————. *Written Trade Agreements in Collective Bargaining,* chap. 7, "The Coal Industry," pp. 93–114. Washington: G.P.O., 1940.

NEARING, SCOTT. *Anthracite.* Philadelphia: John C. Winston, 1915.

NELSON, JAMES. *The Mine Workers' District 50.* New York: Exposition Press, 1955.

NEWELL, ARTHUR. *A Knight of the Toilers* (a novel). Philadelphia: F. L. Marsh, 1905.

NICHOLS, FRANCES H. "Children of the Coal Shadow." *McClure's Magazine,* Vol. XX, February 1903, pp. 435–444.

O'MALLEY, MICHAEL. *Miner's Hill* (a novel). New York: Harper, 1962.

PARKER, GLEN L. *The Coal Industry: A Study in Social Control.* Washington: American Council on Public Affairs, 1940.

PERLMAN, SELIG, and PHILIP TAFT. *History of Labor in the United States, 1896–1932,* pp. 20–30, 326–342, 469–488, 562–571, 593–595, 610–614. New York: Macmillan, 1935.

PERRIGO, H. W. *Factional Strife in District No. 12, United Mine Workers of America, 1919–1933.* Ph.D. Thesis, University of Wisconsin, 1933.

PIERSON, FRANK C. *Collective Bargaining Systems,* pp. 39–45, 170–198. Washington: American Council on Public Affairs, 1942.

PINKOWSKI, EDWARD. *John Siney, the Miners' Martyr.* Philadelphia: Sunshine Press, 1963.

POLAKOV, WALTER N. "Sufficient unto Himself Is the Coal Digger." *Labor and Nation,* May–June 1947, pp. 28–29.

POLLARD, SPENCER D. *Some Problems of Democracy in the Government of Labor Unions, with Special Reference to the United Mine Workers of America and the United Automobile Workers of America.* Ph.D. Thesis, Harvard University, 1940.

PORTER, EUGENE O. "The Colorado Coal Strike of 1913—An Interpretation." *The Historian,* Vol. XII, Autumn 1949, pp. 3–27.

RASKIN, A. H. "Secrets of John L. Lewis' Great Power." *New York Times Magazine,* October 5, 1952, pp. 15, 59.

ROBERTS, PETER. *Anthracite Coal Communities: A Study of the Demography, the Social, Educational, and Moral Life of the Anthracite Regions.* New York: Macmillan, 1904.

—————. *The Anthracite Coal Industry: A Study of the Economic Conditions and Relations of the Co-operative Forces in the Development of the Anthracite Coal Industry of Pennsylvania.* New York: Macmillan, 1901.

ROCHESTER, ANNA. *Labor and Coal.* New York: International Publishers, 1931.

ROE, MARY A. (C. M. Cornwall, pseud.). *Free, Yet Forgiving Their Own Chains* (a novel). New York: Dodd, Mead, 1876.

ROOD, HENRY E. *The Company Doctor* (a novel). Springfield, Mass.: Merriam, 1895.

ROOSEVELT, THEODORE. *Autobiography,* chap. 12, "Social and Industrial Justice" (anthracite strike, 1902). New York: Macmillan, 1919.

ROSEN, GEORGE. *The History of Miners' Diseases, a Medical and Social Interpretation.* New York: Schuman's, 1943.

ROSS, MALCOLM H. *Machine Age in the Hills.* New York: Macmillan, 1933.

ROY, ANDREW. *A History of the Coal Miners of the United States, from the Development of the Mines to the Close of the Anthracite Strike of 1902.* Columbus, Ohio: J. L. Trauger, 1907.

RYAN, FREDERICK L. *The Rehabilitation of Oklahoma Coal Mining Communities.* Norman: University of Oklahoma Press, 1935.

SCHLEGEL, MARVIN W. "The Workingmen's Benevolent Association: First Union of Anthracite Miners." *Pennsylvania History,* Vol. X, October 1943, pp. 243–267.

SEIDMAN, JOEL, et al. *The Worker Views His Union,* chap. 2, "Coal Miners: Unionism as a Tradition." Chicago: University of Chicago Press, 1958.

SELEKMAN, BEN M., and MARY VANKLEECK. *Employes' Representation in Coal Mines: A Study of the Industrial Representation Plan of the Colorado Fuel and Iron Company.* New York: Russell Sage Foundation, 1924.

SHEPPARD, MURIEL EARLEY. *Cloud by Day: The Story of Coal and Coke and People.* Chapel Hill: University of North Carolina Press, 1947.

SIMPSON, ALEXANDER G. *The Life of a Miner in Two Hemispheres.* New York: Abbey Press, 1903.

SINCLAIR, UPTON. *King Coal* (a novel of unorganized coal mining camps of Colorado). New York: Macmillan, 1917.

SOMERS, GERALD G. *Experience under National Wage Agreements: Grievance Settlement in Coal Mining.* Morgantown: West Virginia University Press, 1953.

SUFFERN, ARTHUR E. *The Coal Miners' Struggle for Industrial Status.* New York: Macmillan, 1926.

—————. *Conciliation and Arbitration in the Coal Industry of America.* Boston: Houghton Mifflin, 1915.

SULZBERGER, C. L. *Sit Down with John L. Lewis.* New York: Random House, 1938.

TIPPETT, THOMAS. *Horse Shoe Bottoms* (a novel of Illinois miners in the 1870's). New York: Harper, 1935.

TRACHTENBERG, ALEXANDER. *The History of Legislation for the Protection of Coal Miners in Pennsylvania, 1824–1915.* New York: International Publishers, 1942.

U.S. ANTHRACITE COAL STRIKE COMMISSION. *Report to the President on the Anthracite Coal Strike of May-October, 1902.* Washington: G.P.O., 1903.

U.S. BOARD OF INQUIRY ON THE LABOR DISPUTE IN THE BITUMINOUS COAL INDUSTRY. *In Re Coal Operators (and others) and United Mine Workers of America (Ind.), March 31, 1948.* Labor Arbitration Reports, Bureau of National Affairs, Washington, 9 LA 1016.

——————. *The Labor Dispute in the Bituminous Coal Industry.* Washington: G.P.O., 1950.

U.S. COAL MINES ADMINISTRATION. *A Medical Survey of the Bituminous Coal Industry.* Washington: G.P.O., 1947.

U.S. COMMISSION ON INDUSTRIAL RELATIONS (1912). *The Colorado Coal Miners' Strike.* (As reported in vols. 7 and 8.) Washington: G.P.O., 1916.

——————. *Further Proceedings Relating to the Colorado Strike, Large Foundations and Industrial Control.* Washington: G.P.O., 1916.

——————. *Rockefeller Interests in Colorado.* Washington: G.P.O., 1916.

U.S. CONGRESS. HOUSE. Committee on Education and Labor. *Welfare of Miners.* Washington: G.P.O., 1947.

U.S. CONGRESS. HOUSE. Committee on Labor. *Investigation of Wages and Working Conditions in the Coal-Mining Industry.* Washington: G.P.O., 1922.

U.S. CONGRESS. HOUSE. Committee on Mines and Mining. *Report on the Colorado Strike Investigations Made under House Resolution 387,* Document 1630. Washington: G.P.O., 1915.

VAN KLEECK, MARY. *Miners and Management: A Study of the Collective Agreement between the United Mine Workers of America and the Rocky Mountain Fuel Company, and an Analysis of the Problem of Coal in the United States.* New York: Russell Sage Foundation, 1934.

WALSH, WILLIAM J. *The United Mine Workers of America as an Economic and Social Force in the Anthracite Territory.* Washington: National Capital Press, 1931.

WARE, NORMAN J. *The Labor Movement in the United States, 1860–1895.* "The Miners," pp. 209–221. New York: Appleton, 1929.

WARNE, COLSTON E. "Industrial Relations in Coal," chap. 15, *Labor in Postwar America,* Colston E. Warne, ed. Brooklyn: Remsen Press, 1949.

WARNE, FRANK J. *The Coal-Mine Workers: A Study in Labor Organization.* New York: Longmans, Green, 1905.

——————. *The Slav Invasion and the Mine Workers: A Study in Immigration.* Philadelphia: Lippincott, 1904.

WATKINS, HAROLD M. *Coal and Men: An Economic and Social Study of the British and American Coal Fields* (with a forward by Professor John R. Commons). London: Allen and Unwin, 1934.

WECHSLER, JAMES A. *Labor Baron: A Portrait of John L. Lewis.* New York: William Morrow, 1944.

WEINBERG, EDGAR, ROBERT E. MALAHOFF, and ROBERT T. ADAMS. *Technological Change and Productivity in the Bituminous Coal Industry, 1920–60.* Washington: G.P.O., 1962.

WEST, GEORGE P. (U.S. Commission on Industrial Relations, 1912.) *Report on the Colorado Strike.* Washington: G.P.O., 1915.

WEST, HERBERT F., ed. *The Autobiography of Robert Watchorn.* Oklahoma City: The Robert Watchorn Charities, Ltd., 1959.

WICKERSHAM, EDWARD D. *Opposition to the International Officers of the United Mine Workers of America, 1919–1933.* Ph.D. Thesis, Cornell University, 1951.

WIEBE, ROBERT H. "The Anthracite Strike of 1902: A Record of Confusion." *The Mississippi Valley Historical Review,* Vol. XLVIII, No. 2, September 1961, pp. 229–251.

WIECK, EDWARD A. *The American Miners' Association: A Record of the Origin of Coal Miners' Unions in the United States.* New York: Russell Sage Foundation, 1940.

——————. *The Miners' Case and the Public Interest: A Documented Chronology* (with introduction by Mary Van Kleeck). New York: Russell Sage Foundation, 1947.

——————. *Preventing Fatal Explosions in Coal Mines: A Study of Recent Major Disasters in the United States as Accompaniments of Technological Change.* New York: Russell Sage Foundation, 1942.

WILLIAMS, BEN AMES. *Owen Glen* (a novel). Boston: Houghton Mifflin, 1950.

WILSON, JOHN M. *The Dark and the Damp: An Autobiography.* New York: Dutton, 1951.

WORMSER, RICHARD. *All's Fair* (a novel). New York: Modern Age Books, 1937.

YOUNG, DALLAS M. "Origin of the Progressive Mine Workers of America." *Journal of the Illinois State Historical Society,* Vol . XL, September 1947, pp. 313–330.

Communications

BARBASH, JACK. *Unions and Telephones.* New York: Harper, 1952.

CHAMBERLAIN, NEIL W. *The Union Challenge to Management Control,* Appendix D, pp. 317–329. New York: Harper, 1948.

DAVIS, PEARCE, and HENRY J. MEYER, eds. *Labor Dispute Settlements in the Telephone Industry, 1942–1945.* Washington: Bureau of National Affairs, 1946.

KENNEDY, J. C. "Sidelights on the Telegraphers' Strike." *Journal of Political Economy,* Vol. 15, 1907, pp. 548–551.

"Labor Unions in Transportation and Communications Industries." *Monthly Labor Review,* Vol. 70, No. 3, March 1950, pp. 275–278.

MCISAAC, ARCHIBALD M. *The Order of Railroad Telegraphers: A Study in*

Trade Unionism and Collective Bargaining. Princeton: Princeton University Press, 1933.

MAYER, HENRY. "The National Telephone Strike." *Labor and Nation,* July-August 1947, pp. 13–17.

MAYER, HENRY, AND ABRAHAM WEINER. "The New Jersey Telephone Company Case." *Industrial and Labor Relations Review,* Vol. 1, No. 3, April 1948, pp. 492–499.

SEGAL, MELVIN J. "Industrial Relations in Communications," chap. 19, *Labor in Postwar America,* Colston E. Warne, ed. Brooklyn: Remsen Press, 1949.

SEIDMAN, JOEL, *et al. The Worker Views His Union,* chap. 7, "Telephone Workers: White-Collar Unionism." Chicago: University of Chicago Press, 1958.

ULRIKSSON, VIDKUNN. *The Telegraphers: Their Craft and Their Unions.* Washington: Public Affairs Press, 1953.

U.S. COMMISSION ON INDUSTRIAL RELATIONS (1912). *Reports,* vol. 10, "Commercial Telegraph Companies," pp. 9291–9541. Washington: G.P.O., 1916.

U.S. CONGRESS. SENATE. Committee on Labor and Public Welfare. Subcommittee on Labor and Labor-Management Relations. *Communist Domination of Certain Unions,* pp. 43–58. Washington: G.P.O., 1951.

——————. ——————. *Labor-Management Relations in the Bell Telephone System,* hearings. Washington: G.P.O., 1950.

——————. ——————. *Labor-Management Relations in the Bell Telephone System,* Report No. 139. Washington: G.P.O., 1951.

Construction

BATES, HARRY. *Bricklayers' Century of Craftsmanship.* Washington: Bricklayers, Masons and Plasterers International Union, 1955.

BERTRAM, GORDON, and SHERMAN J. MAISEL. *Industrial Relations in the Construction Industry, the Northern California Experience.* Berkeley: Institute of Industrial Relations, University of California, 1955.

"Big Bill Retires." *Time,* Vol. LVIII, No. 27, December 31, 1951, pp. 11–12.

BLUM, SOLOMON. "Trade-Union Rules in the Building Trades," chap. X, *Studies in American Trade Unionism,* Jacob H. Hollander and George E. Barnett, eds. New York: Henry Holt, 1907.

"Building-Trades Bargaining Plan in Southern California." *Monthly Labor Review,* Vol. 70, No. 1, January 1950, pp. 14–18.

BUILDING TRADES EMPLOYERS' ASSOCIATION OF THE CITY OF NEW YORK. Committee on Welfare Funds. *A Review of Welfare Funds in the New York City Building Trades.* New York: The Association, 1951.

CHRISTIE, ROBERT A. *Empire in Wood: A History of the United Brotherhood of Carpenters and Joiners of America.* Cornell Studies in Industrial and Labor Relations, Vol. 7. Ithaca: New York State School of Industrial and Labor Relations at Cornell University, 1956.

COVINGTON, J. E. "Union Security Elections in the Building and Construction Industry under the Taft-Hartley Act." *Industrial and Labor Relations Review*, Vol. 4, No. 4, July 1951, pp. 543–555.

DEIBLER, FREDERICK S. *The Amalgamated Wood Workers' International Union of North America*. Bulletin 511. Madison: University of Wisconsin, 1912.

DERBER, MILTON. "Case Study 5, Building Construction," *Labor-Management Relations in Illini City*, Vol. 1. Champaign: Institute of Labor and Industrial Relations, University of Illinois, 1953.

DIDONATO, PIETRO. *Christ in Concrete* (a novel). Indianapolis: Bobbs-Merrill, 1939.

DUNLOP, JOHN T., and ARTHUR D. HILL. *Wage Adjustment Board: Wartime Stabilization in the Building and Construction Industry*. Cambridge: Harvard University Press, 1950.

"Fifty Years of Peace" (Building Trades Employers' Association of the City of New York). *Fortune*, February 1953, pp. 84–86.

GALENSON, WALTER. *The CIO Challenge to the AFL*, chap. 16, "The Building Trades," pp. 514–529. Cambridge: Harvard University Press, 1960.

GILPATRICK, THOMAS V. *A Case Study of Labor Relations in a Construction Company in a Midwestern Community*. M.S. Thesis, University of Illinois, 1947.

GRANT, LUKE. *National Erectors' Association and International Association of Bridge and Structural Ironworkers*. Washington: G.P.O., 1915. (Report issued by the U.S. Commission on Industrial Relations.)

HABER, WILLIAM. "Building Construction," chap. 4, *How Collective Bargaining Works*, Harry A. Millis, research director. New York: Twentieth Century Fund, 1945.

————. *Industrial Relations in the Building Industry*. Cambridge: Harvard University Press, 1930.

————, and HAROLD LEVINSON. *Labor Relations and Productivity in the Building Trades*. Ann Arbor: Bureau of Industrial Relations, University of Michigan, 1956.

HARRIS, HERBERT. *American Labor*, pp. 149–172. New Haven: Yale University Press, 1938.

HICHBORN, FRANKLIN. *The System as Uncovered by the San Francisco Graft Prosecution*. San Francisco: J. H. Barry, 1915.

HOROWITZ, MORRIS A. *The Structure and Government of the Carpenters' Union*. New York: John Wiley & Sons, 1962.

HOSKING, WILLIAM GEORGE. *A Study of Area Wage Structure and Wage Determination in the Building Construction Industry of Central New York State, 1942–1951*. Ph.D. Thesis, Cornell University, 1955.

ILLINOIS GENERAL ASSEMBLY. Joint Building Investigation Commission. *Report of Illinois Building Investigation Commission* (Dailey Commission). Springfield: Illinois State Register, 1923.

INTERNATIONAL UNION OF OPERATING ENGINEERS. *Fifty Years of Progress, 1896–1946*. Washington: The Union, 1946. (Reprinted from *International Engineer*, Vol. 89, No. 12.)

MCMAHON, EARL J., ed. and comp. *The Chicago Building Trades Council,*

Yesterday and Today. Chicago: Chicago and Cook County Building and Construction Trades Council, 1945.

MANGAN, JOHN. *History of the Steam Fitters' Protective Association of Chicago*. Chicago: The Association, 1930.

MERCEY, ARCH. *The Laborer's Story, 1903–1953*. Washington: International Hod Carriers', Building and Common Laborers' Union of America (AFL), 1954.

MINTON, BRUCE (Richard Bransten, pseud.), and JOHN STUART. *Men Who Lead Labor* (William Hutcheson). New York: Modern Age Books, 1937.

MONTGOMERY, R. E. *Industrial Relations in the Chicago Building Trades*. Chicago: University of Chicago Press, 1927.

"More Trouble in Paradise." *Fortune*, November 1946, pp. 154–159, 215–225.

NATIONAL JOINT BOARD FOR SETTLEMENT OF JURISDICTIONAL DISPUTES. "The Agreement Establishing a National Joint Board for the Settlement of Jurisdictional Disputes in Building and Construction Industries." *Industrial and Labor Relations Review*, Vol. 2, No. 3, April 1949, pp. 411–415.

NEW YORK STATE. Joint Legislative Committee on Housing (C. C. Lockwood, chairman). *Final Report*. Legislative Document 48. Albany: State Library, 1923.

PARTRIDGE, BELLAMY (Thomas Bailey, pseud.). *Big Freeze* (a novel). New York: Thomas Y. Crowell, 1948.

RADDOCK, MAXWELL. *Portrait of an American Labor Leader: William L. Hutcheson*. New York: American Institute of Social Science, 1955.

ROSE, WILLIAM T. "Daredevil Tradition Dates Back More Than Three Centuries: Mohawk Indians Are World Famous For Their Skills in 'High Steel'." *Industrial Bulletin*, Vol. 40, No. 10, October 1961, pp. 21–24.

RYAN, F. L. *Industrial Relations in the San Francisco Building Trades*. Norman: University of Oklahoma Press, 1936.

SCHEUCH, RICHARD. "Labor Policies in Residential Construction." *Industrial and Labor Relations Review*, Vol. 6, No. 3, April 1953, pp. 378–382.

SCOTT, LEROY. *The Walking Delegate* (a novel). New York: Doubleday, Page, 1905.

SEIDMAN, HAROLD. *Labor Czars*. New York: Liveright, 1938. (Chapters II, V, VI, VII, X.)

SEIDMAN, JOEL, et al. *The Worker Views His Union*, chap. 3, "Plumbers: Craft-conscious Unionism." Chicago: University of Chicago Press, 1958.

SHAW, FRANK L. *The Building Trades*. Cleveland: Survey Committee of the Cleveland Foundation, 1916.

SHELDON, HORACE E. *Union Security and the Taft-Hartley Act in the Buffalo Area*. Research Bulletin 4. Ithaca: New York State School of Industrial and Labor Relations at Cornell University, 1949.

SILVER, HENRY D. "Making a Living in Rochester: The Diary of Henry D. Silver, 1906–1914." *Rochester History*, Vol. XV, No. 4, October 1953.

SKIDMORE, HUBERT. *Hawk's Nest* (a novel). New York: Doubleday, Doran, 1941.

SOBOTKA, STEPHEN P. *The Influence of Unions on Wages and Earnings of*

Labor in the Construction Industry. Ph.D. Thesis, University of Chicago, 1952.

STRAND, KENNETH T. *Jurisdictional Disputes in Construction: The Causes, the Joint Board, and the NLRB.* Pullman: Bureau of Economic and Business Research, School of Economics and Business, Washington State University, 1961.

STRAUB, ADELBERT G., JR. *Whose Welfare? A Report on Union and Employer Welfare Plans in New York.* Albany: State of New York Insurance Department, 1954.

STRAUSS, GEORGE. "Business Agents in the Building Trades: A Case Study in a Community." *Industrial and Labor Relations Review,* Vol. 10, No. 2, January 1957, pp. 237–251.

──────. "Control by the Membership in Building Trades Unions." *American Journal of Sociology,* Vol. 61, No. 6, May 1956, pp. 527–535.

──────. *Unions in the Building Trades.* Buffalo: University of Buffalo, 1958.

U.S. COMMISSION ON INDUSTRIAL RELATIONS (1912). *Reports,* Vol. 2, "Building Trades of New York City," pp. 1581–1799. Washington: G.P.O., 1916.

──────. *Reports,* Vol. 6, "Labor Conditions in Construction Camps," pp. 5087–5168. Washington: G.P.O., 1916.

──────. *Reports,* Vol. 6, "The Painters' Strike in San Francisco," pp. 5473–5484. Washington: G.P.O., 1916.

U.S. CONGRESS. HOUSE. Committee on Education and Labor. *Construction Site Picketing.* Washington: G.P.O., 1960.

──────. ──────. *Northern New Jersey Jurisdictional Disputes in the A.F. of L. Building Trades.* Washington: G.P.O., 1947.

U.S. CONGRESS. SENATE. Committee on Labor and Public Welfare. Subcommittee on Labor and Labor-Management Relations. *To Amend the National Labor Relations Act, 1947 with Respect to the Building and Construction Industry.* Washington: G.P.O., 1951.

──────. ──────. *Labor-Management Relations in the Bonneville Power Administration.* Washington: G.P.O., 1951.

U.S. INDUSTRIAL COMMISSION (1898). *Reports,* Vol. 7, "Report on the Relations and Conditions of Capital and Labor Employed in Manufactures and General Business." *Digest,* pp. 136–149. Washington: G.P.O., 1901.

VON RHAU, HENRY. *Fraternally Yours* (a novel). Boston: Houghton Mifflin, 1949.

WARE, NORMAN J. *The Labor Movement in the United States, 1860–1895,* "The Carpenters," pp. 231–236. New York: Appleton, 1929.

WHITCOMB, ROBERT. *Talk United States!* (a novel). New York: Harrison Smith and Robert Haas, 1935.

WHITNEY, NATHANIEL R. *Jurisdiction in American Building-Trades Unions.* Baltimore: Johns Hopkins Press, 1914.

ZAUSNER, PHILIP. *Unvarnished: The Autobiography of a Union Leader* (Brotherhood of Painters, Decorators, and Paperhangers of America, New York District Council No. 9). New York: Brotherhood Publishers, 1941.

Education

AMERICAN FEDERATION OF TEACHERS, COMMISSION ON EDUCATIONAL RECONSTRUCTION. *Organizing the Teaching Profession.* Glencoe: Free Press, 1955.

DEITCH, JOSEPH. "Man On a Hot Seat" (New York City teachers' strike, April 11, 1962). *Saturday Review,* May 19, 1962, p. 55.

EKLUND, JOHN M. *Collective Negotiations Between Boards of Education and Teachers in the Determination of Personnel Policy in the Public Schools.* Ph.D. Thesis, Columbia University, 1954.

FORDYCE, WELLINGTON G. *The Origin and Development of Teachers Unions in the United States.* Ph.D. Thesis, Ohio State University, 1945.

HECHINGER, FRED M. "The Story Behind the Strike" (New York City teachers' strike, April 11, 1962). *Saturday Review,* May 19, 1962, pp. 54, 56, 78.

HERRICK, MARY. "Research in the Problems of Organized Teachers." *Proceedings of the Tenth Annual Meeting of the Industrial Relations Research Association,* September 5–7, 1957, pp. 249–253. Madison: The Association, 1958.

LONDON, JACK. "Barriers to the Development of Effective Personnel Practice in Public School Organization." *Educational Administration and Supervision,* Vol. 43, No. 2, February 1957, pp. 83–93.

—————. "The Development of a Grievance Procedure in the Public Schools." *Educational Administration and Supervision,* Vol. 43, No. 1, January 1957, pp. 1–18.

OAKES, RUSSELL C. *Public and Professional Reactions to Teachers' Strikes, 1918–1954.* Ph.D. Thesis, New York University, 1958.

PEARSE, ROBERT F. *Studies in White-Collar Unionism: The Development of a Teachers' Union.* Ph.D. Thesis, University of Chicago, 1950.

ROBINSON, AILEEN W. *A Critical Evaluation of the American Federation of Teachers.* Chicago: American Federation of Teachers, 1934.

SCHIFF, ALBERT. *A Study and Evaluation of Teachers' Strikes in the United States.* Ph.D. Thesis, Wayne State University, 1953.

SEYMOUR, HAROLD. "Should College Professors Organize into Unions? Divided, the Profession Weighs the Pros and Cons of Unionism." *Industrial Bulletin,* Vol. 41, No. 1, January 1962, pp. 17–20.

YABROFF, BERNARD, AND LILY MARY DAVID. "Collective Bargaining and Work Stoppages Involving Teachers." *Monthly Labor Review,* Vol. 76, No. 5, May 1953, pp. 475–479.

Electrical and Electronic

ANDERSON, F. J. "The Red Electric Machine: Behind the Matles Mask." *Plain Talk,* September 1947.

BRIGHT, ARTHUR A., JR. *The Electric-Lamp Industry: Technological Change and Economic Development from 1800 to 1947.* New York: Macmillan, 1949.

BROACH, HOWELL H. *Union Progress in New York: Story of the Moderni-*

zation of Union Structure and Business Methods in the Electrical Field. New York: International Brotherhood of Electrical Workers, 1929.

DEAN, LOIS. "Union Activity and Dual Loyalty." *Industrial and Labor Relations Review,* Vol. 7, No. 4, July 1954, pp. 526–536.

DERBER, MILTON. "Electrical Products," chap. 14, *How Collective Bargaining Works,* Harry A. Millis, research director. New York: Twentieth Century Fund, 1945.

FORD, MATTHEW. "Commie-Day in Clifton, New Jersey. *Plain Talk,* September 1947.

GALENSON, WALTER. *The CIO Challenge to the AFL,* chap. 5, "The Electrical and Radio Manufacturing Industries," pp. 239–265. Cambridge: Harvard University Press, 1960.

HARRINGTON, MICHAEL. "Catholics in the Labor Movement: A Case History." *Labor History,* Vol. 1, No. 3, Fall 1960, pp. 231–263.

HARRISON, CHARLES YALE. "Van Arsdale's Tight Little Island." *The Reporter,* April 11, 1950, pp. 11–14. (Local 3, IBEW.)

History of the Westinghouse Strike, East Pittsburgh, Pennsylvania. (No author indicated.) Turtle Creek, Pa.: Foley & Pierce, 1914.

"How a Business Agent Runs His Local." *Business Week,* October 20, 1956, pp. 92–98.

JULIANELLE, J. A. "Purge in Bridgeport, Connecticut." *Plain Talk,* September 1947.

"Labor: Father of the Twenty-Five-Hour Week." *Fortune,* March 1962, pp. 189–194.

MACHINE RESEARCH CORPORATION. *Plant City Reactions to Electrical Workers' Strike.* Princeton: The Corporation, 1946.

MARSH, CHARLES F. *Trade Unionism in the Electric Light and Power Industry.* Urbana: University of Illinois, 1930.

MULCAIRE, MICHAEL. *The International Brotherhood of Electrical Workers: A Study in Trade Union Structure and Functions.* Washington: Catholic University of America, 1923.

OZANNE, ROBERT WILLARD. *The Effect of Communist Leadership on American Trade Unions,* chap. 3. Ph.D. Thesis, University of Wisconsin, 1954.

"The Passing of Marion Hedges." *John Herling's Labor Letter,* January 17, 1959, pp. 3–4.

PETTINGILL, STUART A., and VINCENT ARKELL. "Electronics Employment and Labor Force." *Monthly Labor Review,* Vol. 76, No. 10, October 1953, pp. 1049–1054.

RASKIN, A. H. "Labor's Welfare State: The New York Electrical Workers." *The Atlantic Monthly,* Vol. 211, No. 4, April 1963, pp. 37–44.

SAPOSS. DAVID J. *Communism in American Unions,* part IV, chap. 22, pp. 227–236. New York: McGraw-Hill, 1959.

SEIDMAN, HAROLD. *Labor Czars,* chap. IX, "Electrical Workers Local 3," pp. 127–146. New York: Liveright, 1938.

SELIGMAN, DANIEL. "UE: The Biggest Communist Union." *American Mercury,* Vol. 69, July 1949, pp. 35–45.

"Union Receiver." *Business Week,* January 31, 1948, pp. 74–76.

U.S. CONGRESS. HOUSE. Committee on Education and Labor. *Investigation of Communist Infiltration into Labor Unions which Serve the Industries of the United States: The United Electrical, Radio and Machine Workers of America, CIO.* Washington: G.P.O., 1948.

U.S. INDUSTRIAL COMMISSION (1898). *Reports,* vol. 7, "Report on the Relations and Conditions of Capital and Labor Employed in Manufactures and General Business." *Digest,* pp. 151–152. Washington: G.P.O., 1901.

VELIE, LESTER. "The Union That Gives More to the Boss." *Reader's Digest,* January 1956, pp. 126–130.

WEBER, ARNOLD R. "Craft Representation in Industrial Unions." *Proceedings of the Fourteenth Annual Meeting of the Industrial Relations Research Association,* December 28–29, 1961, pp. 82–92. Madison, Wisconsin: The Association, 1962.

Food and Allied Products

APPEL, JOHN C. "The Unionization of Florida Cigarmakers and the Coming of the War with Spain." *Hispanic American Historical Review,* Vol. XXXVI, February 1956, pp. 38–49.

ARMOUR AND COMPANY; UNITED PACKINGHOUSE FOOD AND ALLIED WORKERS, AFL-CIO; AND AMALGAMATED MEAT CUTTERS AND BUTCHER WORKMEN OF NORTH AMERICA, AFL-CIO. Automation Committee. *Progress Report: Automation Committee.* Chicago: The Committee, June 19, 1961.

BELSKY, JOSEPH. *I, the Union: Being the Personalized Trade Union Story of the Hebrew Butcher Workers of America.* Yonkers: Raddock, 1953.

BLUM, FRED H. *Toward a Democratic Work Process: The Hormel-Packinghouse Workers' Experiment.* New York: Harper, 1954.

CARVER, ARTHUR H. *Personnel and Labor Problems in the Packing Industry.* Chicago: The University of Chicago Press, 1928.

COREY LEWIS. *Meat and Man: A Study of Monopoly, Unionism, and Food Policy.* New York: Viking Press, 1950.

DERBER, MILTON. "Case Study 1—Grain Processing." *Labor-Management Relations in Illini City,* Vol. 1. Champaign: Institute of Labor and Industrial Relations, University of Illinois, 1953.

EDDY, ARTHUR J. *Ganton and Company* (a novel). Chicago: McClurg, 1908.

GALENSON, WALTER. *The CIO Challenge to the AFL,* chap. 10, "The Meat Industry," pp. 349–378. Cambridge: Harvard University Press, 1960.

GARSIDE, EDWARD B. *Cranberry Red* (a novel). New York: Little, Brown, 1938.

GREENE, JOSIAH E. *Not in Our Stars* (a novel). New York: Macmillan, 1945.

HANNA, HILTON E., and JOSEPH BELSKY. *Picket and the Pen: The "Pat" Gorman Story.* Yonkers: American Institute of Social Science, 1960.

HERBST, ALMA. *The Negro in the Slaughtering and Meat Packing Industry in Chicago.* Ph.D. Thesis, University of Chicago, 1930.

HOPE, JOHN II. 'The Self-Survey of the Packinghouse Union: A Technique for Effecting Change.' "Trade Unions and Minority Problems." *The Journal of Social Issues,* Vol. IX, No. 1, 1953.

MCDONALD, GRACE L. (Margaret Graham, pseud.). *Swing Shift* (a novel). New York: Citadel, 1951.

MAURER, FLEISHER & ASSOCIATES, INC., WASHINGTON, D.C. *Union with a Heart: International Union of United Brewery, Flour, Cereal, Soft Drink and Distillery Workers of America, 75 Years of a Great Union, 1886–1961.* Cincinnati: International Union of United Brewery, Flour, Cereal, Soft Drink and Distillery Workers of America, 1961.

MONTGOMERY, LOUISE. *The American Girl in the Stockyards District.* Chicago: University of Chicago Press, 1913.

O'BRIEN, HOWARD V. *New Men for Old* (a novel). New York: Kennerley, 1914.

OZANNE, ROBERT WILLARD. *The Effect of Communist Leadership on American Trade Unions.* Ph.D. Thesis, University of Wisconsin, 1954.

PURCELL, THEODORE V. *Blue Collar Man: Patterns of Dual Allegiance in Industry.* Cambridge: Harvard University Press, 1960.

——————. *The Worker Speaks His Mind on Company and Union.* Cambridge: Harvard University Press, 1953.

RANDALL, ROGER L. "Labor Agreements in the West Coast Fishing Industry: Restraint of Trade or Basis of Industrial Stability?" *Industrial and Labor Relations Review,* Vol. 3, No. 4, July 1950, pp. 514–541.

SAPOSS, DAVID J. *Communism in American Unions,* pp. 119–270 *passim.* New York: McGraw-Hill, 1959.

SEIDMAN, HAROLD. *Labor Czars,* chap. XII, "The Markets," pp. 185–198. New York: Liveright, 1938.

SEIDMAN, JOEL. "Unity in Meat Packing: Problems and Prospects," chap. II, *New Dimensions in Collective Bargaining,* H. W. Davey, H. S. Kaltenborn, and S. H. Ruttenberg, eds. New York: Harper, 1959.

SINCLAIR, UPTON B. *The Jungle* (a novel). New York: Doubleday, Doran, 1906.

THOMPSON, CARL W. "Labor in the Packing Industry." *Journal of Political Economy,* Vol. 15, February 1907, pp. 88–107.

UNITED PACKINGHOUSE WORKERS OF AMERICA. *20 Years with UPWA.* Chicago: The Union, October 1957.

U.S. COMMISSION ON INDUSTRIAL RELATIONS (1912). *Reports,* vol. 4, "Life and Labor Conditions of Chicago Stockyards Employees," pp. 3459–3531. Washington: G.P.O., 1916.

U.S. CONGRESS. HOUSE. Committee on Education and Labor. *Communist Infiltration of Maritime and Fisheries Unions.* Washington: G.P.O., 1948.

——————. ——————. *Labor Practices in the Food Industry.* Washington: G.P.O., 1948.

WARE, NORMAN J. *The Labor Movement in the United States, 1860–1895,* "The Cigar Makers," pp. 258–279. New York: Appleton, 1929.

WITTE, EDWIN E. "Industrial Relations in Meat Packing," chap. 22, *Labor in Postwar America,* Colston E. Warne, ed. Brooklyn: Remsen Press, 1949.

Independent Organizations

BOW, FRANK T. *Independent Labor Organizations and the National Labor Relations Act.* New York: Prentice-Hall, 1940.

"The Case for the Local Independent Union." *Personnel,* November 1955, pp. 226–233.

MARSHALL, F. RAY. "Independent Unions in the Gulf Coast Petroleum Refining Industry—The Esso Experience." *Labor Law Journal,* Vol. 12, No. 9, September 1961, pp. 823–840.

REZLER, JULIUS. "Labor Organization at Du Pont: A Study in Independent Local Unionism." *Labor History,* Vol. 4, No. 2, Spring 1963, pp. 178–195.

SHOSTAK, ARTHUR B. *America's Forgotten Labor Organization: A Survey of the Role of the Single-Firm Independent Union in American Industry.* Princeton: Industrial Relations Section, Department of Economics, Princeton University, 1962.

TROY, LEO. "Local Independent and National Unions: Competitive Labor Organizations." *The Journal of Political Economy,* October 1960, pp. 487–506.

——————. *Local Independent Unionism: Two Case Studies.* New Brunswick, New Jersey: Institute of Management and Labor Relations, Rutgers State University, 1961.

——————. "Local Independent Unions and the American Labor Movement." *Industrial and Labor Relations Review,* Vol. 14, No. 3, April 1961, pp. 331–349. ("Communication" by Philip Taft, pp. 102–106; "Reply" by Leo Troy, pp. 106–110. Vol. 15, No. 1, October 1961.)

U.S. BUREAU OF LABOR STATISTICS. *Characteristics of Company Unions, 1935.* Washington: G.P.O., 1937.

——————. *Unaffiliated Local and Single-Employer Unions in the United States, 1961.* Washington: G.P.O., 1962.

U.S. CONGRESS. HOUSE. Committee on Education and Labor. *Labor-Management Reform Legislation,* Part 3. "Statement of J. W. Dunnebeck, President, International Society of Skilled Trades, Linden, Michigan," pp. 1157–1181; "Statement of Joseph Gritter, Secretary, Christian Labor Association of the United States of America," pp. 1198–1212. Washington: G.P.O., 1959.

Iron, Steel, and Metal

ALBERY, FAXON F. D. *Michael Ryan, Capitalist* (a novel). Columbus, Ohio: Rowfant, 1913.

AMERICAN MANAGEMENT ASSOCIATION. *Labor Relations in United States Steel,* Personnel Series No. 164. New York: The Association, 1955.

ATTAWAY, WILLIAM. *Blood on the Forge* (a novel). New York: Doubleday, Doran, 1941.

BAUDER RUSSELL. *Industrial Relations in the Machinery and Jobbing Branch of the Foundry Industry.* (Unpublished manuscript, University of Wisconsin Library.)

BELL, THOMAS. *Out of This Furnace* (a novel). Boston: Little, Brown, 1941.

BELMAN, ALBERT A. "Wage Chronology No. 11: Aluminum Company of America, 1939–1950." *Monthly Labor Review,* Vol. 71, No. 6, December 1950, pp. 688–692.

BRODY, DAVID. *Steelworkers in America: The Nonunion Era.* Cambridge: Harvard University Press, 1960.

BROMFIELD, LOUIS. *The Green Bay Tree* (a novel). New York: Grosset and Dunlap, 1927.

BROOKS, ROBERT R. R. *As Steel Goes,...Unionism in a Basic Industry.* New Haven: Yale University Press, 1940.

BYINGTON, M. F. *Homestead: The Households of a Mill Town.* New York: Charities Publication Committee, 1910.

CALDWELL, JANET TAYLOR. *Strong City* (a novel). New York: Scribner's, 1942.

CHAMBERLAIN, JOHN. "Philip Murray." *Life,* Vol. 20, No. 6, February 11, 1946, pp. 78–80, 82, 84, 86, 89–90.

CLOSE, K. "Steel Makers: 1937–1947." *Survey Graphic,* March 1947.

COLEMAN, GLEN M. *The Growth of Management-Labor Understanding in the Steel Industry of Western Pennsylvania, with Special Emphasis on Job Security and Seniority.* Ph.D. Thesis, University of Pittsburgh, 1953.

CROWELL, F. ELISABETH. "Painter's Row and the Commons." *Charities and the Commons* (later known as *Survey Graphic*), Vol. 21, No. 19, February 6, 1909, pp. 899–910.

DAUGHERTY, CARROLL R., M. G. DECHAZEAU, and S. S. STRATTON. *The Economics of the Iron and Steel Industry.* New York: McGraw-Hill, 1937.

DAVID, HENRY. "Upheaval at Homestead," chap. 7, *America in Crisis,* Daniel Aaron, ed. New York: Knopf, 1952.

DAVIS, HORACE B. *Labor and Steel.* New York: International Publishers, 1933.

DAVIS, JAMES J. *The Iron Puddler: My Life in the Rolling Mills and What Came of It.* New York: Grosset and Dunlap, 1922.

DEVYVER, FRANK T. "Collective Bargaining in Steel," chap. 16, *Labor in Postwar America,* Colston E. Warne, ed. Brooklyn: Remsen Press, 1949.

FACT FINDING BOARD. *Steel Producing Subsidiaries of U.S. Steel Corp. and United Steelworkers of America (CIO),* February 25, 1946. Labor Arbitration Reports, Bureau of National Affairs, Washington, 1 LA 630.

FEDERAL COUNCIL OF THE CHURCHES OF CHRIST IN AMERICA. Commission on the Church and Social Service. *Report of Special Committee...Con-*

cerning the Industrial Situation in South Bethlehem, Pennsylvania. New York: The Council, 1912.

FEDERAL COUNCIL OF CHURCHES OF CHRIST IN AMERICA. Research Department. *The Twelve Hour Day in the Steel Industry.* New York: The Council, 1923.

FISHER, THOMAS R. *Industrial Disputes and Federal Legislation, with Special Reference to the Railroad, Coal, Steel and Automobile Industries in the U.S. since 1900.* New York: Columbia University Press, 1940.

FITCH, JOHN. *The Steel Workers.* New York: Charities Publications, 1911.

FOSTER, WILLIAM Z. *The Great Steel Strike and Its Lessons.* New York: Huebsch, 1920.

——————. *The Steel Workers and the Fight for Labor's Rights.* New York: New Century Publishers, 1952.

——————. *Unionizing Steel.* New York. Workers Library, 1936.

GALENSON, WALTER. *The CIO Challenge to the AFL,* chap. 2, "The Organization of Steel," pp. 75–122. Cambridge: Harvard University Press, 1960.

——————. *The Unionization of the American Steel Industry.* Berkeley: University of California, Institute of Industrial Relations Reprint No. 84, 1956.

GARRATY, JOHN A. "The United States Steel Corporation Versus Labor: The Early Years." *Labor History,* Vol. 1, No. 1, Winter 1960, pp. 3–38.

GOULD, HELEN M. "Aliquippa" (Steel Strike, 1946). *Labor and Nation,* April-May 1946, pp. 27–30.

GREENE, JOSIAH E. *The Man with One Talent* (a novel). New York: McGraw-Hill, 1951.

GROGAN, WILLIAM. *John Riffe of the Steelworkers: American Labor Statesman.* New York: Coward-McCann, 1959.

GROSSMAN, JONATHAN. "Co-Operative Foundries." *New York History,* Vol. XXIV, April 1943, pp. 196–210.

——————. "The Molders' Struggle Against Contract Prison Labor." *New York History,* Vol. XXIII, October 1942, pp. 449–457.

GULICK, CHARLES A. *Labor Policy of the United States Steel Corporation.* New York: Columbia University Press, 1924.

GUTMAN, HERBERT G. "An Iron Workers' Strike in the Ohio Valley, 1873–1874." *The Ohio Historical Quarterly,* Vol. 68, No. 4, October 1959, pp. 353–370.

——————. "Two Lockouts in Pennsylvania 1873–1874." *The Pennsylvania Magazine of History and Biography,* Vol. LXXXIII, No. 3, July 1959, pp. 307–326.

HALPER, ALBERT. *The Foundry* (a novel). New York: Viking Press, 1934.

HARBISON, FREDERICK H. "Steel," chap 10, *How Collective Bargaining Works,* Harry A. Millis, research director. New York: Twentieth Century Fund, 1945.

——————, and ROBERT C. SPENCER. "The Politics of Collective Bargaining: The Postwar Record in Steel." *American Political Science Review,* Vol. 48, No. 3, September 1954, pp. 705–720.

HARRIS, CYRIL. *The Trouble at Hungersford* (a novel). Boston: Little, Brown, 1952.

HARVEY, G. B. M. *Henry Clay Frick*. New York and London: Scribner's, 1928.

INTERCHURCH WORLD MOVEMENT OF NORTH AMERICA. *Public Opinion and the Steel Strike*. New York: Harcourt, Brace, 1921.

——————. *Report on the Steel Strike of 1919*. New York: Harcourt, Brace, 1920.

"It Happened in Steel: Story of the M. C. Taylor Labor Formula." *Fortune*, May 1937, pp. 91–94.

JENSEN, VERNON H. *Heritage of Conflict: Labor Relations in the Nonferrous Metals Industry up to 1930*. Ithaca: Cornell University Press, 1950.

——————. *Nonferrous Metals Industry Unionism, 1932–1954*. Ithaca: New York State School of Industrial and Labor Relations, Cornell University, 1954.

KELLY, GEORGE E., and EDWIN BEACHLER. *Man of Steel: The Story of David J. McDonald*. New York: North American Book Co., 1954.

LAHNE, HERBERT J. "The Welder's Search for Craft Recognition." *Industrial and Labor Relations Review*, Vol. 11, No. 4, July 1958, pp. 591–607.

LEE, HARRY. *Sir and Brother* (a novel). New York: Appleton-Century-Crofts, 1948.

LEVIN, MEYER. *Citizens* (a novel). New York: Viking Press, 1940.

LEVINSON, HAROLD M. *Collective Bargaining in the Steel Industry: Pattern Setter or Pattern Follower?* Ann Arbor: Institute of Labor and Industrial Relations, University of Michigan-Wayne State University, 1962.

McCAFFREE, KENNETH M. *Bargaining in the Metal Trades in the Northwest*. Washington: U.S. Bureau of Labor Statistics, 1957.

McSORLEY, EDWARD. *Our Own Kind*. New York: Harper, 1946.

MANN, HENRY. *Adam Clarke* (a novel). New York: Popular Book Co., 1904.

MARTIN, JAMES M. *Which Way, Sirs, the Better?* (a novel). Boston: Arena, 1895.

MILLER, J. WADE. *Sharon Steel Corporation and United Steelworkers of America*. Washington: National Planning Association, 1949.

MURRAY, ROBERT K. "Communism and the Great Steel Strike of 1919." *Mississippi Valley Historical Review*, Vol. XXXVIII, December 1951, pp. 445–466.

NATIONAL LABOR RELATIONS BOARD. Division of Economic Research. *Written Trade Agreements in Collective Bargaining*, chap. 12, "The Steel Industry," pp. 189–209. Washington: G.P.O., 1940.

O'CONNOR, HARVEY. *Steel-Dictator*. New York: John Day, 1935.

OLDS, MARSHALL. *Analysis of the Interchurch World Movement Report on the Steel Strike*. New York: G. P. Putnam, 1922.

O'MALLEY, MICHAEL. *Miners Mill* (a novel). New York: Harper, 1962.

PALMER, FRANK L. *Spies in Steel: An Exposé of Industrial War*. Denver: Labor Press, 1928.

RAIMON, ROBERT L. "Affluence, Collective Bargaining and Steel." *Labor Law Journal*, November 1960, pp. 979–986.

ROBINSON, JESSE S. *The Amalgamated Association of Iron, Steel, and Tin Workers*. Baltimore: Johns Hopkins Press, 1920.

ROSS, CLINTON. *The Silent Workman* (a novel). New York: Putnam, 1886.

SAKOLSKI, A. M. "The Finances of the Iron Molders' Union." *Studies in American Trade Unionism*, Jacob H. Hollander and George E. Barnett, eds., pp. 83–107. New York: Holt, 1906.

SAPOSS, DAVID J. *Communism in American Unions*, pp. 119–270 *passim*. New York: McGraw-Hill, 1959.

—————. *Organization of Steel Workers*. New York: Bureau of Industrial Research, 1921.

SCOTT, LEROY. *The Walking Delegate* (a novel). New York: Doubleday, Page, 1905.

SEIDMAN, JOEL, *et al. The Worker Views His Union*, chap. 4, "Steel Workers: Militant Unionism," chap. 5, "Metal Workers: Factionalism and Conflict." Chicago: University of Chicago Press, 1958.

SELEKMAN, BEN M. *Employes' Representation in Steel Works: A Study of the Industrial Representation Plan of the Minnequa Steel Works of the Colorado Fuel and Iron Company*. New York: Russell Sage Foundation, 1924.

SELTZER, GEORGE. "The United Steelworkers and Unionwide Bargaining." *Monthly Labor Review*, Vol. 84, No. 2, February 1961, pp. 129–136.

SHULTZ, GEORGE P., and ROBERT P. CRISARA. *The LaPointe Machine Tool Company and United Steelworkers of America*. Washington: National Planning Association, 1952.

SINCLAIR, UPTON. *Little Steel* (a novel). New York: Farrar and Rinehart, 1938.

SMITH, WILLIAM DALE. *A Multitude of Men* (a novel). New York: Simon and Shuster, 1959.

'STEEL NEGOTIATION DOCUMENTS.' *Monthly Labor Review*, Vol. 82, No. 12, December 1959: George W. Taylor, "Remarks upon Conclusion of Steel Board Testimony," pp. 1330–1332; "The Steel Board's Report to the President," pp. 1333–1341; "The Supreme Court's Ruling in the Injunction Appeal," pp. 1342–1344; "The Kaiser-Steelworkers Agreement," pp. 1345–1346; and "A Long-Range Plan for Preventing Bargaining Crises," p. 1347.

"Steelworkers Are Tough and Their Union Is the Best Organized in the C.I.O." *Life*, February 4, 1946.

"Steelworkers Want Wartime Justice." *Fortune*, February 1944, pp. 164–166.

STIEBER, JACK. "Occupational Wage Differentials in the Basic Steel Industry." *Industrial and Labor Relations Review*, Vol. 12, No. 2, January 1959, pp. 167–181.

—————. *The Steel Industry Wage Structure: A Study of the Joint Union-Management Job Evaluation Program in the Basic Steel Industry*. Cambridge: Harvard University Press, 1959.

STOCKTON, FRANK T. *The International Molders' Union of North America.* Baltimore: Johns Hopkins Press, 1921.

STOWELL, MYRON R. *Fort Frick: Or the Siege of Homestead.* Pittsburgh: Pittsburgh Printing Company, 1893.

STRAUS, DONALD B. "Laws Won't Stop Strikes." *Harper's,* July 1, 1952, pp. 21–27.

TILLETT, DOROTHY S. (John Stephen Strange, pseud.). *Angry Dust* (a novel). New York: Doubleday, 1946.

TILOVE, ROBERT. *Collective Bargaining in the Steel Industry.* Philadelphia: University of Pennsylvania Press, 1948.

TROUTMANN, WILLIAM E., and PETER HAGBOLDT. *Hammers of Hell* (a novel). Chicago: New World Press, 1921.

ULMAN, LLOYD. *The Government of the Steel Workers' Union.* New York: John Wiley, 1962.

UNITED STATES, defendant. *The Steel Seizure Case* (Youngstown Sheet and Tube Co. *et al.* vs. Charles Sawyer), House Document No. 534, Parts I and II. Washington: G.P.O., 1952.

U.S. BOARD OF INQUIRY ON THE 1959 LABOR DISPUTE IN THE STEEL INDUSTRY. *Final Report.* Washington: The Board, January 6, 1960.

————. *Report to the President Submitted by the Board of Inquiry under Executive Orders 10843 and 10848 Pursuant to the "National Emergencies" Sections of the Labor Management Relations Act, 1947.* Washington: The Board, October 19, 1959.

U.S. BUREAU OF LABOR. *Report on Conditions of Employment in the Iron and Steel Industry in the United States,* Senate Document No. 110. Washington: G.P.O., 1911–1913.

U.S. BUREAU OF LABOR STATISTICS. *Work Stoppages: Basic Steel Industry, 1901–1958.* Washington: G.P.O., 1959.

U.S. COMMISSION ON INDUSTRIAL RELATIONS (1912). *Reports,* vol. 3, "The Metal Trades of Philadelphia," pp. 2817–2927. Washington: G.P.O., 1916.

U.S. CONGRESS. HOUSE. Committee on Education and Labor. *Investigation of Riot at Shakespeare Company, Kalamazoo, Michigan.* Washington: G.P.O., 1948.

————. ————. *Investigation of the Wage Stabilization Board.* Washington: G.P.O., 1952.

U.S. CONGRESS. HOUSE. Committee on the Judiciary. *Investigation of the Employment of Pinkerton Detectives in Connection with the Labor Troubles at Homestead, Pennsylvania.* Washington: G.P.O., 1892.

U.S. CONGRESS. SENATE. Committee on Labor and Public Welfare. Subcommittee on Labor and Labor-Management Relations. *Disputes Functions of the Wage Stabilization Board.* Washington: G.P.O., 1952.

————. ————. *National Emergency Labor Disputes.* Washington: G.P.O., 1952.

————. ————. Committee on the Judiciary. *Relationship Between Teamsters Union and Mine, Mill & Smelter Workers.* Washington: G.P.O., 1962.

U.S. Department of Labor. *Collective Bargaining in the Basic Steel Industry: A Study of the Public Interest and the Role of Government*. Washington: G.P.O., 1961.

U.S. Industrial Commission (1898). *Reports,* vol. 7, "Report on the Relations and Conditions of Capital and Labor Employed in Manufactures and General Business." *Digest,* pp. 84–85, 152–159, 382–398. Washington: G.P.O., 1901.

"United Steelworkers of America." *Fortune,* November 1946, pp. 142–144, 252–264.

Vorse, Mary H. *Men and Steel*. New York: Boni and Liveright, 1920.

Walker, Charles R. *Bread and Fire* (a novel). Boston: Houghton Mifflin, 1927.

——————. *Steel, the Diary of a Furnace Worker*. Boston: Atlantic Monthly Press, 1922.

——————. *Steeltown: An Industrial Case History of the Conflict between Progress and Security*. New York: Harper, 1950.

Ware, Norman J. *The Labor Movement in the United States, 1860–1895,* "The Iron and Steel Workers," pp. 228–231. New York: Appleton, 1929.

Weber, Arnold R. "Craft Representation in Industrial Unions." *Proceedings of the Fourteenth Annual Meeting of the Industrial Relations Research Association,* December 28–29, 1961, pp. 82–92. Madison: The Association, 1962.

Westin, Alan F. *The Anatomy of a Constitutional Law Case: Youngstown Sheet and Tube Co. v. Sawyer; the Steel Seizure Decision*. New York: Macmillan, 1958.

White, Victor. *Peter Domanig in America: Steel* (a novel). Indianapolis: Bobbs-Merrill, 1954.

Young, Ernest W. *Comments on the Interchurch Report on the Steel Strike of 1919*. Boston: R. G. Badger, 1921.

Zinke, George W. *Minnequa Plant of Colorado Fuel and Iron Corporation and Two Locals of United Steelworkers of America*. Washington: National Planning Association, 1951.

Leather and Fur

Brown, Leo C., S. J. *Union Policies in the Leather Industry*. Cambridge: Harvard University Press, 1947.

Burt, Edward W. *The Shoe-Craft: Its Organization*. Boston: The Everett Press, 1917.

Commons, J. R. *Labor and Administration,* chap. XIV, "American Shoemakers, 1648–1895," pp. 219–266. New York: Macmillan, 1913.

Davis, Horace B. *Shoes: The Workers and the Industry*. New York: International Publishers, 1940.

Foner, Philip S. *The Fur and Leather Workers Union*. Newark, New Jersey: Nordan Press, 1950.

GALSTER, AUGUSTA E. *The Labor Movement in the Shoe Industry, Especially in Philadelphia.* New York: Ronald, 1924.

HALL, JOHN PHILIP. "The Knights of St. Crispin in Massachusetts, 1869–1878." *Journal of Economic History,* Vol. XVIII, June 1958, pp. 161–175.

JETER, GOETZE. *The Strikers* (a novel about a shoe factory in New England during the 1930's). Philadelphia: Stokes, 1937.

LEITER, ROBERT D. "The Fur Workers Union." *Industrial and Labor Relations Review,* Vol. 3, No. 2, January 1950, pp. 163–186.

LESCOHIER, DON D. *The Knights of St. Crispin, 1867–1874: A Study in the Industrial Causes of Trade Unionism.* Madison: University of Wisconsin, 1910.

MCNEILL, GEORGE E., ed. *The Labor Movement: The Problem of Today,* pp. 209–213. New York: M. W. Hazen, 1892. (An account of the Brockton strike of 1885 and the settlement reached based upon the "Philadelphia Rules," so-called from their previous adoption and use by the Philadelphia Shoe manufacturers and operatives.)

MORGAN, J. W. "The History of Labor Relations in the Leather Industry;" "Labor Union Development in the Tanning Industry;" "The Leather Union Now a Potent Industry Force;" "Communism in the Leather Labor Unions;" "Communist Tactics in the Leather Unions;" "Combatting Communism in Leather Unions;" "The T-H Act and the Leather Industry;" "The Unions are Held Responsible;" "Recent Effects of the T-H Act in the Leather Industry." *Leather and Shoes,* June 1, July 10, July 24, August 14, August 28, September 11, September 25, October 9, October 23, 1948.

NESTOR, AGNES. *Brief History of the International Glove Workers Union of America.* Chicago: The Union, 1942.

NORTON, THOMAS L. *Trade Union Policies in the Massachusetts Shoe Industry, 1919–1929.* New York: Columbia University Press, 1932.

SAPOSS, DAVID J. *Communism in American Unions,* pp. 119–270 *passim.* New York: McGraw-Hill, 1959.

SHULTZ, GEORGE P. *Pressures on Wage Decisions: A Case Study in the Shoe Industry.* New York: Published jointly by the Technology Press of the Massachusetts Institute of Technology and Wiley, 1951. (The Brotherhood of Shoe and Allied Craftsmen, an independent union).

TWENTIETH CENTURY ASSOCIATION, BOSTON. *The Strike of the Shoe Workers in Marlboro, Mass., November 14, 1898–May 5, 1899*...Boston: Boston Co-operative Press, 1900.

U.S. INDUSTRIAL COMMISSION (1898). *Reports,* vol. 7, "Report on the Relations and Conditions of Capital and Labor Employed in Manufactures and General Business." *Digest,* pp. 176–180. Washington: G.P.O., 1901.

WALINSKY, OSSIP, ed. *Industrial Peace in Action: Thirty Years of Collective Bargaining in the Pocketbook Industry of New York.* New York: Pocketbook Workers Union, 1948.

WARE, NORMAN J. *The Labor Movement in the United States, 1860–1895,* "The Shoemakers." pp. 200–209. New York: Appleton, 1929.

WARNER, WILLIAM L., and J. O. LOW. *The Social System of the Modern Factory: The Strike, a Social Analysis.* New Haven: Yale University Press, 1947.

Lumber, Woodworking, Paper, Pulp

ALLEN, RUTH A. *East Texas Lumber Workers: An Economic and Social Picture.* Austin: University of Texas Press, 1961.

BURNS, MATTHEW J. *History of the Papermakers.* Albany: n.p., 1922. Microfilm in Library of New York State School of Industrial and Labor Relations made from typewritten copy.

CANTWELL, ROBERT. *Land of Plenty* (a novel about a strike of lumber workers in the West during the 1930's). New York: Farrar and Rinehart, 1934.

COLMAN, LOUIS. *Lumber* (a novel about strikes in a lumber mill town in the Northwest). Boston: Little, Brown, 1931.

DEIBLER, FREDERICK S. *The Amalgamated Wood Workers' International Union of America: A Historical Study of Trade Unionism in Its Relation to the Development of an Industry.* Madison: University of Wisconsin, 1912.

DOERFLINGER, WILLIAM M. *Shantymen and Shantyboys: Songs of Sailor and Lumberman.* New York: Macmillan, 1951.

ELIEL, PAUL. "Industrial Peace and Conflict: A Study of Two Pacific Coast Industries" (Paper and Pulp). *Industrial and Labor Relations Review,* Vol. 2, No. 4, July 1949, pp. 477–501.

ENGBERG, GEORGE B. "Collective Bargaining in the Lumber Industry of the Upper Great Lakes States." *Agricultural History,* Vol. XXIV, October 1950, pp. 205–211.

——————. "Lumber and Labor in the Lake States." *Minnesota History,* Vol. XXXVI, March 1959, pp. 153–166.

FLEMING, R. W., and EDWIN E. WITTE. *Marathon Corporation and Seven Labor Unions.* Washington: National Planning Association, 1950.

GALENSON, WALTER. *The CIO Challenge to the AFL,* chap. 11, "The Lumber Industry," pp. 379–408. Cambridge: Harvard University Press, 1960.

GLOCK, MARGARET S. *Collective Bargaining in the Pacific Northwest Lumber Industry.* Berkeley: Institute of Industrial Relations, University of California, 1955.

GOODSTEIN, ANITA SHAFER. "Labor Relations in the Saginaw Valley Lumber Industry, 1865–1885." *Bulletin of the Business Historical Society,* Vol. XXVII, December 1953, pp. 193–221.

HAPGOOD, HUTCHINS. *The Spirit of Labor* (a novel). New York: Duffield, 1907.

HARRIS, CYRIL. *The Trouble at Hungersford* (a novel). Boston: Little, Brown, 1952.

HART, ALAN. *In the Lives of Men* (a novel). New York: Norton, 1937.

INDUSTRIAL WORKERS OF THE WORLD. *The Lumber Industry and Its Workers.* Chicago: The Union, 1921.

JENSEN, VERNON H. "Industrial Relations in the Lumber Industry," chap. 24, *Labor in Postwar America*, Colston E. Warne, ed. Brooklyn: Remsen Press, 1949.

―――――. *Lumber and Labor.* New York: Farrar and Rinehart, 1945.

KERR, CLARK, and ROGER RANDALL. *Crown Zellerbach and the Pacific Coast Pulp and Paper Industry and International Brotherhood of Pulp, Sulphite and Paper Mill Workers and International Brotherhood of Paper Makers.* Washington: National Planning Association, 1948.

MACDONALD, ROBERT M. "Unionism and the Wage Structure in the United States Pulp and Paper Industry," *The Evolution of Wage Structure,* Lloyd G. Reynolds and Cynthia H. Taft, pp. 99–166. New Haven: Yale University Press, 1956.

MAHER, RICHARD A. *Gold Must Be Tried by Fire* (a novel about paper mill workers around 1915). New York: Macmillan, 1917.

MORGAN, MURRAY C. (Cromwell Murray, pseud.). *The Viewless Winds* (a novel about labor-capital conflict in an Oregon logging town during the 1930's). New York: Dutton, 1949.

MYERS, CHARLES A., and GEORGE P. SHULTZ. *Nashua Gummed and Coated Paper Company and Seven AFL Unions.* Washington: National Planning Association, 1950.

RANDALL, ROGER. *Labor Relations in the Pulp and Paper Industry of the Pacific Northwest.* Portland, Oregon: Northwest Regional Council, 1942.

SAPOSS, DAVID J. *Communism in American Unions,* pp. 119–270 *passim.* New York: McGraw-Hill, 1959.

TELLER, CHARLOTTE. *The Cage* (a novel about lumber workers in Chicago during the 1880's). New York: Appleton, 1907.

TODES, CHARLOTTE. *Labor and Lumber.* New York: International Publishers, 1931.

TYLER, ROBERT L. "The United States Government as Union Organizer: The Loyal Legion of Loggers and Lumbermen." *Mississippi Valley Historical Review,* Vol. XLVII, December 1960, pp. 434–451.

WEATHERWAX, CLARA. *Marching! Marching!* (a novel about lumber workers in the Northwest during the 1930's). New York: John Day, 1935.

WEBER, ARNOLD R. "Craft Representation in Industrial Unions." *Proceedings of the Fourteenth Annual Meeting of the Industrial Relations Research Association,* December 28–29, 1961, pp. 82–92. Madison: The Association, 1962.

Machinist

BLACK-LISTED MACHINIST. *Capital and Labor.* Chicago: Publisher Unknown, 1902.

DAHLHEIMER, H. *A History of the Mechanics Educational Society of America in Detroit from Its Inception in 1933 through 1937.* Detroit: Mechanics Educational Society of America, 1951.

GALENSON, WALTER. *The CIO Challenge to the AFL,* chap. 15, "The Machinists," pp. 495–513. Cambridge: Harvard University Press, 1960.

GROVES, HAROLD M. *The Machinist in Industry.* (Unpublished manuscript, University of Wisconsin Library.)

HEDGES, MARION HAWTHORNE. *The Iron City* (a novel). New York: Boni and Liveright, 1919.

INTERNATIONAL ASSOCIATION OF MACHINISTS. *Half a Century with the International Association of Machinists.* Washington: The Union, 1938.

————.*Machinists on the March, 1888–1950.* Washington: The Union, May, 1950.

JACOBS, PAUL. "Mr. Hayes Settles a Local Disturbance." *The Reporter Magazine,* April 2, 1959, pp. 18–21.

KERR, CLARK, and GEORGE HALVERSON. *Lockheed Aircraft Corporation and International Association of Machinists.* Washington: National Planning Association, 1949.

LICHLITER, MARCELLUS D. *History of the Junior Order United American Mechanics of the United States of North America.* Philadelphia: Lippincott, 1908.

NATIONAL LABOR RELATIONS BOARD. Division of Economic Research. *Written Trade Agreements in Collective Bargaining,* chap. 10, "The Machinists," pp. 149–166. Washington: G.P.O., 1940.

"No-Raid Agreement between UAW and IAM." *Monthly Labor Review,* Vol. 70, No. 3, March 1950, pp. 278–279.

PERLMAN, MARK. *Democracy in the International Association of Machinists.* New York: John Wiley, 1962.

————. *The Machinists: A New Study in American Trade Unionism.* Cambridge: Harvard University Press, 1961.

WARD, ESTOLV. *The Piecard* (a novel). New York: Associated Authors, 1954.

WEBSTER, HENRY K. *An American Family: A Novel of Today.* Indianapolis: Bobbs-Merrill, 1918.

WHARTON, A. O. "Fifty Years of the Machinists Union." *Labor Information Bulletin,* Vol. V, No. 5, May 1938, pp. 1–4.

Metal Mining

DAVIDSON, LALLAH S. *South of Joplin* (a novel about lead miners and the CIO in Missouri, Oklahoma, and Kansas during the 1930's). New York: Norton, 1939.

DELLI QUADRI, CARMEN LEONARD. *Labor Relations on the Mesabi Range.* M.A. Thesis, University of Colorado, 1944.

ELLIOTT, RUSSELL R. "Labor Troubles in the Mining Camp at Goldfield, Nevada, 1906–1908." *Pacific Historical Review,* Vol. XIX, November 1950, pp. 369–384.

————. *Radical Labor in the Nevada Mining Booms, 1900–1920.* Carson City, Nevada: State Printing Office, 1961.

FOOTE, MARY H. *Coeur d'Alene* (a novel about a labor war between a mining syndicate and a union based on Coeur d'Alene riots). Boston: Houghton Mifflin, 1894.

GARLAND, HAMLIN. *Hesper* (a novel about Colorado miners striking for a nine-hour day around 1900). New York: Harper, 1903.

GAZZAM, JOSEPH P. "The Leadville Strike of 1896." *Bulletin of the Missouri Historical Society,* Vol. VII, October 1950, pp. 89–94.

HURT, WALTER. *The Scarlet Shadow* (a novel about the Cripple Creek Strike around 1900). Girard, Kansas: Appeal to Reason, 1907.

JENSEN, VERNON H. *Heritage of Conflict: Labor Relations in the Nonferrous Metals Industry Up to 1930.* Ithaca: Cornell University Press, 1950.

——————. *Nonferrous Metals Industry Unionism, 1932–1954.* Ithaca: New York State School of Industrial and Labor Relations, Cornell University, 1954.

LANGDON, EMMA F. *The Cripple Creek Strike: A History of Industrial Wars in Colorado, 1903–4–5.* Denver: Great Western, 1904–1905.

——————. *Labor's Greatest Conflict: The Formation of the Western Federation of Miners, a Brief Account of the Rise of the United Mine Workers of America.* Denver: Great Western, 1908.

OZANNE, ROBERT W. *The Effect of Communist Leadership on American Trade Unions,* Chapter 3 (Mine, Mill and Smelter Workers Union). Ph.D. Thesis, University of Wisconsin, 1954.

PETERSEN, WILLIAM J. "Regulating the Lead Miners." *Palimpsest,* Vol. XVII, June 1936, pp. 185–200.

RASTALL, BENJAMIN M. *The Labor History of the Cripple Creek District.* Madison: University of Wisconsin, 1908.

ROOSEVELT, THEODORE. *Autobiography,* chap. XIII, "Social and Industrial Justice" (Western Federation of Miners). New York: Macmillan, 1919.

SAPOSS, DAVID J. *Communism in American Unions,* pp. 119–270 *passim.* (Mine, Mill and Smelter Workers Union). New York: McGraw-Hill, 1959.

SHELDON, CHARLES M. *His Brother's Keeper* (a novel about Western iron miners based on events in an actual strike during the 1890's). Boston: Congregational Sunday-School and Publishing Society, 1896.

STAVIS, BARRIE. *The Man Who Never Died: A Play About Joe Hill.* New York: Haven Press, 1954.

SULLIVAN, WILLIAM A. "The 1913 Revolt of the Michigan Copper Miners." *Michigan History,* Vol. 43, No. 3, September 1959, pp. 3–23.

U.S. COMMISSION ON INDUSTRIAL RELATIONS (1912). *Final Report and Testimony,* Vol. XI, pp. 10569–10572 (Western Federation of Miners). Washington: G.P.O., 1916.

U.S. CONGRESS. SENATE. Committee on Labor and Public Welfare. Subcommittee on Labor and Labor-Management Relations. *Communist Domination of Certain Unions,* pp. 97–100 (Mine, Mill and Smelter Workers Union). Washington: G.P.O., 1951.

——————. ——————. Committee on the Judiciary. *Relationship Between*

Teamsters Union, and Mine, Mill & Smelter Workers. Washington, G.P.O., 1962.

WOOD, FREMONT. *The Introductory Chapter to the History of the Trials of Moyer, Haywood, and Pettibone.* Caldwell, Idaho: Caxton, 1931.

Music and Entertainment

BAKER, ROBERT O. *The International Alliance of Theatrical Stage Employes and Moving Picture Machine Operators of the United States and Canada.* Lawrence, Kansas: The Author, 1933.

CHRISTENSON, C. LAWRENCE. "Chicago Service Trades," chap. 15, *How Collective Bargaining Works,* Harry A. Millis, research director (Motion Picture Machine Operators of Chicago and Musicians of Chicago). New York: Twentieth Century Fund, 1945.

COMMONS, JOHN R. *Labor and Administration,* "The Musicians of St. Louis and New York." New York: Macmillan, 1913.

COUNTRY, VERN. "The Organized Musicians." *University of Chicago Law Review.* Part I: Vol. 16, No. 1, Autumn 1948, pp. 56–85; Part II: Vol. 16, No. 2, Winter 1949, pp. 239–297.

FAULKENDER, ROBERT EDGAR. *Historical Development and Basic Policies of the Actors Equity.* Ph.D. Thesis, University of Pittsburgh, 1954.

HARDING, ALFRED. *The Revolt of the Actors.* New York: William Morrow, 1929.

LEITER, ROBERT D. *The Musicians and Petrillo.* New York: Bookman Associates, 1953.

LOFT, ABRAM. *Musicians Guild and Union: A Consideration of the Evolution of Protective Organization among Musicians.* Ph.D. Thesis, Columbia University, 1950.

LUNDE, ANDERS S. "The American Federation of Musicians and the Recording Ban." *Public Opinion Quarterly,* Vol. 12, No. 1, Spring 1948, pp. 45–56.

MAHER, JEWEL G. *Analysis of Organization and Collective Bargaining by Radio Artists* (AFRA). Ph.D. Thesis, University of Chicago, 1951.

MENDE, ROBERT. *Spit and the Stars.* New York: Rinehart, 1949.

MILLER, MERLE. *The Judges and the Judged* (Report for the American Civil Liberties Union). Garden City: Doubleday, 1952.

PEARLIN, LEONARD I., and HENRY E. RICHARDS. "Equity: A Study of Union Democracy," *Labor and Trade Unionism: An Interdisciplinary Reader,* Walter Galenson and Seymour Lipset, eds., pp. 265–281. New York: Wiley, 1960.

ROSS, MURRAY. *Stars and Strikes: Unionization of Hollywood.* New York: Columbia University Press, 1941.

SAPOSS, DAVID J. *Communism in American Unions,* chapters 4–9, pp. 19–81. New York: McGraw-Hill, 1959.

SEIDMAN, HAROLD. *Labor Czars,* chap. XI, "The Motion Picture Operators," pp. 172–184. New York: Liveright, 1938.

U.S. CONGRESS. HOUSE. Committee on Education and Labor. *Economic Conditions in the Performing Arts.* Washington: G.P.O., 1962.

———————. ———————. *Investigation of Associated Actors and Artistes of American and Affiliated Unions.* Washington: G.P.O., 1948.

———————. ———————. *Investigation of James C. Petrillo, The American Federation of Musicians, et al.* Washington: G.P.O., 1947.

———————. ———————. *Jurisdictional Disputes in the Motion Picture Industry.* Washington: G.P.O., 1948.

———————. ———————. *Restrictive Union Practices of the American Federation of Musicians.* Washington: G.P.O., 1948.

———————. ———————. Committee on Un-American Activities. *Communist Methods of Infiltration (Entertainment).* Washington: G.P.O., 1954.

———————. ———————. *Hearings Regarding the Communist Infiltration of the Motion Picture Industry.* Washington: G.P.O., 1947.

U.S. CONGRESS. SENATE. Committee on Government Operations. Permanent Subcommittee on Investigations. *American Guild of Variety Artists.* Washington: G.P.O., 1962.

U.S. INDUSTRIAL COMMISSION (1898). *Reports,* vol. 7, "Report on the Relations and Conditions of Capital and Labor Employed in Manufactures and General Business." *Digest* pp. 198–199. Washington: G.P.O., 1901.

Newspapers

ALLEN, WALTER M. "A Survey of the Extent of Unionization of Daily Newspaper Pressrooms by the I.P.P. & A.U. of N.A." *Proceedings of the Tenth Annual Meeting of the Industrial Relations Research Association,* September 5–7, 1957, pp. 254–259. Madison: The Association, 1958.

BENDINER, ROBERT. "One for All—and All for Nothing." *Reporter,* April 2, 1959, pp. 13–17.

BROWN, BERNARD D. "Labor's Shotgun Wedding." *New Leader,* Vol. XLVI, No. 8, April 15, 1963, pp. 16–17.

BURNS, ROBERT K. "Daily Newspapers," chap. 2, *How Collective Bargaining Works,* Harry A. Millis, research director. New York: Twentieth Century Fund, 1945.

HARRIS, HERBERT. *American Labor,* pp. 173–192 (Newspaper Guild). New Haven: Yale University Press, 1938.

MINTON, BRUCE B. (Richard Bransten, pseud.), and JOHN STUART. *Men Who Lead Labor* (Biography of Heywood Broun). New York: Modern Age Books, 1937.

MURASKEN, ESTELLE. *Newswriters' Unions in English-Speaking Countries.* New York: U.S. Works Progress Administration, 1937. (Mimeo.).

"The Nation: Labor" (New York City Newspaper Strike, December 1962–March 1963). *Time,* Vol. LXXXI, No. 9, March 1, 1963, pp. 13–17.

NATIONAL LABOR RELATIONS BOARD. Division of Economic Research. *Collective Bargaining in the Newspaper Industry.* Washington: G.P.O., 1939.

SAPOSS, DAVID J. *Communism in American Unions,* pp. 119–270 *passim.* (Newspaper Guild). New York: McGraw-Hill, 1959.

Printing and Publishing

BAKER, ELIZABETH F. "The Development of the International Printing Pressmen and Assistants' Union." *Proceedings of the Tenth Annual Meeting of the Industrial Relations Research Association,* September 5–7, 1957, pp. 156–162. Madison: The Association, 1958.

――――――. *Displacement of Men by Machines: Effects of Technological Change in Commercial Printing.* New York: Columbia University Press, 1933.

――――――. *Printers and Technology: A History of the International Printing Pressmen and Assistants' Union.* New York: Columbia University Press, 1957.

――――――. "The Printing Foreman—Union Man: A Historical Sketch." *Industrial and Labor Relations Review,* Vol. 4, No. 2, January 1951, pp. 223–235.

――――――. "The Printing Pressroom Foreman—Union Man: A Case Study." *Industrial and Labor Relations Review,* Vol. 4, No. 3, April 1951, pp. 367–385.

BARNETT, GEORGE. *The Printers: A Study in American Trade Unionism.* Cambridge: American Economic Association, 1909.

BROWN, EMILY C. "Book and Job Printing," chap. 3, *How Collective Bargaining Works,* Harry A. Millis, research director. New York: Twentieth Century Fund, 1945.

BURNS, ROBERT K. "Industrial Relations in Printing," chap. 18, *Labor in Postwar America,* Colston E. Warne, ed. Brooklyn: Remsen Press, 1949.

CLARK, FLORENCE ELIZABETH. *The Printing Trades and Their Workers.* Scranton: International Text Books, 1932.

CORKERY, JAMES P. "Wage Chronology No. 16: Chicago Printing, 1939–50." *Monthly Labor Review,* Vol. 73, No. 1, July 1951, pp. 49–56.

DENKER, DAVID. "The Printers: Craft Unionism." *Current History,* July 1954, pp. 26–30.

FEIN, MARVIN. *The International Typographical Union 1910–29.* (Unpublished manuscript, University of Wisconsin.)

GALENSON, WALTER. *The CIO Challenge to the AFL,* chap. 17, "Printing and Publishing," pp. 530–565. Cambridge: Harvard University Press, 1960.

HARD, WILLIAM. "The Typographical Union—Model for All." *The Reader's Digest,* June 1943, pp. 1–5.

HOAGLAND, HENRY E. *Collective Bargaining in the Lithographic Industry.* New York: Columbia University Press, 1917.

INTERNATIONAL PRINTING PRESSMEN AND ASSISTANTS' UNION OF NORTH AMERICA. *History of the Suit of the Chicago Printing Pressmen's Union against the Officers of the International Printing Pressmen and Assistants' Union of North America* (pamphlet). Chicago: The Union, 1919.

KOVNER, JOSEPH. "Basic Issue Between ITU and the T-H Law." *Labor and Nation,* January-February 1948, pp. 13-14.

LAMPMAN, BEN HUR. *Tramp Printer.* Portland, Oregon: Metropolitan, 1934.

LEESE, CHARLES. *Collective Bargaining among Photo-Engravers in Philadelphia.* Philadelphia: University of Pennsylvania Press, 1929.

LIPSET, SEYMOUR M., MARTIN A. TROW, and JAMES S. COLEMAN. *Union Democracy: The Internal Politics of the International Typographical Union.* Glencoe, Ill.: Free Press, 1956.

LOFT, JACOB. "Backgrounds and Perspectives in the Printers-Publishers Fight." *Labor and Nation,* March-April 1948, pp. 19–20, 48.

————. *The Printing Trades.* New York: Farrar and Rinehart, 1944.

LYNCH, JAMES M. *Epochal History of the International Typographical Union.* Indianapolis: International Typographical Union, 1925.

MUNSON, FRED C. *Labor Relations in the Lithographic Industry.* Cambridge: Harvard University Press, 1963.

NATIONAL LABOR RELATIONS BOARD. Division of Economic Research. *Written Trade Agreements in Collective Bargaining,* chap. 4, "The Printing Industry," pp. 49–62. Washington: G.P.O., 1940.

PASCHELL, WILLIAM. "The International Typographical Union." *Monthly Labor Review,* Vol. 74, No. 5, May 1952, pp. 493–498.

PERLMAN, SELIG, and PHILIP TAFT. *History of Labor in the United States, 1896–1932,* pp. 51–60, 456–460, 497–499. New York: Macmillan, 1935.

PORTER, ARTHUR R., JR. *Job Property Rights: A Study of the Job Controls of the International Typographical Union.* New York: King's Crown Press, 1954.

POWELL, LEONA M. *The History of the United Typothetae of America.* Chicago: University of Chicago Press, 1926.

RAYMOND, MARGARET T. *Bend in the Road* (a novel). New York: Longmans, Green, 1934.

ROSE, WILLIAM T. "New York Union Advertises to Tell Its Story: Lithographers Condemn Featherbedding, Welcome Automation as Tool for Progress." *Industrial Bulletin,* Vol. 41, No. 3, March 1962, pp. 3–7.

SEYBOLD, JOHN W. *The Philadelphia Printing Industry: A Case Study.* Philadelphia: University of Pennsylvania Press, 1949.

SOFFER, BENSON. "The Role of Union Foremen in the Evolution of the International Typographical Union." *Labor History,* Vol. 2, No. 1, Winter 1961, pp. 62–81.

STEVENS, GEORGE A. *New York Typographical Union No. 6: A Study of a Modern Trade Union and Its Predecessors.* Albany: New York State Department of Labor, 1913.

STEWART, ETHELBERT. "A Documentary History of the Early Organizations of Printers." *Bulletin of the Bureau of Labor,* Document 61, pp. 857–1033. Washington: G.P.O., 1905.

TRACY, GEORGE A. *History of the Typographical Union: Its Beginnings, Progress and Development, Its Beneficial and Educational Features together with a Chapter on the Early Organization of Printers.* Indianapolis: International Typographical Union, 1913.

U.S. CONGRESS. HOUSE. Committee on Education and Labor. *Chicago ITU-Publishers Dispute.* Washington: G.P.O., 1948.

—————. —————. *The Philadelphia Record Case.* Washington: G.P.O., 1947.

U.S. INDUSTRIAL COMMISSION (1898). *Reports,* vol. 7, "Report on the Relations and Conditions of Capital and Labor Employed in Manufactures and General Business." *Digest,* pp. 171–175. Washington: G.P.O., 1901.

VAN KLEECK, MARY. *Women in the Bookbinding Trade.* New York: Survey Associates, 1913.

WARE, NORMAN J. *The Labor Movement in the United States, 1860–1895,* "The Printers," pp. 236–242. New York: Appleton, 1929.

Public Service

THE AMERICAN ASSEMBLY. *The Federal Government Service: Its Character, Prestige, and Problems,* chap. 4, pp. 139–145. New York: Graduate School of Business, Columbia University, 1954.

AMERICAN CIVIL LIBERTIES UNION. *Policy Statement on Civil Rights in Government Employment.* New York: American Civil Liberties Union, April 13, 1959.

AMERICAN FEDERATION OF LABOR AND CONGRESS OF INDUSTRIAL ORGANIZATIONS, GOVERNMENT EMPLOYEES COUNCIL. *Report of the American Bar Association Committee on Labor Relations of Governmental Employees.* Washington: The Council, 1955.

ANDERSON, ARVID. "Labor Relations in the Public Service." *Labor Law Journal,* November 1961, pp. 1069–1094.

BAARSLAG, KARL. *History of the National Federation of Post Office Clerks.* Washington: National Federation of Post Office Clerks, 1945.

BERGER, HARRIET F. "The Grievance Process in the Philadelphia Public Service." *Industrial and Labor Relations Review,* Vol. 13, No. 4, July 1960, pp. 568–580.

CALIFORNIA, UNIVERSITY OF. Bureau of Governmental Research. *Organized Public Employee Relations: An Annotated Bibliography of Periodical Literature.* Los Angeles: The Bureau, 1961.

CASE, HARRY L. *Personnel Policy in a Public Agency: The TVA Experience.* New York: Harper, 1955.

CLING, EDWIN LAYNE. *Industrial Labor Relations Policies and Practices in Municipal Government—Milwaukee, Wisconsin.* Ph.D. Thesis, Northwestern University, 1957.

DOHERTY, WILLIAM C. *Mailman, U.S.A.* (history of the National Association of Letter Carriers). New York: David McKay, 1960.

ERRANT, JAMES W. *Trade Unionism in the Civil Service of Chicago, 1895–1930.* Ph.D. Thesis, University of Chicago, 1939.

"Executive Order Governing Procedures of Departments and Agencies of New York State for Resolution of Employee Complaints." *Industrial and Labor Relations Review,* Vol. 4, No. 1, October 1950, pp. 102–109.

GIBBONS, JAMES J. *The International Association of Fire Fighters.* Washington: The Association, 1944.

GODINE, MORTON R. *The Labor Problem in the Public Service: A Study of Political Pluralism.* Cambridge: Harvard University Press, 1951.

GOLDBERG, JOSEPH P. "The Government's Industrial Employees: I—Extent of Employment, Status, Organization." *Monthly Labor Review,* Vol. 77, No. 1, January 1954, pp. 1–6.

—————. "The Government's Industrial Employees: II—Consultation, Bargaining, and Wage Determination." *Monthly Labor Review,* Vol. 77, No. 3, March 1954, pp. 249–256.

HART, WILSON R. *Collective Bargaining in the Federal Civil Service: A Study of Labor-Management Relations in United States Government Employment.* New York: Harper, 1961.

HARVEY, O. L. "The 10-Hour Day in the Philadelphia Navy Yard, 1835–36." *Monthly Labor Review,* Vol. 85, No. 3, March 1962, pp. 258–260.

HERRON, ROBERT. "The Police Strike of 1918." *Bulletin of the Historical and Philosophical Society of Ohio,* Vol. XVII, July 1959, pp. 181–194.

KAMPELMAN, MAX M. "TVA Labor Relations: A Laboratory in Democratic Human Relations." *Minnesota Law Review,* Vol. 30, April 1946, pp. 332–371.

KAPLAN, H. ELIOT. "Concepts of Public Employee Relations." *Industrial and Labor Relations Review,* Vol. 1, No. 2, January 1948, pp. 206–230.

KILLINGSWORTH, CHARLES C. "Grievance Adjudication in Public Employment." *The American Arbitration Journal,* Vol. 13, No. 1, 1958, pp. 3–15.

KLAUS, IDA. "Collective Bargaining by Government Employees." *Proceedings,* Conference on Labor, New York University, 1959, pp. 21–38. New York: M. Bender, 1959.

KRAMER, LEO. *Labor's Paradox—The American Federation of State, County, and Municipal Employees AFL-CIO.* New York: Wiley, 1962.

KRISLOV, JOSEPH. "The Independent Public Employee Association: Characteristics and Functions." *Industrial and Labor Relations Review,* Vol. 15, No. 4, July 1962, pp. 510–520.

—————. "The Union Quest for Recognition in Government Service." *Labor Law Journal,* June 1958, pp. 421–424, and 461.

—————. "The Union Shop, Employment Security, and Municipal Workers." *Industrial and Labor Relations Review,* Vol. 12, No. 2, January 1959, pp. 256–258.

KRUGER, DANIEL H. "Trends in Public Employment." *Proceedings of the Fourteenth Annual Meeting of the Industrial Relations Research Associa-*

tion, December 28–29, 1961, pp. 354–366. Madison: The Association, 1962.

"Labor Relations Program for Employees of the City of New York." *Industrial and Labor Relations Review,* Vol. 12, No. 4, July 1959, pp. 618–625.

LYONS, RICHARD L. "The Boston Police Strike of 1919." *New England Quarterly,* Vol. XX, June 1947, pp. 147–168.

McFADDEN, RICHARD CHARLES. *Labor-Management Relations in the Illinois State Service, 1952.* Urbana: Institute of Labor and Industrial Relations, Cooperating with Institute of Government and Public Affairs, University of Illinois, 1954.

MILLETT, JOHN H. *Public Employee Unionism in Downstate Illinois Municipalities.* Ph.D. Thesis, University of Illinois, 1951.

MIRE, JOSEPH. "Unions in the Public Services." *Labor and Nation,* September-October 1947, pp. 41–42.

NEW YORK CITY DEPARTMENT OF LABOR. *Experience of New York City Municipal Agencies in the Operation of Their Grievance Procedures and Joint Labor Relations Committees.* New York: The Department, 1955.

————. *Studies on the Organizing of Public Employees.* New York: The Department, 1955. (9 numbers in 1 volume.)

NOLAN, LORETTO R., and JAMES T. HALL, JR. "Strikes of Government Employees, 1942–61." *Monthly Labor Review,* Vol. 86, No. 1, January 1963, pp. 52–54.

RHYNE, CHARLES S. *Labor Unions and Municipal Employee Law.* Washington: National Institute of Municipal Law Officers, 1946. *A Supplementary Report,* August 1949.

SAPOSS, DAVID J. *Communism in American Unions,* pp. 119–270 *passim.* New York: McGraw-Hill, 1959.

SCHWEPPE, EMMA. *The Firemen's and Patrolmen's Unions in the City of New York.* New York: King's Crown Press, 1948.

SIMPSON, DOROTHY. *Selected References on Collective Bargaining in the Public Service.* Berkeley: Bureau of Public Administration Library, University of California, 1960.

SMITH, RUSSELL A., and DORIS B. McLAUGHLIN. "Public Employment: A Neglected Area of Research and Training in Labor Relations." *Industrial and Labor Relations Review,* Vol. 16, No. 1, October 1962, pp. 30–44.

SPERO, STERLING D. *Government as Employer.* New York: Remsen Press, 1948.

————. *The Labor Movement in a Government Industry: A Study of Employee Organization in the Postal Service.* New York: Doran, 1924.

STUTZ, ROBERT L. *Collective Dealing by Units of Local Government in Connecticut.* Storrs: Labor-Management Institute, Connecticut University, 1960.

"Trends in Labor Legislation for Public Employees." *Monthly Labor Review,* Vol. 83, No. 12, December 1960, pp. 1293–1296.

U.S. CONGRESS. HOUSE. Committee on Education and Labor. *Investigation of GSI Strike.* Washington: G.P.O., 1948.

U.S. Congress. Joint Committee on Atomic Energy. *Labor Policy in Atomic Energy Plants.* Washington: G.P.O., 1948.

——————. Joint Committee on Labor-Management Relations. *Labor-Management Relations in TVA.* Washington: G.P.O., 1949.

U.S. Congress. Senate. Committee on Labor and Public Welfare. Subcommittee on Labor and Labor-Management Relations. *Communist Domination of Certain Unions,* pp. 111–133 (United Public Workers of America). Washington: G.P.O., 1951.

——————. ——————. *Labor-Management Relations in the Bonneville Power Administration.* Washington: G.P.O., 1951.

U.S. President's Task Force on Employee-Management Relations in the Federal Service. *A Policy for Employee-Management Cooperation in the Federal Service: Report, November 30, 1961.* Washington: U.S. President's Task Force, 1961.

White, Leonard D. "Strikes in the Public Service." *Public Personnel Review,* Vol. 10, January 1949, pp. 3–10.

Ziskind, David. *One Thousand Strikes of Government Employees.* New York: Columbia University Press, 1940.

Rubber

Anthony, Donald. "Rubber Products," chap. 12, *How Collective Bargaining Works,* Harry A. Millis, research director. New York: Twentieth Century Fund, 1945.

Galenson, Walter. *The CIO Challenge to the AFL,* chap. 6, "The Rubber Industry," pp. 266–282. Cambridge: Harvard University Press, 1960.

Jones, Alfred W. *Life, Liberty, and Property: A Story of Conflict and a Measurement of Conflicting Rights.* Philadelphia and New York: Lippincott, 1941.

McKenney, Ruth. *Industrial Valley* (a novel). New York: Harcourt, Brace, 1939.

National Labor Relations Board. Division of Economic Research. *Written Trade Agreements in Collective Bargaining,* chap. 11, "The Rubber Industry," pp. 167–188. Washington: G.P.O., 1940.

Parsons, Edgar A. *Some Economic Aspects of Collective Bargaining in the Rubber Industry.* Ph.D. Thesis, Cornell University, 1950.

Roberts, Harold S. *The Rubber Workers.* New York: Harper, 1944.

Saposs, David J. *Communism in American Unions,* pp. 119–270 *passim.* New York: McGraw-Hill, 1959.

Sobel, Irvin. *Economic Impact of Collective Bargaining upon the Rubber Tire Industry.* Ph.D. Thesis, University of Chicago, 1951.

Thurber, John Newton. *Rubber Workers' History (1935–1955).* Akron: United Rubber, Cork, Linoleum and Plastic Workers of America, 1955.

United Rubber Workers of America. *Five Years: The Story of the United Rubber Workers of America.* Akron: The Union, n.d. (1940?).

"United Rubber Workers of America, 1935–1945." *Monthly Labor Review,* Vol. 62, No. 4, April 1946, pp. 601–606.

Supervision

BAKER, ELIZABETH F. "The Printing Foreman—Union Man: A Historical Sketch." *Industrial and Labor Relations Review*, Vol. 4, No. 2, January 1951, pp. 223–235.

—————. "The Printing Pressroom Foreman—Union Man: A Case Study." *Industrial and Labor Relations Review*, Vol. 4, No. 3, April 1951, pp. 367–385.

CABE, J. CARL. *Collective Bargaining by Foremen*. Urbana: University of Illinois, Institute of Labor and Industrial Relations, September 1947.

—————. *Foremen's Unions: A New Development in Industrial Relations*. Urbana: University of Illinois, Bureau of Economic and Business Research, 1947.

"Collective Bargaining by Supervisory Employees under the Wagner Act." *University of Chicago Law Review*, Vol. 13, No. 3, April 1946, pp. 332–346.

COOPER, HERMAN E. "The Status of Foremen as 'Employees' under the National Labor Relations Act." *Fordham Law Review*, Vol. 15, November 1946, pp. 191–221.

LARROWE, CHARLES P. "A Meteor on the Industrial Relations Horizon: The Foreman's Association of America." *Labor History*, Vol. 2, No. 3, Fall 1961, pp. 259–294.

LEITER, ROBERT DAVID. *The Foreman in Industrial Relations*. New York: Columbia University Press, 1948.

MANN, FLOYD C., and JAMES K. DENT. "The Supervisory: Member of Two Organizational Families." *Harvard Business Review*, Vol. 32, No. 6, November-December 1954, pp. 103–112.

NORTHRUP, H. R. "The Foreman's Association of America." *Harvard Business Review*, Vol. 23, No. 2, Winter 1945, pp. 187–202.

ROSENTHAL, ROBERT J. "Exclusions of Employees under the Taft-Hartley Act." *Industrial and Labor Relations Review*, Vol. 4, No. 4, July 1951, pp. 556–570.

SLICHTER, SUMNER H., ROBERT D. CALKINS, and WILLIAM H. SPOHN. "The Changing Position of Foremen in American Industry." *Advanced Management*, Vol. 10, No. 4, December 1945, pp. 155–161.

SUFRIN, SIDNEY C. "Foremen and Their Social Adjustment." *Industrial and Labor Relations Review*, Vol. 4, No. 3, April 1951, pp. 386–392.

Textiles

ADAMS, SAMUEL H. *Sunrise to Sunset* (a novel). New York: Random House, 1950.

ANDERSON, SHERWOOD. *Beyond Desire* (a novel). New York: Liveright, 1932.

BARKIN, SOLOMON. "Labor Relations in the United States Textile Industry." *International Labor Review*, Vol. LXXV, No. 3, May 1957, pp. 391–411.

BASSO, HAMILTON. *In Their Own Image* (a novel). New York: Scribner, 1935.

BEAL, FRED E. *Proletarian Journey.* New York: Hillman-Curl, 1937.

BELLAMY, CHARLES J. *The Breton Mills* (a novel). New York: Putnam, 1879.

BENJAMIN, CHARLES A. (Published anonymously.) *The Strike in the B----Mill* (a novel). Boston: Ticknor, 1887.

BERNSTEIN, IRVING. *The Lean Years: A History of the American Worker 1920–1933,* "Prologue: Revolt in the Piedmont," pp. 1–43. Boston: Houghton Mifflin, 1960.

BROCK, E. J. *Background and Recent Status of Collective Bargaining in the Cotton Industry of Rhode Island.* Washington: Catholic University of America Press, 1942.

BROOKS, ROBERT R. *The United Textile Workers of America.* New Haven: Yale University Microfilms, 1935.

CAHN, BILL. *Mill Town.* New York: Cameron and Kahn, 1954.

CHURCHILL, WINSTON. *The Dwelling Place of Light* (a novel). New York: Macmillan, 1917.

COLE, DONALD B. "Lawrence, Massachusetts: Model Town to Immigrant City, 1845–1912." *Historical Collections of the Essex Institute,* Vol. XCII, October 1956, pp. 349–375.

COOK, CLAIR M. "Boyd Payton: Saintly Scapegoat." *The Christian Century,* June 14, 1961, pp. 736–738.

CUTHBERT, CLIFTON. *Another Such Victory* (a novel). New York: Hillman-Curl, 1937.

DARGAN, OLIVE T. (Fielding Burke, pseud.). *Call Home the Heart* (a novel). New York: Longmans, Green, 1932.

——————. *A Stone Came Rolling* (a novel). New York: Longmans, Green, 1935.

DAVIS, REBECCA HARDING. *Margaret Howth* (a novel). Boston: Ticknor & Fields, 1862.

DELL, FLOYD. *Diana Stair* (a novel). New York: Farrar and Rinehart, 1932.

DOUGLAS, AMANDA M. *Hope Mills* (a novel). Boston: Lee and Shepard, 1880.

DUNN, ROBERT W., and J. HARDY. *Labor and Textiles.* New York: International Publishers, 1931.

DUNNE, WILLIAM F. *Gastonia, Citadel of the Class Struggle in the South.* New York: Workers Library, 1929.

EBERT, JUSTUS. *The Trial of a New Society.* Cleveland: I.W.W. Publishing Bureau, 1913.

EDMUNDS, MURRELL. *Between the Devil* (a novel). New York: Dutton, 1939.

FAST, HOWARD. *Clarkton* (a novel). New York: Duell, Sloan & Pearce, 1947.

GALENSON, WALTER. *The CIO Challenge to the AFL,* chap. 9, "The Renascence of Textile Unionism," pp. 325–348. Cambridge: Harvard University Press, 1960.

GINGER, RAY. "Labor in a Massachusetts Cotton Mill, 1853–60." *Business History Review*, Vol. XXVIII, March 1954, pp. 67–91.

GRIFFIN, RICHARD W. "Poor White Laborers in Southern Cotton Factories, 1789–1865." *South Carolina Historical Magazine*, Vol. LXI, January 1960, pp. 26–40.

HADCOCK, EDITHA. "Labor Problems in the Rhode Island Cotton Mills—1790–1940." *Rhode Island History*, Vol. XIV, July 1955, pp. 82–85, 88–93; October 1955, pp. 110–119.

HALE, EDWARD E. *How They Lived at Hampton* (a novel). Boston: J. S. Smith, 1888.

HARRIS, HERBERT. *American Labor*, pp. 305–349. New Haven: Yale University Press, 1938.

HUTCHINS, GRACE. *Labor and Silk*. New York: International Publishers, 1929.

JOSEPHSON, HANNAH. *The Golden Threads: New England's Mill Girls and Magnates*. New York: Duell, Sloan and Pearce, 1949.

KELLY, RICHARD. *Nine Lives for Labor*. New York: Praeger, 1956.

KENNEDY, JOHN W. *The General Strike of the Textile Industry, September, 1934*. Master's Thesis, Duke University, 1947.

KENNEDY, THOMAS. *Effective Labor Arbitration: The Impartial Chairmanship of the Full-Fashioned Hosiery Industry*. Philadelphia: University of Pennsylvania Press, 1948.

LAHNE, HERBERT J. *Cotton Mill Worker*. New York: Farrar and Rinehart, 1944.

LARCOM, LUCY. *An Idyl of Work* (a narrative poem based upon her experience in the Lowell Mills). Boston: James R. Osgood, 1875.

—————. *A New England Girlhood*. New York: Corinth Books, 1961 (originally published 1889).

LEFTWICH, RICHARD. *Some Effects of Collective Bargaining on Resource Allocation: The Fullfashioned Hosiery Industry*. Ph.D. Thesis, University of Chicago, 1950.

LUMPKIN, GRACE. *To Make My Bread* (a novel). New York: Macaulay, 1932.

LUMPKIN, KATHERINE D. *Shutdowns in the Connecticut Valley*. Northampton, Mass.: Department of History, Smith College, 1934.

MACDONALD, LOIS. *Southern Mill Hills*. New York: Alex Hillman, 1928.

McMAHON, THOMAS F. *United Textile Workers of America*. New York: Workers Education Bureau Press, 1926.

MIMS, HENRY N., and GUY B. ARTHUR, JR. *Analysis of 31 Southern Textile Labor Contracts*. Toccoa, Ga.: Management Evaluation Services, 1949.

MITCHELL, GEORGE S. *Textile Unionism and the South*. Chapel Hill: University of North Carolina Press, 1931.

MOORE, JOHN T. *The Bishop of Cottontown* (a novel). Philadelphia: Winston, 1906.

MUSTE, A. J. "Not So Long Ago: Autobiography." *Liberation*.

Part 7: "The Lawrence Strike of 1919," Vol. II, No. 11, February 1958, pp. 15–19;

Part 8: "They Can't Weave Wool with Machine Guns," Vol. III, No. 1, March 1958, pp. 16–19;

Part 9: "Nonviolence and the Lawrence Strike," Vol. III, No. 2, April 1958, pp. 16–19;

Part 10: "The Attempt to Build a Union," Vol. III, No. 3, May 1958, pp. 16–18.

NEILL, CHARLES P. *Report on the Strike of Textile Workers in Lawrence, Massachusetts in 1912*, Senate Document No. 870 (U.S. Bureau of Labor Study). Washington: G.P.O., 1912.

NORTON, NANCY P. "Labor in the Early New England Carpet Industry." *Bulletin of the Business Historical Society*, Vol. XXVI, March 1952, pp. 19–26.

NYMAN, RICHMOND C., and ELLIOTT D. SMITH. *Union-Management Cooperation on the "Stretch-Out": Labor Extension at the Pequot Mills.* New Haven: Yale University Press, 1935.

PAGE, DOROTHY MYRA. *Gathering Storm* (a novel). New York: International Publishers, 1932.

——————. *Southern Cotton Mills and Labor.* New York: Workers Library, 1929.

PALMER, GLADYS. *Union Tactics and Economic Change.* Philadelphia: University of Pennsylvania Press, 1932.

PAUL, GEORGE S. *American Velvet Company and Textile Workers Union of America.* Washington: National Planning Association, 1953.

PHILLIPS, EDWARD L. *Collective Bargaining and Craft Unions: An Historical and Analytical Study of a Strike...in the Textile Industry of Fall River, Massachusetts.* Fall River: Loomfixers' Union, 1950.

POPE, LISTON. *Millhands and Preachers: A Study of Gastonia, North Carolina.* New Haven: Yale University Press, 1942.

POTWIN, MARJORIE A. *Cotton Mill People of the Piedmont.* New York: Columbia University Press, 1927.

RANKIN, CARL E. *The University of North Carolina and the Problems of the Cotton Mill Employee.* Ph.D. Thesis, Columbia University, 1938.

RHYNE, JENNINGS J. *Some Southern Cotton Mill Workers and Their Villages.* Chapel Hill: University of North Carolina Press, 1930.

RIEVE, EMIL. "TWUA-CIO." *Labor and Nation,* September-October 1947, p. 30.

ROBINSON, HARRIET H. *Loom and Spindle: Or, Life Among the Early Mill Girls.* New York: Crowell, 1898.

ROGIN, LAWRENCE. *Making History in Hosiery: The Story of the American Federation of Hosiery Workers.* Philadelphia: Federation of Hosiery Workers, 1938.

ROLLINS, WILLIAM. *The Shadow Before* (a novel). New York: McBride, 1934.

SAVAGE, SARAH. *The Factory Girl* (a novel published anonymously "By a Lady"). Boston: Munroe, Francis and Parker, 1814. (In Library of the American Antiquarian Society, Worcester, Mass.)

101

SEIDMAN, JOEL, *et al. The Worker Views His Union,* chap. 6, "Knitting Mill Workers: The Impact of an Organizing Strike." Chicago: University of Chicago Press, 1958.

SELEKMAN, B. M., and OTHERS. *The Clothing and Textile Industries in New York and Its Environs.* New York: Regional Plan of New York and Its Environs, 1925.

SHELDON, CHARLES M. *The Crucifixion of Philip Strong* (a novel). Chicago: McClurg, 1894.

SMITH, THOMAS R. *The Cotton Textile Industry of Fall River, Massachusetts.* New York: King's Crown Press, 1944.

STORROW, CHARLES S. *Report of the Treasurer of the Committee of Relief for the Sufferers by the Fall of the Pemberton Mill in Lawrence, Massachusetts.* New York: Publisher Unknown, 1860.

TABER, GLADYS B. *A Star to Steer By* (a novel). Philadelphia: Macrae Smith, 1938.

TAYLOR, GEORGE W. *The Full-Fashioned Hosiery Worker: His Changing Economic Status.* Philadelphia: University of Pennsylvania Press, 1931.

—————. "Hosiery," chap. 9, *How Collective Bargaining Works,* Harry A. Millis, research director. New York: Twentieth Century Fund, 1945.

TEXTILE WORKERS UNION OF AMERICA. *Almost Unbelieveable: The Story of an Industry, a Union and a Law.* New York: The Union, n.d. (1961).

—————. *Building A Textile Union.* New York: The Union, 1948.

—————. *Half a Million Forgotten People: The Story of the Cotton Textile Workers.* New York: The Union, 1944.

—————. *Taft-Hartleyism in Textiles with Special Reference to Conditions in the Southern Branch of the Industry.* New York: The Union, 1953.

TIPPETT, THOMAS. *Mill Shadows: A Drama of Social Forces in Four Acts.* Katonah, New York: Brookwood Labor College, 1932.

—————. *When Southern Labor Stirs.* New York: J. Cape and H. Smith, 1931.

TURNER, GEORGE K. *The Taskmasters* (a novel). New York: McClure,Phillips, 1902.

U.S. COMMISSION ON INDUSTRIAL RELATIONS (1912). *Reports,* vol. 4, "The Textile Industry in Philadelphia," pp. 3033–3090. Washington: G.P.O., 1916.

U.S. CONGRESS. HOUSE. Committee on Rules. *The Strike at Lawrence, Massachusetts.* House Document No. 671. Washington: G.P.O., 1912.

U.S. CONGRESS. SENATE. Committee on Labor and Public Welfare. Subcommittee on Labor and Labor-Management Relations. *Labor-Management Relations in the Southern Textile Industry.* Washington: G.P.O., 1952.

—————. —————. *Labor-Management Relations in the Southern Textile Manufacturing Industry,* Parts 1 and 2. Washington: G.P.O., 1950 and 1951.

U.S. DEPARTMENT OF LABOR. Bureau of Labor Statistics. *Union Agreements in the Cotton-Textile Industry.* Bulletin 885. Washington: G.P.O., 1947.

U.S. INDUSTRIAL COMMISSION (1898). *Reports,* vol. 7, "Report on the Relations and Conditions of Capital and Labor Employed in Manufactures and General Business." *Digest,* pp. 190–191. Washington: G.P.O., 1901.

UNITED TEXTILE WORKERS OF AMERICA. *The AFL Textile Workers.* Washington: The Union, 1950.

VAN VORST, MARIE. *Amanda of the Mill* (a novel). New York: Dodd-Mead, 1905.

VORSE, MARY H. *The Passaic Textile Strike, 1926–1927.* Passaic, N.J.: General Relief Committee of Textile Strikers, 1927.

————. *Strike!* (a novel). New York: Liveright, 1930.

WALTON, PERRY. *The Story of Textiles.* Boston: Walton Printing Co., 1912.

WARD, ELIZABETH S. PHELPS. *The Silent Partner* (a novel). Boston: Osgood, 1871.

WEISBORD, ALBERT. *Passaic: The Story of a Struggle against Starvation Wages and for the Right to Organize.* Chicago: Daily Worker, 1926.

YABROFF, BERNARD, and ANN J. HERLIHY. "History of Work Stoppages in Textile Industries." *Monthly Labor Review,* Vol. 76, No. 4, April 1953, pp. 367–371.

YELLEN, SAMUEL. *American Labor Struggles* ("The Great Lawrence Strike!"). New York: Harcourt, Brace, 1936.

Transportation—Air

BLUM, ALBERT A. "Fourth Man Out: The Background of the Flight Engineer—Airline Pilot Conflict." *Labor Law Journal,* August 1962, pp. 649–657.

DALE, ERNEST, and ROBERT L. RAIMON. "Management Unionism and Public Policy on the Railroads and the Airlines." *Industrial and Labor Relations Review,* Vol. 11, No. 4, July 1958, pp. 551–571.

KAHN, MARK L. "Wage Determination for Airlines Pilots." *Industrial and Labor Relations Review,* Vol. 6, No. 3, April 1953, pp. 317–336.

KRISLOV, JOSEPH. "Representation Disputes in the Railroad and Airline Industries." *Labor Law Journal,* February 1956, pp. 98–103.

LEIDING, OSCAR. *A Story of the Origin and Progression of the Air Line Pilots Association and of Its Key Figure and Organizer, 1930–1944.* Chicago(?): The Association, 1945.

MATER, DAN H., and GARTH L. MANGUM. "The Integration of Seniority Lists in Transportation Mergers." *Industrial and Labor Relations Review,* Vol. 16, No. 3, April 1963, pp. 343–365.

MODES, ED, ed. *The ALPA Story* (a history and study of the background, functions, and organization of the Air Line Pilots Association). Chicago(?): Air Line Pilots Association, 1954.

OLIVER, ELI L. "Labor Problems of the Transportation Industry." *Law and Contemporary Problems,* Vol. 25, No. 1, Winter 1960, pp. 3-21.

PRICE WESLEY. "Labor's Biggest Wind." *Saturday Evening Post,* August 2, 1947, pp. 25, 117–118.

"Recommendations on the Airlines-Flight Engineers Dispute." *Monthly Labor Review,* Vol. 84, No. 7, July 1961, pp. 750–753.

RUPPENTHAL, KARL M. "Compulsory Retirement of Air Line Pilots." *Industrial and Labor Relations Review,* Vol. 14, No. 4, July 1961, pp. 528–547.

Transportation—Railroads

AFROS, JOHN L. "Guaranteed Employment Plan of Seaboard Railroad." *Monthly Labor Review,* Vol. 65, No. 2, August 1947, pp. 167–171.

AGNEW, ROBERT J. *The Diesel-electric Locomotive and Railway Employees.* Ph.D. Thesis, Massachusetts Institute of Technology, 1953.

ALLEN, RUTH A. *The Great Southwest Strike.* Austin: University of Texas Press, 1942.

ASHLEY, WILLIAM J. *The Railroad Strike of 1894.* Cambridge: The Church Social Union, 1895.

BARNARD, HARRY. *Eagle Forgotten: The Life of John Peter Altgeld.* Indianapolis: Bobbs-Merrill, 1938.

BERNHARDT, JOSHUA. *The Railroad Labor Board: Its History, Activities and Organization.* Baltimore: Johns Hopkins Press, 1923.

BEYER, OTTO. "Union-Management Cooperation in the Railway Industry." *Bulletin of the Taylor Society,* February 1926.

BOYLE, OHIO D. *History of Railroad Strikes: A History of the Railroad Revolt of 1887 . . . .* Washington: Brotherhood Publishing Co., 1935.

BRADLEY, WALTER, comp. *An Industrial War: History of the Missouri and North Arkansas Railroad Strike.* Harrison, Arkansas: Bradley and Russell, 1923.

BRUCE, ROBERT V. *1877: Year of Violence.* New York and Indianapolis: Bobbs-Merrill Co., 1959.

BUREAU OF INFORMATION OF THE EASTERN RAILWAYS. *Wages and Labor Relations in the Railroad Industry, 1900–1941.* New York: The Bureau, 1942.

BURNS, WILLIAM F. *The Pullman Boycott.* St. Paul: McGill, 1894.

CARWARDINE, WILLIAM H. *The Pullman Strike.* Chicago: Charles Kerr, 1894.

CHRISTIE, HUGH K., and JAMES McKINNEY. *The Railway Foreman and His Job.* Chicago: American Technical Society, 1947.

CLEVELAND, GROVER. *The Government in the Chicago Strike of 1894.* Princeton: Princeton University Press, 1913.

COTTRELL, WILLIAM F. *The Railroader.* Stanford, Cal.: Stanford University Press, 1940.

DACUS, J. A. *Annals of the Great Strikes in the United States.* Chicago: L. T. Palmer, 1877.

DALE ERNEST, and ROBERT L. RAIMON. "Management Unionism and Public Policy on the Railroads and the Airlines." *Industrial and Labor Relations Review,* Vol. 11, No. 4, July 1958, pp. 551–571.

DEBS, EUGENE V. *Writings and Speeches of Eugene V. Debs.* New York: Hermitage Press, 1948.

DENISON, THOMAS S. *An Iron Crown: A Tale of the Great Republic* (a novel). Chicago: T. S. Denison, 1885.

DEWSNUP, ERNEST R. *Railway Organization and Working.* Chicago: University of Chicago Press, 1906.

DOWLING, GEORGE T. *The Wreckers* (a novel). Philadelphia: Lippincott, 1886.

FAGAN, J. O. *Labor and the Railroads.* Boston: Houghton Mifflin, 1909.

FISHER, THOMAS R. *Industrial Disputes and Federal Legislation, with Special Reference to the Railroad, Coal, Steel, and Automobile Industries in the U.S. since 1900.* New York: Columbia University Press, 1940.

FORAN, MARTIN A. *The Other Side* (a novel). Cleveland, Ohio: Ingham, Clarke & Co.; Washington, D.C.: Gray & Clarkson, 1886.

FORD, PAUL LEICESTER. *The Honorable Peter Stirling and What People Thought of Him* (a novel). New York: Holt, 1894.

GALENSON, WALTER. *The CIO Challenge to the AFL,* chap. 18, "Railroad Unionism," pp. 566–582. Cambridge: Harvard University Press, 1960.

GINGER, RAY. *Altgeld's America.* New York: Funk & Wagnalls, 1958.

GUTMAN, HERBERT G. "Trouble on the Railroads in 1873–1874: Prelude to the 1877 Crisis?" *Labor History,* Vol. 2, No. 2, Spring 1961, pp. 215–235.

HALL, JOHN A. *The Great Strike on the "Q," with a History of the Organization and Growth of the Brotherhood of Locomotive Firemen, and Switchmen's Mutual Aid Association of North America.* Chicago: Elliott and Beezley, 1889.

HARRIS, HERBERT. *American Labor,* pp. 225–266. New Haven: Yale University Press, 1938.

HARRIS, LEE O. *The Man Who Tramps* (a novel). Indianapolis: Douglass & Carlon, 1878.

HAY, JOHN (published anonymously). *The Bread-Winners* (a novel). New York: Harper, 1884.

HEADLEY, JOEL T. *Pen and Pencil Sketches of the Great Riots: An Illustrated History of the Railroad and Other Great American Riots.* New York: E. B. Treat, 1877.

HENDERSON, JAMES A. "The Railroad Riots in Pittsburgh, Saturday and Sunday, April 21st and 22nd, 1877." *Western Pennsylvania Historical Magazine,* Vol. XI, July 1928, pp. 194–197.

HERRICK, ROBERT. *The Web of Life* (a novel). New York: Macmillan, 1900.

HEYWOOD, EZRA H. *The Great Strike: Its Relation to Labor, Property and Government.* Princeton, Mass.: Cooperative Publishing, 1878.

HOROWITZ, MORRIS A. *Manpower Utilization in the Railroad Industry: An Analysis of Working Rules and Practices.* Boston: Bureau of Business and Economic Research, Northeastern University, 1960.

—————. "The Railroads' Dual System of Payment: A Make-Work Rule?" *Industrial and Labor Relations Review,* Vol. 8, No. 2, January 1955, pp. 177–194.

HORTON, GEORGE R., and H. ELLSWORTH STEELE. "The Unity Issue among Railroad Engineers and Firemen." *Industrial and Labor Relations Review,* Vol. 10, No. 1, October 1956, pp. 48–69.

JAKUBAUSKAS, EDWARD B. "Technological Change and Recent Trends in the Composition of Railroad Employment." *Quarterly Review of Economics & Business,* Vol. 2, No. 4, November 1962, pp. 81–90.

JESSUP, MARY F. *Women in the Railroad Industry during and after World War I,* Historical Studies of Wartime Problems No. 70. Washington: Bureau of Labor Statistics (Division of Historical Studies of Wartime Problems, 1941–1945), 1944. (Mimeo.).

JONES, HARRY E. *Inquiry of the Attorney General's Committee on Administrative Procedure Relating to the National Railroad Adjustment Board— Historical Background and Growth of Machinery Set Up for the Handling of Railroad Labor Disputes, 1888–1940.* Washington: U.S. Department of Justice, 1941.

——————. *Railroad Wages and Labor Relations, 1900–1952: An Historical Survey and Summary of Results.* New York: Bureau of Information of the Eastern Railways, 1953.

KAUFMAN, JACOB JOSEPH. *Collective Bargaining in the Railroad Industry.* New York: King's Crown Press, 1954.

——————. "Emergency Boards Under the Railway Labor Act." *Labor Law Journal,* December 1958, pp. 910–920, 949.

——————. "Government Intervention in Railroad Labor Disputes." *Current Economic Comment,* Vol. 20, No. 3, August 1958, pp. 9–16.

——————. "Grievance Arbitration in the Railroad Industry." *Labor Law Journal,* March 1958, pp. 244–247.

——————. "Grievance Procedure under the Railway Labor Act." *Southern Economic Journal,* Vol. 14, July 1952, pp. 66–78.

——————. "Logic and Meaning of Work Rules on the Railroads." *Proceedings of the Fourteenth Annual Meeting of the Industrial Relations Research Association,* December 28–29, 1961, pp. 378–388. Madison: The Association, 1962.

——————. "Representation in the Railroad Industry." *Labor Law Journal,* July 1955, pp. 437–512.

——————. "Wage Criteria in the Railroad Industry." *Industrial and Labor Relations Review,* Vol. 6, No. 1, October 1952, pp. 119–126.

KEENAN, HENRY F. *The Money-Makers* (a novel). New York: Appleton, 1885.

KRISLOV, JOSEPH. "Representation Disputes in the Railroad and Airline Industries." *Labor Law Journal,* February 1956, pp. 98–103.

"Labor-Management Relations Under the Railway Labor Act, 1934–57." *Monthly Labor Review,* Vol. 81, No. 8, August 1958, pp. 879–881.

"Labor Unions in Transportation and Communications Industries." *Monthly Labor Review,* Vol. 70, No. 3, March 1950, pp. 275–278.

LAZAR, JOSEPH. *Due Process on the Railroads.* Los Angeles: University of California Press, 1953.

——————. *Due Process on the Railroads: Disciplinary Grievance Pro-*

cedures before the National Railroad Adjustment Board. Los Angeles: Institute of Industrial Relations, California University, 1958.

LECHT, LEONARD. *Experience under Railway Labor Legislation.* New York: Columbia University Press, 1955.

LINDSEY, ALMONT. "Paternalism and the Pullman Strike." *American Historical Review,* Vol. XLIV, January 1939, pp. 272–289.

――――――. *The Pullman Strike.* Chicago: University of Chicago Press, 1942.

LOGAN, SAMUEL C. *A City's Danger and Defense: Or, Issues and Results of the Strikes of 1877, Containing the Origin and History of the Scranton City Guard.* Philadelphia: J. B. Rodgers Printing Co., 1887.

McCABE, JAMES D. (Edward W. Martin, pseud.). *The History of the Great Riots.* Philadelphia: National Publishing Co., 1877.

McDONALD, GRACE L. (Margaret Graham, pseud.). *Swing Shift* (a novel). New York: Citadel Press, 1951.

McMURRY, DONALD L. "Federation of the Railroad Brotherhoods, 1889–1894." *Industrial and Labor Relations Review,* Vol. 7, No. 1, October 1953, pp. 73–92.

――――――. *The Great Burlington Railroad Strike of 1888.* Cambridge: Harvard University Press, 1956.

――――――. "Labor Policies of the General Managers' Association of Chicago, 1886–1894." *Journal of Economic History,* Vol. XIII, Spring 1953, pp. 160–178.

――――――. "The Legal Ancestry of the Pullman Strike Injunctions." *Industrial and Labor Relations Review,* Vol. 14, No. 2, January 1961, pp. 235–256.

MANDEL, BERNARD. "The Great Uprising of 1877." *Cigar Makers Official Journal,* December 1953.

――――――. "Notes on the Pullman Boycott." *Explorations in Entrepreneurial History,* Vol. VI, No. 3, February 1954, pp. 184–189.

MANGUM, GARTH L. "Grievance Procedures for Railroad Operating Employees." *Industrial and Labor Relations Review,* Vol. 15, No. 4, July 1962, pp. 474–499.

MANNING, THOMAS G. *The Chicago Strike of 1894: Industrial Labor in the Late Nineteenth Century.* New York: Holt, 1960.

MATER, DAN H. *The Railroad Seniority System: History, Description and Evaluation.* Ph.D. Thesis, University of Chicago, 1942.

――――――, and GARTH L. MANGUM. "The Integration of Seniority Lists in Transportation Mergers." *Industrial and Labor Relations Review,* Vol. 16, No. 3, April 1963, pp. 343–365.

MEYERS, FREDERIC. "Criteria in the Making of Wage Decisions by 'Neutrals': The Railroads as a Case Study." *Industrial and Labor Relations Review,* Vol. 4, No. 3, April 1951, pp. 343–355.

MIDDLETON, P. H. *Railways and Organized Labor.* Chicago: Railway Business Association, 1941.

MINTON, BRUCE B. (Richard Bransten, pseud.), and JOHN STUART. *Men Who*

Lead Labor (biography of A. Philip Randolph). New York: Modern Age Books, 1937.

MISSOURI. Bureau of Labor Statistics and Inspection. *The Official History of the Great Strike of 1886 on the Southwestern Railway System.* Jefferson City: The Bureau, 1887.

MURPHY, FRANK J., S.J. "Agreement on the Railroads—The Joint Railway Conference of 1926." *Labor Law Journal,* September 1960, pp. 823–836, 864.

NATIONAL LABOR RELATIONS BOARD. Division of Economic Research. *Written Trade Agreements in Collective Bargaining,* chap. 8, "The Railway Industry," pp. 115–127. Washington: G.P.O., 1940.

NORRIS, FRANK. *The Octopus* (a novel). Long Island: Garden City Publishing Co., 1901.

NORTHRUP, HERBERT R. "Industrial Relations on the Railroads," chap. 20, *Labor in Postwar America,* Colston Warne, ed. Brooklyn: Remsen Press, 1949.

——————. "The Railway Labor Act and Railway Labor Disputes in Wartime." *American Economic Review,* June 1946.

——————. "Unfair Labor Practice Prevention under the Railway Labor Act." *Industrial and Labor Relations Review,* Vol. 3, No. 3, April 1950, pp. 323–340.

——————, and MARK L. KAHN. "Railroad Grievance Machinery: A Critical Analysis—I." *Industrial and Labor Relations Review,* Vol. 5, No. 3, April 1952, pp. 365–382; II, Vol. 5, No. 4, July 1952, pp. 540–559.

OLIVER, ELI. "Job and Income Security in Railway Mergers and Abandonments." *Automation and Major Technological Change: Collective Bargaining Problems,* papers presented at a conference held under the auspices of the Industrial Union Department, AFL-CIO, April 22, 1958, pp. 21–27.

——————. "Labor Problems of the Transportation Industry." *Law and Contemporary Problems,* Vol. 25, No. 1, Winter 1960, pp. 3–21.

PERSON, CARL E. *The Lizard's Trail: A Story from the Illinois Central and Harrison Lines Strike of 1911 to 1915 Inclusive.* Chicago: Lake Publishing Co., 1918.

PIERSON, FRANK C. *Collective Bargaining Systems,* pp. 36–38. Washington: American Council on Public Affairs, 1942.

PINKERTON, ALLAN. *Strikers, Communists, Tramps and Detectives: Railroad Strike of 1877.* New York: Carleton, 1900.

POLLACK, JEROME. "Workmen's Compensation for Railroad Work Injuries and Diseases." *Cornell Law Quarterly,* Vol. XXXVI, No. 2, Winter 1951.

PRESIDENTIAL RAILROAD COMMISSION. *Report of the Presidential Railroad Commission.* Washington: The Commission, February 1962. (Processed).

PULLMAN, GEORGE M. *The Strike at Pullman.* Cambridge: Church Social Union, 1895.

RAILROAD BROTHERHOOD UNITY MOVEMENT. *Revolt in the Railroad Unions.* Chicago: Publisher Unknown, 1935.

RAILWAY LABOR EXECUTIVES' ASSOCIATION. *Labor and Transportation—*

Program and Objectives of Transportation Labor in the Post-War Period. Washington: The Association, 1946.

SALMONS, CHARLES H., comp. *The Burlington Strike.* Aurora: Bunnell & Ward, 1889.

SAXTON, ALEXANDER P. *Great Midland* (a novel). New York: Appleton-Century-Crofts, 1948.

SHANNON, DAVID A. "Eugene V. Debs: Conservative Labor Editor." *Indiana Magazine of History,* Vol. XLVII, December 1951, pp. 357–364.

SIGMUND, ELWIN W. "Railroad Strikers in Court: Unreported Contempt Cases in Illinois in 1877." *Journal of the Illinois State Historical Society,* Vol. XLIX, Summer 1956, pp. 190–209.

SPENCER, WILLIAM H. *The National Railroad Adjustment Board.* Chicago: University of Chicago Press, 1938.

STOCKETT, JOSEPH NOBLE. *The Arbitral Determination of Railway Wages.* Boston: Houghton Mifflin, 1918.

TROY, LEO. "Labor Representation on American Railways." *Labor History,* Vol. 2, No. 3, Fall 1961, pp. 295–322.

"Twenty Years of Benefit Programs for Railroad Workers." *Monthly Labor Review,* Vol. 79, No. 7, July 1956, pp. 815–817.

UHL, ALEXANDER. *Trains and the Men Who Run Them.* Washington: Public Affairs Institute, 1954.

U.S. ATTORNEY GENERAL'S COMMITTEE ON ADMINISTRATIVE PROCEDURE. *Railroad Retirement Board.* Washington: The Committee, 1939.

—————. *Railway Labor: The National Railroad Adjustment Board and the National Mediation Board.* Washington: The Committee, 1940.

U.S. COMMISSION ON INDUSTRIAL RELATIONS (1912). *Reports,* vol. 11, "Conditions of Labor on the Pennsylvania Railroad," pp. 10067–10449. Washington: G.P.O., 1916.

—————. *Reports,* vol. 10, "Harriman Railroad System Strike," pp. 9697–10066. Washington: G.P.O., 1916.

—————. *Reports,* vol. 10, "Pullman Employees," pp. 9543–9695. Washington: G.P.O., 1916.

U.S. CONGRESS. HOUSE. Committee on Education and Labor. *Investigation of Communist Influence in the Bucyrus-Erie Strike.* Washington: G.P.O., 1948.

U.S. CONGRESS. SENATE. Committee on Interstate Commerce. *Government Investigation of Railway Disputes.* Washington: G.P.O., 1917.

—————. —————. Committee on Labor and Public Welfare. Subcommittee on Labor and Labor-Management Relations. *Labor Dispute between the Railroad Carriers and Four Operating Railroad Brotherhoods.* Washington: G.P.O., 1951.

U.S. DEPARTMENT OF LABOR. Bureau of Labor Statistics. *Employment Outlook in Railroad Occupations,* Bulletin 961. Washington: G.P.O., 1949.

—————. —————. *Use of Federal Power in Settlement of Railway Labor Disputes,* Bulletin 303. Washington: G.P.O., 1922.

U.S. EIGHT-HOUR COMMISSION. *Report of the Eight-Hour Commission.* Washington: G.P.O., 1918. See especially Appendix VI, "Railway Wage Schedules and Agreements," by William Z. Ripley, and Appendix VII, "Employment Conditions in Road and Yard Service," by Victor S. Clark.

U.S. EMERGENCY BOARD, 1943 (Carriers and Employees, Diesel-Electric Operators). *Transcript of Proceedings of the National Railway Labor Panel Emergency Board. So-Called "Diesel Case."* New York: Eastern Printing Corp., 1943.

U.S. EMERGENCY BOARD, 1943 (Carriers and Employees, Non-Operating). *Transcript of Proceedings of the National Railway Labor Panel Emergency Board. Union Shop Wage Increase Case.* New York: Eastern Printing Corp., 1943.

U.S. EMERGENCY BOARD, 1943 (Carriers and Employees, Operating). *Transcript of Proceedings of the National Railway Labor Panel Emergency Board. Wage Increase Case.* New York: Eastern Printing Corp., 1943.

U.S. NATIONAL MEDIATION BOARD. *Administration of the Railway Labor Act by the National Mediation Board, 1934–1957.* Washington: G.P.O., 1958.

——————. *Fifteen Years under the Railway Labor Act, Amended, and the National Mediation Board, 1934–1949.* Washington: G.P.O., 1950.

——————. *Labor Relations in the Railroad Industry.* Washington: G.P.O., 1940.

U.S. STRIKE COMMISSION. *Report on the Chicago Strike of June-July, 1894,* Senate Executive Document No. 7. Washington: G.P.O., 1895.

VARG, PAUL A. "The Political Ideas of the American Railway Union." *The Historian,* Vol. X, Spring 1948, pp. 85–100.

WARD, FRANK B. *The United States Railroad Labor Board and Railway Labor Disputes.* Philadelphia: University of Pennsylvania Press, 1929.

WARMAN, CY. *Snow on the Headlight* (a novel). New York: Appleton, 1899.

WHITTAKER, FREDERICK. *Nemo, King of the Tramps; or, The Romany Girl's Vengeance. A Story of the Great Railroad Riots* (a novel). New York: M. J. Ivers & Co., 1881.

WISH, HARVEY. "The Pullman Strike: A Study in Industrial Warfare." *Journal of the Illinois State Historical Society,* Vol. XXXII, September 1939, pp. 288–312.

WOLF, HARRY D. *The Railroad Labor Board.* Chicago: University of Chicago Press, 1927.

——————. "Railroads," chap. 7, *How Collective Bargaining Works,* Harry A. Millis, research director. New York: Twentieth Century Fund, 1945.

WOOD, LOUIS A. *Union-Management Cooperation on the Railroads.* New Haven: Yale University Press, 1931.

YEARLEY, CLIFTON K., JR. "The Baltimore and Ohio Railroad Strike of 1877." *Maryland Historical Magazine,* Vol. LI, September 1956, pp. 188–211.

CARMEN

CHRISTIE, HUGH K. *The Carman's Helper.* Chicago: Trade Educational Bureau of the Brotherhood of Railway Carmen of America, 1920.

HOGAN, EDMOND K. *The Work of the Railway Carman.* Kansas City, Mo.: Brotherhood of Railway Carmen of America, 1921.

PAINTER, LEONARD. *Through 50 Years with the Brotherhood of Railway Carmen of America.* Kansas City, Mo.: Brotherhood of Railway Carmen of America, 1941.

CLERKS

HENIG, HARRY. *The Brotherhood of Railway Clerks.* New York: Columbia University Press, 1937.

CONDUCTORS

ROBBINS, EDWIN C. *Railway Conductors: A Study in Organized Labor.* New York: Columbia University Press, 1914.

LOCOMOTIVE ENGINEERS

BROOKS, HAROLD C. "Story of the Founding of the Brotherhood of Locomotive Engineers." *Michigan History Magazine,* Vol. XXVII, October-December 1943, pp. 611–619.

FULTON, JUSTIN D. *Sam Hobart.* New York: Funk & Wagnalls, 1883. See especially Chapter VIII, "The Brotherhood of Locomotive Engineers," pp. 83–109.

RICHARDSON, REED C. *The Locomotive Engineer: 1863–1963, A Century of Railway Labor Relations and Work Rules.* Ann Arbor: Bureau of Industrial Relations, University of Michigan, 1963.

STEVENSON, GEORGE JAMES. *The Brotherhood of Locomotive Engineers and Its Leaders, 1863–1920.* Ph.D. Thesis, Vanderbilt University, 1954.

LOCOMOTIVE FIREMEN AND ENGINEMEN

BROTHERHOOD OF LOCOMOTIVE FIREMEN AND ENGINEMEN. *Fiftieth Anniversary, Brotherhood of Locomotive Firemen and Enginemen, December 1, 1873–December 1, 1923.* Kansas City, Mo.: The Brotherhood, 1923.

——————. "Historical Sketch, 1873–1947." *Brotherhood of Locomotive Firemen and Enginemen's Magazine,* Vol. 123, No. 1, July 1947, pp. 17–49.

——————. *An Historical Sketch of the Brotherhood.* Cleveland: The Brotherhood, 1937.

FEDERAL COUNCIL OF THE CHURCHES OF CHRIST IN AMERICA. Department of Research and Education. *The Enginemen's Strike on the Western Maryland Railroad.* New York: Davis Press, 1927.

HOROWITZ, MORRIS A. "The Diesel Firemen Issue on the Railroads." *Industrial and Labor Relations Review,* Vol. 13, No. 4, July 1960, pp. 550–558.

MAINTENANCE OF WAY

BROTHERHOOD OF MAINTENANCE OF WAY EMPLOYEES. *Pictorial History, 1877-1951*. Detroit: The Brotherhood, 1952.

HERTEL, DENVER WILLARD. *History of the Brotherhood of Maintenance of Way Employees: Its Birth and Growth, 1877–1955*. Washington: Ransdell, 1955.

SHOPMEN

AMERICAN FEDERATION OF LABOR. Railway Employees' Department. *The Case of the Railway Shopmen: A Brief Statement of Facts Concerning the Controversies Which Precipitated the Strike*. Washington: The Department, 1922.

SIGNALMEN

BROTHERHOOD OF RAILROAD SIGNALMEN OF AMERICA. *50 Years of Railroad Signaling: A History of the Brotherhood of Railroad Signalmen of America*. Chicago: The Brotherhood, n.d.

FAGAN, J. O. *Confessions of a Railroad Signalman*. Boston: Houghton Mifflin, 1908.

SLEEPING CAR PORTERS

BRAZEAL, BRAILSFORD. *The Brotherhood of Sleeping Car Porters: Its Origin and Development*. New York: Harper, 1946.

TELEGRAPHERS

McISAAC, ARCHIBALD M. *The Order of Railroad Telegraphers: A Study in Trade Unionism and Collective Bargaining*. Princeton: Princeton University Press, 1933.

TRAINMEN

McCALEB, WALTER F. *Brotherhood of Railroad Trainmen: With Special Reference to the Life of Alexander F. Whitney*. New York: Boni and Liveright, 1936.

SEIDMAN, JOEL. *The Brotherhood of Railroad Trainmen: The Internal Political Life of a National Union*. New York: Wiley, 1962.

"Trainmen: When They Fight, the U.S. Is Involved." *Business Week*, October 10, 1953, pp. 170–173.

U.S. CONGRESS. HOUSE. Committee on Labor. *Investigation of the Causes of Labor Disputes*, Part II, "General Labor Conditions" (Testimony of A. F. Whitney). Washington: G.P.O., 1946.

WHITNEY, ALEXANDER F. *Report of A. F. Whitney, President, Brotherhood of Railroad Trainmen, on Railroad Rules-Wage Movement, U.S., 1944–45–46.* Cleveland: Brotherhood of Railroad Trainmen, 1946.

Transportation—Teamsters

BARRY, DESMOND A., and JOHN E. RASCO. *Too Hot to Handle.* Garden City: Doubleday, 1962.

"Beck and Reuther." *The Reporter,* July 5, 1949, pp. 4–7.

BELL, JOHN F. "The Teamsters: Big Unionism." *Current History,* Vol. 27, July 1954, pp. 36–41.

BERNSTEIN, IRVING. "The Politics of the West Coast Teamsters and Truckers." *Proceedings of the Tenth Annual Meeting of the Industrial Relations Research Association,* September 5–7, 1957, pp. 12–34. Madison: The Association, 1958.

BOFFO, LOUIS S. "Study 4, Trucking," *Labor-Management Relations in Illini City,* Vol. 1. Champaign: University of Illinois Press, 1953.

BOWERS, ROBERT S. *The International Brotherhood of Teamsters and a Theory of Jurisdiction.* Ph.D. Thesis, University of Wisconsin, 1951.

DEARMOND, FREDERICK F. *Managers vs. Teamsters: The New Tactics in Labor Bargaining.* Springfield, Mo.: Mycroft Press, 1959.

EDDY, ARTHUR J. *Ganton and Company* (a novel). Chicago: McClurg, 1908.

FEINSINGER, NATHAN P. *Collective Bargaining in the Trucking Industry.* Philadelphia: University of Pennsylvania Press, 1949.

GALENSON, WALTER. *The CIO Challenge to the AFL,* chap. 14, "The Teamsters," pp. 459–494. Cambridge: Harvard University Press, 1960.

GILLINGHAM, J. B. *The Teamsters Union on the West Coast.* Berkeley: Institute of Industrial Relations, University of California, 1956.

HASS, ERIC. *Dave Beck, Labor Merchant.* New York: New York Labor News Co., 1955.

HILL, SAMUEL. *Teamsters and Transportation: Employee-Employer Relationships in New England.* Washington: American Council on Public Affairs, 1942.

HOSTETTER, GORDON L., and THOMAS Q. BEESLEY. *It's a Racket!* Chicago: Les Quin, 1929.

INDUSTRIAL RELATIONS COUNSELORS. *A Profile of the Teamsters Union.* New York: Industrial Relations Counselors, 1961.

INTERNATIONAL BROTHERHOOD OF TEAMSTERS. Joint Council No. 13. *The Name is Hoffa.* St. Louis: The Council, 1956.

JACOBS, PAUL. "The World of Jimmy Hoffa." *The Reporter.* Part I, January 24, 1957, pp. 13–18; Part II, February 7, 1957, pp. 10–17.

KERR, CLARK. "Collective Bargaining on the Pacific Coast." *Monthly Labor Review,* Vol. 64, No. 4, April 1947, pp. 650–674.

LEITER, ROBERT D. "The Relationship Between Structure and Policy in the Teamsters Union." *Proceedings of the Tenth Annual Meeting of the Indus-*

trial Relations Research Association, September 5–7, 1957, pp. 148–155. Madison: The Association, 1958.

LENS, SIDNEY. "Dave Beck's Teamsters: Sour Note in Labor Harmony." *Harper's,* February 1956, pp. 74–82.

McCLELLAN, JOHN L. (as told to Beverly Smith, Jr.). "What We Learned about Labor Gangsters." *Saturday Evening Post.* Part I, May 3, 1958, pp. 22–23; Part II, May 10, 1958, p. 35.

MARTIN, JOHN B. *Jimmy Hoffa's Hot.* Greenwich, Connecticut: Fawcett, 1959.

MILK DRIVERS AND DAIRY EMPLOYEES UNION, LOCAL 471. *Status of Free Men.* Minneapolis: The Union, 1947.

MILLER, JOE. "Dave Beck Comes Out of the West." *The Reporter,* December 8, 1953, pp. 20–23.

NEUBERGER, RICHARD. *Our Promised Land.* New York: Macmillan, 1939.

ROBINSON, ROBERT M. "San Francisco Teamsters at the Turn of the Century." *California Historical Society Quarterly,* Vol. XXXV, March 1956, pp. 59–69; June 1956, pp. 145–153.

ROMER, SAM. *The International Brotherhood of Teamsters: Its Government and Structure.* New York: Wiley, 1962.

——————. "The Teamster Monitors and the Administration of the International Union." *Proceedings of the Spring Meeting of the Industrial Relations Research Association,* May 4 and 5, 1961. Reprinted from *Labor Law Journal,* July 1961, pp. 604–613.

ROSE, ARNOLD. "The Influence of a Border City Union on the Race Attitudes of Its Members." *The Journal of Social Issues,* Vol. 9, No. 1, 1953.

——————. *Union Solidarity: The Internal Cohesion of a Labor Union* (Local 688, St. Louis, IBT). Minneapolis: University of Minnesota Press, 1952.

SCHNEPP, GERALD J., and ISABELLE MORELLO. "Approaches to the Industry Council Idea in the U.S." *Industrial Relations* (Quebec, Canada), Vol. 9, September 1954, pp. 381–394.

SEIDMAN, HAROLD. *Labor Czars,* chap. XII, "The Markets," pp. 185–198. New York: Liveright, 1938.

SHEFFERMAN, NATHAN (written in collaboration with Dale Kramer). *The Man in the Middle.* Garden City: Doubleday, 1961.

STRAUB, ADELBERT G., JR. *Whose Welfare? A Report on Union and Employer Welfare Plans in New York.* (See sections on Locals 804 and 805, IBT.) Albany: State of New York Insurance Department, 1954.

"Teamsters' Dave Beck." *Fortune,* Vol. 38, December 1948, pp. 191–198.

"Teamsters Drive Tests the Hard-Boiled Approach." *Business Week,* September 8, 1956, pp. 60–70.

"Teamsters Face Their Judges." *Business Week,* September 7, 1957, pp. 171–172.

"Teamsters Strengthen Dave Beck's Hand." *Business Week,* March 31, 1956, pp. 156–158.

"Teamster Union Welfare, Pension Plans." *Industrial Bulletin,* June 1954, pp. 19–20.

TOBIN, DAN. "As to Being One's Brothers' Keeper." *Teamster,* June 1948.

U.S. CONGRESS. SENATE. Committee on Government Operations. *James R. Hoffa and Continued Underworld Control of New York Teamster Local 239.* Washington: G.P.O., 1962.

————. ————. Committee on the Judiciary. *Relationship Between Teamsters Union and Mine, Mill & Smelter Workers.* Washington: G.P.O., 1962.

VOTAW, ALBERT N. "The Teamsters and the Hoods." *The New Leader,* May 14, 1951, pp. 6–7.

WALKER, CHARLES R. *American City: A Rank and File History* (Minneapolis truck drivers strike of 1934). New York: Farrar & Rinehart, 1937.

Transportation—Urban

AMALGAMATED ASSOCIATION OF STREET, ELECTRIC RAILWAY AND MOTOR COACH EMPLOYEES OF AMERICA. "Golden Jubilee." *Motorman, Conductor and Motor Coach Operator,* Vol. 50, No. 9, September 1942 (entire issue).

DUNCAN, DAVID. *Serpent's Egg* (a novel about a bus driver in California during World War II). New York: Macmillan, 1949.

FABER, GUSTAV. *And Then Came T.W.U.: The Brooklyn Trolley Strike.* New York: Transport Workers Union of America, CIO, 1950.

FLEMING, RALPH D. *Labor Conditions and Wages in Street Railway, Motor and Wagon Transportation Services in Cleveland.* Menasha, Wis.: Banta, 1916.

HUBERMAN, LEO. *The Great Bus Strike.* New York: Modern Age, 1941.

KHEEL, THEODORE W., and J. K. TURCOTT. *Transit and Arbitration: A Decade of Decisions* and *The Path to Transit Peace.* Englewood Cliffs: Prentice-Hall, 1960.

LAWRENCE, JAMES S. "T.W.U.-Transit Authority Compromise on Issue: Agreement Between Labor, Management Smooths Shuttle Train Differences." *Industrial Bulletin,* Vol. 41, No. 3, March 1962, pp. 8–11, 15.

MACDONALD, LOIS, BRUNO STEIN, and PETER FREUND. *The Grievance Process in New York City Transit.* New York: Graduate School of Public Administration and Social Service, New York University, 1956.

MCGINLEY, JAMES J. *Labor Relations in the New York Rapid Transit Systems, 1904–1944.* New York: King's Crown Press, 1949.

NEW YORK (STATE) BOARD OF INQUIRY ON ROCHESTER TRANSIT WORK STOPPAGE. *Final Report to the Industrial Commissioner from Board of Inquiry on Rochester Transit Work Stoppage, May 1–May 23, 1952.* Rochester(?): The Board(?), 1952.

————. *Proceedings in the Matter of the Arbitration between the Rochester Transit Corporation and Local 282 of Amalgamated Association of Street, Electric Railway and Motor Coach Employees of America.* Rochester (?): The Board (?), 1952.

ODETS, CLIFFORD. *Waiting for Lefty,* and *Till the Day I Die* (2 plays). New York: Covici-Friede, 1935.

[OLIPHANT, HERMAN]. *Interborough Rapid Transit Company against William Green, et al., Brief for Defendants.* New York: Workers Education Bureau Press, 1928.

SAPOSS, DAVID J. *Communism in American Unions,* pp. 119–270 *passim.* New York: McGraw-Hill, 1959.

SCHMIDT, EMERSON P. *Industrial Relations in Urban Transportation.* Minneapolis: University of Minnesota Press, 1937.

SUSSNA, EDWARD. "Collective Bargaining on the New York City Transit System, 1940–1957." *Industrial and Labor Relations Review,* Vol. 11, No. 4, July 1958, pp. 518–533.

TOURGEE, ALBION W. *Murvale Eastman, Christian Socialist* (a novel about horsecar drivers in an Eastern city during the 1880's). New York: Fords, Howard, and Hulbert, 1890.

U.S. COMMISSION ON INDUSTRIAL RELATIONS (1912). *Reports,* vol. 3, "The Cooperative Plan of the Philadelphia Rapid Transit Co.," pp. 2731–2816. Washington: G.P.O., 1916.

U.S. INDUSTRIAL COMMISSION (1898). *Reports,* vol. 7, "Report on the Relations and Conditions of Capital and Labor Employed in Manufactures and General Business." *Digest,* pp. 200–202. Washington: G.P.O., 1901.

WEINBERG, J. "Priests, Workers and Communists: What Happened in a New York Transit Workers Union." *Harpers,* Vol. 197, November 1948, pp. 49–56.

YOUNG, DALLAS M. "Fifty Years of Labor Arbitration in Cleveland Transit." *Monthly Labor Review,* Vol. 83, No. 5, May 1960, pp. 464–471.

Transportation—Water and Longshoring

ALBION, ROBERT G. *Maritime and Naval History: An Annotated Bibliography.* Mystic, Conn.: Marine Historical Association, 1955.

ALBRECHT, ARTHUR E. *The International Seamen's Union of America,* Bulletin 342, Bureau of Labor Statistics. Washington: G.P.O., 1923.

ANDERSON, THOMAS. *Here Comes Pete Now* (a novel). New York: Random House, 1961.

AUERBACK, JEROLD S. "Progressives at Sea: The La Follette Act of 1915." *Labor History,* Vol. 2, No. 3, Fall 1961, pp. 344–360.

AXTELL, SILAS B., comp. *A Symposium on Andrew Furuseth.* New Bedford, Mass.: Darwin Press, 1948.

BARNES, CHARLES B. *The Longshoremen.* New York: Russell Sage Foundation, 1915.

BELL, DANIEL. *The End of Ideology: On the Exhaustion of Political Ideas in the Fifties,* chap. 9, "The Racket-Ridden Longshoremen: The Web of Economics and Politics." New York: Collier Books, 1961.

—————. "Last of the Business Rackets." *Fortune,* June 1951, pp. 89–91, 193–203.

—————. "Some Aspects of the New York Longshore Situation." *Proceedings of the Seventh Annual Meeting of the Industrial Relations Research Association,* December 28–30, 1954, pp. 298–304. Madison: The Association, 1955.

BISSELL, RICHARD. *A Stretch on the River* (a novel). Boston: Little, Brown, 1950.

BOYER, RICHARD O. *The Dark Ship* (a novel). Boston: Little, Brown, 1947.

BRISSENDEN, PAUL F. *Employment System of the Lake Carriers' Association.* Bulletin 235, Bureau of Labor Statistics. Washington: G.P.O., 1918.

BROWN, GILES T. "The West Coast Phase of the Maritime Strike of 1921." *Pacific Historical Review,* Vol. XIX, November 1950, pp. 385–396.

CATHERWOOD, MARTIN P., DEAN ALFANGE, and JOHN P. BOLAND. *Final Report to the Industrial Commissioner, State of New York, from Board of Inquiry on Longshore Industry Work Stoppage, October-November 1951, Port of New York.* Albany: State of New York, 1952.

CHEVALIER, HAAKON M. *For Us the Living* (a novel). New York: Knopf, 1948.

"CIO to Sea." *Time,* Vol. XXX, No. 3, July 19, 1937, pp. 12–14.

CLARK, WILLIAM H. *Ships and Sailors: The Story of Our Merchant Marine.* Boston: Page, 1938.

COMMONS, JOHN R. "The Longshoremen of the Great Lakes," chap. 15, *Labor and Administration.* New York: Macmillan, 1913.

DOERFLINGER, WILLIAM M. *Shantymen and Shantyboys: Songs of Sailor and Lumberman.* New York: Macmillan, 1951.

DUNNE, WILLIAM F. *The Great San Francisco General Strike.* New York: Workers Library Publishers, 1934.

ELIEL, PAUL. "Industrial Peace and Conflict: A Study of Two Pacific Coast Industries." *Industrial and Labor Relations Review,* Vol. 2, No. 4, July 1949, pp. 477–501.

—————. *The Waterfront and General Strikes.* San Francisco: Hooper Printing Co., 1934.

"Employment Conditions in the Longshore Industry." *Industrial Bulletin,* Vol. 31, February 1952, pp. 7–14.

FACT-FINDING BOARD. *In re Waterfront Employers Association of the Pacific Coast...and International Longshoremen's and Warehousemen's Union (CIO), May 13, 1946.* Labor Arbitration Reports, Vol. 3, pp. 165-181. Washington: Bureau of National Affairs, 1946.

FAIRLEY, LINCOLN. "The ILWU-PMA Mechanization and Modernization Agreement." *Proceedings of the Spring Meeting of the Industrial Relations Research Association,* May 4–5, 1961. Reprinted from *Labor Law Journal,* July 1961, pp. 664–680.

FALL, JAMES. *British Merchant Seamen in San Francisco, 1892–1898.* London: Publisher Unknown, 1899.

FARNAM, H. W. "The Seamen's Act of 1915." *American Labor Legislation Review,* Vol. 6, No. 1, March 1916, pp. 41–60.

FRANCIS, ROBERT E. *A History of Labor on the San Francisco Waterfront.* Ph.D. Thesis, University of California, 1934.

FURUSETH, ANDREW. "The Seamen's Act and Its Critics." *American Labor Legislation Review*, Vol. 6, No. 1, March 1916, pp. 61–68.

GALENSON, WALTER. *The CIO Challenge to the AFL*, chap. 13, "The Maritime Industry," pp. 427–458. Cambridge: Harvard University Press, 1960.

GOLDBERG, JOSEPH P. "Collective Bargaining in Maritime Shipping Industry." *Monthly Labor Review*, Vol. 71, No. 3, September 1950, pp. 332–337.

——————. *The Maritime Story: A Study in Labor-Management Relations.* Cambridge: Harvard University Press, 1958.

——————. "Seamen and the International Labor Organization." *Monthly Labor Review*, Vol. 81, No. 9, September 1958, pp. 974–981.

GORTER, WYTZE, and GEORGE H. HILDEBRAND. *The Pacific Coast Maritime Shipping Industry, 1930–1948*, 2 vols. Berkeley: University of California Press, 1954.

GROAT, GEORGE G. *An Introduction to the Study of Organized Labor in America.* New York: Macmillan, 1926.

HARRISON, CHARLES YALE. "Stalin's American Merchant Marine." *American Mercury*, Vol. 51, October 1940, pp. 135–144.

HAVIGHURST, WALTER. *Pier 17* (a novel). New York: Macmillan, 1935.

HEALEY, JAMES C. *Foc's'le and Glory-Hole, A Study of the Merchant Seaman and His Occupation.* New York: Merchant Marine Publishing Association, 1936.

HERZOG, DONALD ROSWELL. *A Study of Labor Relations Relating to American Seamen in the Maritime Industry.* Ph.D. Thesis, University of Iowa, 1955.

HIELD, WAYNE. "What Keeps Harry Bridges Going?" *Labor and Nation*, Vol. VIII, No. 1, January-March 1952, pp. 38–40.

HOAGLAND, HENRY E. *Wage Bargaining on the Vessels of the Great Lakes.* Urbana: University of Illinois Press, 1917.

HOHMAN, ELMO P. *The American Whaleman: A Study of Life and Labor in the Whaling Industry.* New York: Longmans, Green, 1928.

——————. *History of American Merchant Seamen.* Hamden, Conn.: The Shoe String Press, 1956.

——————. "Labor Problems in the Merchant Marine." *Proceedings of the Fourteenth Annual Meeting of the Industrial Relations Research Association*, December 28–29, 1961, pp. 346–353. Madison: The Association, 1962.

——————. "Maritime Labor Economics as a Determinant of the Structure and Policy of Seamen's Unions." *Proceedings of the Tenth Annual Meeting of the Industrial Relations Research Association*, September 5–7, 1957, pp. 163–170. Madison: The Association, 1958.

——————. "Maritime Labor in the U.S." *International Labour Review*, Vol. 38, August and September 1938.

——————. "Work and Wages of American Merchant Seamen." *Industrial and Labor Relations Review*, Vol. 15, No. 2, January 1962, pp. 221–229.

HUBERMAN, LEO. *The National Maritime Union—What It Is, What It Does.* New York: National Maritime Union, 1943.

INTERNATIONAL JURIDICAL ASSOCIATION. *Report on the Status and Working*

Conditions of Seamen in the American Merchant Marine. New York: Publisher Unknown, 1936.

INTERNATIONAL LONGSHOREMEN'S ASSOCIATION, AFL. *Answer of the International Longshoremen's Association, AFL, to the Report of the New York State Crime Commission Dealing with the Waterfront of the Port of New York Submitted to the Governor and the Members of the Legislature of the State of New York.* New York: The Association, 1953.

————. *The ILA Program to Improve and Further Stabilize Labor and Industrial Conditions in the Port of New York* (submitted to Board of Inquiry, December 1951). New York: Waldman and Waldman (Louis and Seymour), Attorneys, 1951. (Mimeo.).

INTERNATIONAL LONGSHOREMEN'S AND WAREHOUSEMEN'S UNION. *The ILWU Story.* San Francisco: The Union, 1955.

————. *Union Busting: New Model: The Case Against the Coast Guard Screening Program.* San Francisco: The Union, 1951.

JENSEN, VERNON H. "Decasualization of Employment on the New York Waterfront." *Industrial and Labor Relations Review,* Vol. 11, No. 4, July 1958, pp. 534–550.

————. "Dispute Settlement in the New York Longshore Industry." *Industrial and Labor Relations Review,* Vol. 10, No. 4, July 1957, pp. 588–608.

————. "Hiring Practices and Employment Experience of Longshoremen in the Port of New York." *International Labour Review,* Vol. LXXVII, No. 4, April 1958, pp. 1–28.

JOHNSON, ALVIN S. "Andrew Furuseth." *New Republic,* November 11, 1916.

JOHNSON, MALCOLM. *Crime on the Labor Front.* New York: McGraw-Hill, 1950.

KELLER, MARVEL. *Decasualization of Longshore Work in San Francisco.* Philadelphia: Works Project Administration, National Research Project, 1939.

KELLEY, FLORENCE. "The LaFollette Law from the Consumers League Point of View." *Proceedings of the Academy of Political Science,* Vol. 6, October 1915, pp. 90–96.

KENNEDY, P. B. "The Seamen's Act." *Annals of the American Academy of Political and Social Science,* Vol. 63, January 1916, pp. 232–243.

KERR, CLARK. "Collective Bargaining on the Pacific Coast" (Seafaring). *Monthly Labor Review,* Vol. 64, No. 4, April 1947, pp. 650–674.

KILLINGSWORTH, CHARLES C. "The Modernization of West Coast Longshore Work Rules." *Industrial and Labor Relations Review,* Vol. 15, No. 3, April 1962, pp. 295–306. Fairley, Lincoln. "West Coast Longshore Work Rules." Vol. 16, No. 1, October 1962, pp. 134–135. Killingsworth, Charles C. "Reply." pp. 135–136.

KOSSORIS, MAX D. "Working Rules in West Coast Longshoring." *Monthly Labor Review,* Vol. 84, No. 1, January 1961, pp. 1–10.

LAFOLLETTE, ROBERT. "The American Sailor, a Free Man." *The Survey,* Vol. 34, May 1, 1915.

LANG, F. J. *Maritime: An Historical Sketch—A Worker's Program.* New York: Pioneer, 1945.

LARROWE, CHARLES P. *Maritime Labor Relations on the Great Lakes.* East Lansing: Labor and Industrial Relations Center, Michigan State University, 1959.

—————. *Shape-Up and Hiring Hall: A Comparison of Hiring Methods and Labor Relations on the New York and Seattle Waterfronts.* Berkeley: University of California Press, 1955.

"Legislative Recommendations of the New York Waterfront Commission." *Monthly Labor Review,* Vol. 84, No. 5, May 1961, pp. 510–512.

LIBRARY OF CONGRESS. *Andrew Furuseth, a Bibliographical List.* Washington: The Library, 1942.

LIEBES, RICHARD A. *Longshore Labor Relations on the Pacific Coast, 1934–1942.* Ph.D. Thesis, University of California, 1943.

McFEE, W. "Seagoing Soviets: Will Communist Waterfronters Take Over Our Merchant Marine?" *Saturday Evening Post,* September 21, 1940, p. 27ff.

MALM, F. THEODORE. "Wage Differentials in Pacific Coast Longshoring." *Industrial and Labor Relations Review,* Vol. 5, No. 1, October 1951, pp. 33–49.

MARITIME LABOR BOARD. *Report to the President and to the Congress. March 1, 1940.* Washington: G.P.O., 1940.

"The Maritime Unions." *Fortune,* September 1937, pp. 123–128, 132–137.

MARTIN, HARRY. *Merchant Marine Machinations.* New York: Merchant Manuals Distributing Co., 1949.

MEARS, ELIOT GRINNELL. *Maritime Trade of Western United States.* Stanford: Stanford University Press, 1935.

MINTON, BRUCE B. (Richard Bransten, pseud.), and JOHN STUART. *Men Who Lead Labor* (biography of Harry Bridges). New York: Modern Age Books, 1937.

NATIONAL LABOR RELATIONS BOARD. Division of Economic Research. *Written Trade Agreements in Collective Bargaining,* chap. 9, "The Maritime Industry," pp. 127–148. Washington: G.P.O., 1940.

NATIONAL MARITIME UNION. *This Is the NMU: A Picture History of the National Maritime Union of America, CIO.* New York: W. R. Gottlieb, 1954.

NEW YORK STATE CRIME COMMISSION. *Record of the Public Hearing Held by Governor Thomas E. Dewey on the Recommendations of the New York State Crime Commission for Remedying Conditions on the Waterfront of the Port of New York.* (June 8 and 9, 1953.) New York: Publishers Printing Co., 1953.

NEW YORK STATE SCHOOL OF INDUSTRIAL AND LABOR RELATIONS, CORNELL UNIVERSITY. *Longshore Industry with Emphasis on the Situation in New York City.* Urbana: Institute of Labor and Industrial Relations, University of Illinois (Industrial Relations Libraries Exchange Bibliographies No. 810 and Cornell List, NYSSILR, No. 87, mimeographed), April 30, 1953.

"New York's Waterfront." *Fortune,* December 1949, pp. 210–213.

NORRIS, CHARLES G. *Flint* (a novel). New York: Doubleday, Doran, 1944.

Norris, Martin J. *The Law of Seamen.* New York: Baker, Voorhis, 1951.

Ogg, Elizabeth. *Longshoremen and Their Homes.* New York: Greenwich House, 1939.

Ozanne, Robert Willard. *The Effect of Communist Leadership on American Trade Unions,* chap. 3, "Marine Cooks and Stewards." Ph.D. Thesis, University of Wisconsin, 1954.

Pacific Maritime Association. *Analysis of Strikes and Work Stoppages in the West Coast Maritime Industry.* San Francisco: The Association, 1952. (ILR Microfilm No. 65.)

Palmer, Dwight L. *Pacific Coast Maritime Labor.* Ph.D. Thesis, Stanford University, 1936.

Phelps, E. A. M., ed. *The Open Shop, a Debate* (between Andrew Furuseth and W. G. Merritt). New York: Wilson, 1920.

Phleger, Herman. *Pacific Coast Longshoremen's Strike of 1934.* San Francisco(?):Publisher Unknown,1934(?).

"Polluted Port." *Fortune,* December 1953, pp. 64–68.

Poole, Ernest. *The Harbor* (a novel). New York: Macmillan, 1915.

Raymond, Allen. *Waterfront Priest* (Rev. John M. Corridan, S.J.). New York: Holt, 1955.

Record, Jane Cassels. "The Rise and Fall of a Maritime Union." *Industrial and Labor Relations Review,* Vol. 10, No. 1, October 1956, pp. 81–92.

Robinson, Donald. "How Our Seamen Bounced the Commies." *Saturday Evening Post,* December 25, 1948.

Ryan, Edwin. *One Clear Call* (a novel). New York: Macmillan, 1962.

Ryan, Paul W. (Mike Quin, pseud.). *The Big Strike* (Pacific Coast Longshoremen's strike, 1934). Olema, Calif.: Olema Publishing Co., 1949.

—————. *On the Drumhead: A Selection from the Writings of Mike Quin.* San Francisco: Pacific Publishing Foundation, 1948.

Rygg, A. N. "Andrew Furuseth." *American-Scandinavian Review,* Vol. XXVI, June 1938, pp. 123–133.

Sanderson and Porter, Engineers and Constructors. *Study of the Port of New York.* New York: New York Crime Commission, 1953.

Saposs, David J. *Communism in American Unions,* pp. 119–270 *passim.* New York: McGraw-Hill, 1959.

Schneider, Betty V., and Abraham Siegel. *Industrial Relations in the Pacific Coast Longshore Industry.* Berkeley: Institute of Industrial Relations, University of California, 1956.

Schulberg, Budd. "How One Pier Got Rid of the Mob." *New York Times Magazine,* September 27, 1953, pp. 17, 58–60.

—————. "Joe Docks, Forgotten Man of the Waterfront." *New York Times Magazine,* December 28, 1952, pp. 3, 28–30.

—————. *Waterfront* (a novel). New York: Random House, 1955.

Seafarers International Union of North America. *The Seafarers in World War II.* San Francisco: The Union, 1951.

"Settlement of Hawaiian Longshoremen's Strike." *Monthly Labor Review,* Vol. 69, No. 6, December 1949, pp. 653–656.

"Seven Seamen." *Fortune,* September 1937, pp. 121–122, 130–132.

SKLAR, GEORGE, and PAUL PETERS. *Stevedore* (a play). New York: Covici-Friede, 1934.

SMITH, FRANCIS H. *Tom Grogan* (a novel). Boston: Houghton Mifflin, 1896.

STANDARD, WILLIAM L. *Merchant Seamen: A Short History of Their Struggles.* New York: International Publishers, 1947.

STURM, HERMAN M. "Postwar Labor Relations in the Maritime Industry," chap. 21, *Labor in Postwar America,* Colston Warne, ed. Brooklyn: Remsen Press, 1949.

SWANSTROM, EDWARD E. *The Waterfront Labor Problem: A Study in Decasualization and Unemployment Insurance.* New York: Fordham University Press, 1938.

TAFT-HARTLEY BOARD OF INQUIRY. *In re Maritime Industry (Atlantic Coast Employers) and International Longshoremen's Assn. (AFL). Final Report of Board of Inquiry, October 21, 1948.* Labor Arbitration Reports, Vol. 11, pp. 388–393. Washington: Bureau of National Affairs, 1949.

TAFT, PHILIP. "Problems of Labor Relations in the Maritime Industry." *American Seamen,* Winter 1941.

————. "Strife in the Maritime Industry." *Political Science Quarterly,* Vol. 54, June 1939, pp. 216–236.

————. "The Unlicensed Seafaring Unions." *Industrial and Labor Relations Review,* Vol. 3, No. 2, January 1950, pp. 187–212.

TANK, HERB. *Communists on the Water Front.* New York: New Century, 1946.

TAYLOR, PAUL SCHUSTER. *The Sailor's Union of the Pacific.* New York: Ronald Press, 1923.

————, and NORMAN GOLD. "San Francisco and the General Strike." *Survey Graphic,* September 1934.

TRAVERS, ROBERT. *A Funeral for Sabella* (a novel). New York: Harcourt, Brace, 1952.

TURNBULL, JOHN G. *Labor-Management Relations on the Mississippi Waterway System.* Minneapolis: University of Minnesota Press, 1951.

UHLINGER, CHARLES W. *Bibliography on History of Labor in the American Merchant Marine, 1850–1915.* (Manuscript, New York State Maritime College.)

————. *Collective Bargaining on Government Operated Vessels in World War II.* (Mimeographed manuscript, New York State Maritime College.)

U.S. BOARD OF INQUIRY ON THE LABOR DISPUTE INVOLVING LONGSHOREMEN AND ASSOCIATED OCCUPATIONS IN THE MARITIME INDUSTRY ON THE ATLANTIC AND GULF COAST. *Report to the President by the Board of Inquiry Appointed October 6, 1959.* Washington: The Board, 1959.

U.S. COMMISSION ON INDUSTRIAL RELATIONS (1912). *Reports,* vol. 3, "The Dock Workers of New York City," pp. 2051–2212. Washington: G.P.O., 1916.

U.S. CONGRESS. HOUSE. Committee on Education and Labor. *Communist Infiltration of Maritime Fisheries Unions.* Washington: G.P.O., 1948.

——————. ——————. *Hiring Practices, Maritime Industry*. Washington: G.P.O., 1949.

——————. ——————. *Hiring Seamen*. Washington: G.P.O., 1949.

——————. ——————. *Investigation of Communist Infiltration into Labor Unions Which Serve the Industries of the United States, the International Fishermen and Allied Workers of America, CIO*. Washington: G.P.O., 1948.

——————. ——————. *Investigation of Steamship Unions*. Washington: G.P.O., 1948.

——————. ——————. Committee on Merchant Marine and Fisheries. *Labor-Management Problems of the American Merchant Marine*. Washington: G.P.O., 1955.

——————. ——————. Committee on Un-American Activities. *Communist Activities among Seamen and on Waterfront Facilities*, pp. 1747–1854. Hearings, Part I. Washington: G.P.O., 1960.

U.S. CONGRESS. SENATE. Committee on Interstate and Foreign Commerce. *Waterfront Investigation*. Hearings, 2 parts. Washington: G.P.O., 1953.

——————. ——————. Committee on Labor and Public Welfare. Subcommittee on Labor and Labor-Management Relations. *Communist Domination of Certain Unions*. Washington: G.P.O., 1951.

——————. ——————. *Labor-Management Relations in the East Coast Oil Tanker Industry*. Washington: G.P.O., 1950 and 1951.

——————. ——————. *The Marine Cooks and Stewards Union*. Washington: G.P.O., 1953.

——————. ——————. *Maritime Hiring Halls*. Washington: G.P.O., 1950, 1951, and 1952.

——————. ——————. *West Coast Maritime Industry*. Washington: G.P.O., 1948.

——————. ——————. Committee on the Judiciary. *Scope of Soviet Activity in the United States, Commission on the Waterfront*. Hearings. Washington: G.P.O., 1956.

U.S. MARITIME ADMINISTRATION. *Guide to Seafaring Collective Bargaining*. Washington: G.P.O., 1959.

——————. *Review of Labor-Management Relations in the Maritime Industry and the Subsidization of Seamen Wages*. Washington: The Administration, 1955. (Processed).

U.S. NATIONAL ARCHIVES. *Preliminary Inventory of the Records of the Maritime Labor Board*. Washington: National Archives, 1949.

VARNEY, H. L. "Sovietizing Our Merchant Marine." *American Mercury*, Vol. 44, May 1938, pp. 31–43.

WALDMAN, LOUIS, and SEYMOUR WALDMAN. *Final Report on Survey of ILA Locals*. New York: ILA, 1952.

WATERFRONT COMMISSION OF NEW YORK HARBOR. *Waterfront Commission Act*. New York: The Commission, 1953. (Mimeo.).

"Waterfront Mess." *Fortune*, April 1953, pp. 94–98.

WEINTRAUB, HYMAN G. *Andrew Furuseth: Emancipator of the Seamen.* Berkeley: University of California Press, 1959.

WHALEN, ROBERT G. "Two Generals Patrol the Docks." *New York Times Magazine,* November 29, 1953, p. 20.

WOLLETT, DONALD H., and ROBERT J. LAMPMAN. "The Law of Union Factionalism—The Case of the Sailors." *Stanford Law Review,* Vol. 4, No. 2, February 1952.

YELLEN, SAMUEL. *American Labor Struggles* (Longshoremen, San Francisco). New York: Harcourt, Brace, 1936.

White Collar and Service

FINANCE

BAKER, HELEN. *Current Policies in Personnel Relations in Banks.* Princeton: Industrial Relations Section, Princeton University, 1940.

BELL, THOMAS. *There Comes a Time* (a novel). Boston: Little, Brown, 1946.

GROAT, MARGARET SCHAER. *Collective Bargaining in Wall Street.* M.S. Thesis, Cornell University, 1948.

MASSE, BENJAMIN L. "The Strike on Wall Street." *America,* April 24, 1948.

GENERAL

"Aiming at White-Collar Target." *Business Week,* May 12, 1956, pp. 169–171.

BAMBRICK, JAMES J., and HAROLD STIEGLITZ. *White Collar Unionization: Union Strategy and Tactics, Analysis of Contracts, Problems after Unionization.* New York: National Industrial Conference Board, 1949.

BOLLENS, LEO F. *White Collar or Noose? The Occupation of Millions.* New York: North River Press, 1947.

BRUNER, DICK. "Why White Collar Workers Can't Be Organized." *Harper's,* August 1957, pp. 44–50.

BURNS, ROBERT K. *Unionization of the White Collar Worker.* New York: American Management Association, 1947.

CHICAGO UNIVERSITY, INDUSTRIAL RELATIONS CENTER. *Studies in White Collar Unionism.* Chicago: The Center, 1954.

CRONER, FRITZ. "Salaried Employees in Modern Society." *International Labour Review,* Vol. LXIX, No. 2, February 1954, pp. 97–110.

Developments in White Collar Unionism: A Panel Discussion by Harold J. Gibbons, Everett M. Kassalow, and Joel Seidman. Chicago: A. G. Bush Library, Industrial Relations Center, University of Chicago, 1962.

DOWD, DOUGLAS F. "The White Collar Worker." *Monthly Review,* July-August 1958, pp. 127–133.

KASSALOW, EVERETT M. *Automation and Technological Change: A Challenge to the American Labor Movement.* Boston: June 27, 1958. (Mimeo.).

MICHIGAN UNIVERSITY, BUREAU OF INDUSTRIAL RELATIONS. *Attitudes of White-Collar Workers Toward Unionization* by Robert J. Doolan; and *Experiences with White-Collar Unions* by T. S. Nurnberger. Ann Arbor: The Bureau, 1959.

MILLS, C. WRIGHT. *White Collar: The American Middle Classes.* New York: Oxford University Press, 1951.

SAPOSS, DAVID J. *Communism in American Unions,* pp. 119–270 *passim.* New York: McGraw-Hill, 1959.

SOLOMON, BENJAMIN. "The Problems and Areas of Union Expansion in the White-Collar Sector." *Proceedings of the Ninth Annual Meeting of the Industrial Relations Research Association,* December 28–29, 1956, pp. 238–243. Madison: The Association, 1957.

STRAUSS, GEORGE. "White Collar Unions Are Different." *Harvard Business Review,* September-October 1954, pp. 73–82.

"A Union Target: The White-Collar Worker." *Business Week,* February 7, 1948, pp. 88–94.

OFFICE

AHERN, EILEEN. *Survey of Personnel Practices in Unionized Offices.* New York: American Management Association, 1948.

AMERICAN MANAGEMENT ASSOCIATION. *Collective Bargaining in the Office.* New York: The Association, 1948.

BECKER, ESTHER R., and EUGENE F. MURPHY. *The Office in Transition: Meeting the Problems of Automation.* New York: Harper, 1957. (See especially Chapter 13, "The Future of White Collar Unionization.")

LAWRENCE, JOSEPHINE. *Sound of Running Feet* (a novel about an attempt to form a union among real estate clerks in the 1930's). Philadelphia: Stokes, 1937.

LUBIN, JOHN F. *Clerical and Office Unionism in the United States: The Unit for Collective Bargaining.* Ph.D. Thesis, University of Pennsylvania, 1956.

PELL, ORLIE. *The Office Worker—Labor's Side of the Ledger.* New York: League for Industrial Democracy, October 1938.

PROSSER, WILLIAM H. *Nine to Five* (a novel). Boston: Little, Brown, 1953.

RICE, ELMER. *The Adding Machine: A Play in Seven Scenes.* New York: Samuel French, 1929.

SULLIVAN, DANIEL. "Labor Looks to Enlisting White Collar Workers: Office Employes International Union has 15,000 Members in New York State." *Industrial Bulletin,* Vol. 39, No. 12, December 1960, pp. 15–19.

U.S. CONGRESS. SENATE. Committee on Labor and Public Welfare. Subcommittee on Labor and Labor-Management Relations. *Communist Domination of Certain Unions,* pp. 3–18 (United Office and Professional Workers of America). Washington: G.P.O., 1951.

PROFESSIONAL

AFL-CIO, INDUSTRIAL UNION DEPARTMENT. *Summary Report and Conclusion of IUD Seminar; Collective Bargaining Problems of Professional and Technical Workers in Industry, Harvard University, January 14–17, 1960.* Washington: The Department, January 1960. (Mimeo.).

BAMBRICK, JAMES J., JR., ALBERT A. BLUM, and HERMINE ZAGAT. *Unionization among American Engineers.* New York: National Industrial Conference Board, 1956.

BOUGHTON, V. T. "Engineering Societies and Unions." *Civil Engineering,* October 1939, pp. 418–419.

CULLEY, JACK F. *A Primer on Engineering Unionism,* Reprint Series No. 12. Iowa City: Bureau of Labor and Management, Iowa University, 1959.

DVORAK, ELDON J. "Will Engineers Unionize?" *Industrial Relations,* Vol. 2, No. 3, May 1963, pp. 45–65.

ENGINEERING SOCIETIES LIBRARY. *Bibliography on Unionization of Professional Engineers.* New York: The Library, 1954. (Processed).

FINER, HERMAN. *Administration and the Nursing Services.* New York: Macmillan, 1952.

FISHER, WALDO E. "Collective Bargaining for Engineers." *Engineering and Science Monthly,* June 1946, pp. 24–25.

GOLDSTEIN, BERNARD. "The Perspective of Unionized Professionals." *Social Forces,* May 1959, pp. 323–327.

————. "Some Aspects of the Nature of Unionism Among Salaried Professionals in Industry," *Labor and Trade Unionism: An Interdisciplinary Reader,* Walter Galenson and Seymour Lipset, eds., pp. 329–336. New York: Wiley, 1960.

————, and BERNARD P. INDIK. "Unionism as a Social Choice: The Engineers' Case." *Monthly Labor Review,* Vol. 86, No. 4, April 1963, pp. 365–369.

GREENWOOD, DAVID C. *The Engineering Profession and Unionization.* Washington: Public Affairs Press, 1960.

HANSEN, W. LEE. "Professional Engineers: Salary Structure Problems." *Industrial Relations,* Vol. 2, No. 3, May 1963, pp. 33–44.

KORNHAUSER, WILLIAM. *Scientists in Industry, Conflict and Accommodation.* Berkeley and Los Angeles: University of California Press, 1962.

KRUGER, DANIEL H. "Bargaining and the Nursing Profession." *Monthly Labor Review,* Vol. 84, No. 7, July 1961, pp. 699–705.

MICHIGAN STATE UNIVERSITY, LABOR AND INDUSTRIAL RELATIONS CENTER. *Effective Utilization of Engineering Personnel.* East Lansing: The Center, 1957.

MYERS, HUGH L. "The Engineer and Organized Labor." *Cornell Engineer,* Vol. 11, No. 6, March 1946, pp. 13–14, 32–36.

NATIONAL SOCIETY OF PROFESSIONAL ENGINEERS. *Tabulation of Unions Representing Engineering and Technical Employees.* Washington: The Society, 1959.

NORTHRUP, HERBERT R. "Collective Bargaining by Professional Societies," chap. 6, *Insights into Labor Issues,* Richard A. Lester and Joseph Shister, eds., pp. 134–162. New York: Macmillan, 1948.

ORRELL, HERBERT M. "Engineers Turn to Unionism." *The Nation,* Vol. 174, June 21, 1952, p. 605.

PECKWORTH, H. F. *The Engineer and Collective Bargaining.* New York: American Society of Civil Engineers, July 1943.

PRINCETON UNIVERSITY, INDUSTRIAL RELATIONS SECTION. *Personnel Management and the Professional Employee.* Princeton: The Section, 1957.

RIEGEL, JOHN W. *Collective Bargaining as Viewed by Unorganized Engineers and Scientists.* Ann Arbor: Bureau of Industrial Relations, Michigan University, 1959.

SHEA, T. E. "The Implications of Engineering Unionism—Western Electric Experience." *Research Management,* Autumn 1959, pp. 149–157.

SOMERS, GERALD G. "Small Establishments and Chemicals." *Proceedings of the Ninth Annual Meeting of the Industrial Relations Research Association,* December 28–29, 1956, pp. 248–255. Madison: The Association, 1957.

STRAUSS, GEORGE. "Professionalism and Occupational Associations." *Industrial Relations,* Vol. 2, No. 3, May 1963, pp. 7–31.

TAFT, EVERETT. "Unions among Engineers." *Proceedings of the Ninth Annual Meeting of the Industrial Relations Research Association,* December 28–29, 1956, pp. 244–247. Madison: The Association, 1957.

U.S. CONGRESS. HOUSE. Special Committee on Un-American Activities. *Investigation of Un-American Propaganda Activities in the United States,* pp. 703–718 (Federation of Architects, Engineers, Chemists and Technicians). Washington: G.P.O., 1944.

WALTON, RICHARD E. *The Impact of the Professional Engineering Union: A Study of Collective Bargaining among Engineers and Scientists and Its Significance for Management.* Boston: Graduate School of Business Administration, Harvard University, 1961.

RETAIL, WHOLESALE, DEPARTMENT STORES

ALLAWAY, RICHARD. *Four Analytical Approaches Toward an Understanding of the Decision-Making Process in Three Retail Unions.* Ph.D. Thesis, Cornell University, June 1950.

BAKER, HELEN, and ROBERT R. FRANCE. *Personnel Administration and Labor Relations in Department Stores: An Analysis of Developments and Practices.* Princeton: Industrial Relations Section, Princeton University, August 1950.

BEDOLIS, ROBERT A. "Miracle on Astor Place: The District 65 Story." *The Nation,* September 25, 1954, 255–257.

ESTEY, MARTEN S. "Patterns of Union Membership in Retail Trades." *Industrial and Labor Relations Review,* Vol. 8, No. 4, July 1955, pp. 557–564.

——————. *Some Factors Influencing Labor Organizations in the Retail Trades.* Princeton: Princeton University, 1952.

GREENBERG, MAX. "The Retail, Wholesale and Department Store Union." *AFL-CIO American Federationist,* Vol. 66, No. 6, July 1959, pp. 23–25.

HALPER, ALBERT. *The Chute* (a novel). New York: Viking, 1937.

————. *The Little People* (a novel). New York: Harper, 1942.

HARRINGTON, MICHAEL. *The Retail Clerks.* New York: Wiley, 1962.

HEALY, PAUL F. "He Runs a White-Collar Union." *Saturday Evening Post,* March 16, 1957, pp. 49, 125–126.

HOWARD, GEORGE (Jason Striker, pseud.). *Haste to Succeed* (a novel). New York: Appleton-Century-Crofts, 1961.

HUGHES, RUPERT. *Miss 318 and Mr. 37* (a novel). New York: Revell, 1912.

KIRSTEIN, GEORGE G. *Stores and Unions: A Study of the Growth of Unionism in Dry Goods and Department Stores.* New York: Fairchild, 1950.

LA DAME, MARY. *The Filene Store: A Study of Employees' Relation to Management in a Retail Store.* New York: Russell Sage Foundation, 1930.

SAPOSS, DAVID J. *Communism in American Unions,* pp. 119–270 *passim.* New York: McGraw-Hill, 1959.

SEIDMAN, HAROLD. *Labor Czars,* chap. XII, "The Markets," pp. 185–198, chap. XIII, "Assorted Rackets," pp. 199–213. New York: Liveright, 1938.

U.S. COMMISSION ON INDUSTRIAL RELATIONS (1912). *Reports,* vol. 3, "The Department Stores of New York City," pp. 2213–2410. Washington: G.P.O., 1916.

U.S. INDUSTRIAL COMMISSION (1898). *Reports,* vol. 7, "Report on the Relations and Conditions of Capital and Labor Employed in Manufactures and General Business." *Digest,* pp. 17–27. Washington: G.P.O., 1901.

ZUGSMITH, LEANE. *A Time to Remember* (a novel). New York: Random House, 1936.

SERVICES

BUILDING SERVICE EMPLOYEES INTERNATIONAL UNION, AFL, LOCAL 32B. *Going Up!: The Story of 32B.* New York: The Union, 1955.

CHRISTENSON, C. LAWRENCE. "Chicago Service Trades," chap. 15, *How Collective Bargaining Works,* Harry A. Millis, research director, pp. 806–868. New York: Twentieth Century Fund, 1945.

DEARMOND, FRED. *The Laundry Industry.* New York: Harper, 1950.

"Employment in Social Welfare and Related Organizations." *Monthly Labor Review,* Vol. 77, No. 10, October 1954, pp. 1126—1129.

FISHER, WILLIAM. *The Waiters* (a novel). Cleveland and New York: World, 1953.

HALL, WILLIAM S. *Journeymen Barbers' International Union of America.* Baltimore: Johns Hopkins Press, 1936.

HEPTON, ESTELLE. *Battle for the Hospitals: A Study of Unionization in Non-profit Hospitals.* Ithaca: New York State School of Industrial and Labor Relations, Cornell University, March 1963.

HOROWITZ, MORRIS A. *The New York Hotel Industry: A Labor Relations Study.* Cambridge: Harvard University Press, 1960.

JOSEPHSON, MATTHEW. *Union House, Union Bar: The History of the Hotel and Restaurant Employees and Bartenders' International Union (AFL-CIO)*. New York: Random House, 1956.

KENNEDY, VAN DUSEN. *Arbitration in the San Francisco Hotel and Restaurant Industries*. Philadelphia: University of Pennsylvania, 1952.

KOCHERY, DAVIS R., and GEORGE STRAUSS. "The Nonprofit Hospital and the Union." *Buffalo Law Review*, Vol. 9, No. 2, Winter 1960, pp. 255–282.

"Local 144: 'A Miniature U.N.'" (health and welfare). *Industrial Bulletin*, Vol. 42, No. 3, March 1963, pp. 16–18.

NESTEL, LOUIS P. *Labor Relations in the Laundry Industry in Greater New York*. New York: Claridge, 1950.

RUBIN, JAY, and M. J. OBERMEIER. *Growth of a Union: The Life and Times of Edward Flore*. New York: Historical Union Association, 1943.

RUSS, GEORGE L. "The Insurance Agents Are Sold on Unionism." *American Federationist*, Vol. 16, December 1954, pp. 22–23.

SAPOSS, DAVID J. *Communism in American Unions* (hotel, restaurant, bar), Part II, chaps. 10–12, pp. 82–115. New York: McGraw-Hill, 1959.

SCHERER, JOSEPH. *Collective Bargaining in the Service Industries: A Study of the Year-Round Hotels*. Ph.D. Thesis, University of Chicago, 1951.

——————. "The Union Impact on Wages: The Case of the Year-Round Hotel Industry." *Industrial and Labor Relations Review*, Vol. 9, No. 2, January 1956, pp. 213–224.

SEIDMAN, HAROLD. *Labor Czars*, chap. XIII, "Assorted Rackets," pp. 199–213 (hotel, restaurant, bar). New York: Liveright, 1938.

SLOCUM, JOHN HOWARD. *A Study of the Labor Relations of Selected Colleges and Universities and Their Maintenance Employees*. Ph.D. Thesis, Cornell University, 1950.

STIGLER, GEORGE J. *Domestic Servants in the United States, 1900–1940*. New York: National Bureau of Economic Research, 1946.

U.S. COMMISSION ON INDUSTRIAL RELATIONS (1912). *Reports*, vol. 4, "Conditions of Employment of Waiters and Cooks," pp. 3533–3536. Washington: G.P.O., 1916.

U.S. INDUSTRIAL COMMISSION (1898). *Reports*, vol. 14 (includes a special report on domestic service). Washington: G.P.O., 1901.

WHYTE, WILLIAM F. *Human Relations in the Restaurant Industry*. New York: McGraw-Hill, 1948.

Index

Bedolis, Robert A., 127
Beesley, Thomas Q., 23, 113
Behen, David M., 32
Bell, Daniel, 15, 24, 27, 116, 117
Bell, John F., 113
Bell, Thomas, 79, 124
Bellamy, Charles J., 99
Belman, Albert A., 79
Belsky, Joseph, 76
Bendiner, Robert, 91
Benjamin, Charles A., 99
Bennett, Harry, 50
Berger, Harriet F., 94
Berglund, Abraham, 36
Berman, Edward, 13
Berman, Hyman, 59
Bernhardt, Joshua, 104
Bernstein, Irving, 15, 17, 20, 22, 27, 50, 62, 99, 113
Bernstein, Leonard, 34
Bers, Melvin K., 46
Bertram, Gordon, 70
Beshoar, Barron B., 62
Beyer, Otto, 104
Bezanson, A., 63
Biemiller, Andrew J., 30
"Big Bill Retires," 70
Billington, Ray Allen, 46
Bimba, Anthony, 4, 8
Bing, A., 17
Bisno, Beatrice, 56, 59
Bissell, Richard P., 39, 56, 117
Black, J. William, 1
Black-Listed Machinist, 87
Blackwood, George D., 51
Blankenhorn, Heber, 62
Bliss, W. D. P., 5, 16
Bloch, Herman D., 25
Bloch, Joseph W., 57
Bloch, Louis, 62
Bloomberg, Warner, Jr., 27
Blum, Albert A., 1, 30, 103, 126
Blum, Fred H., 76
Blum, Solomon, 70
Boffo, Louis S., 113
Boland, John P., 117
Bolino, August C., 27
Bollens, Leo F., 124
Bonnett, C. E., 13
Bonosky, Phillip, 51
Bookbinder, Hyman H., 56
Boone, Gladys, 16
Bornet, Vaughn D., 17
Bortz, Nelson M., 51
Boucher, Arline, 8
Boughton, V. T., 126
Bow, Frank T., 78
Bowers, Robert S., 113
Boyer, Richard O., 117
Boyle, Ohio D., 104
Bradley, Walter, 104
Brandeis, Louis D., 16
Braun, Kurt, 56
Braverman, Harry, 30

Brazeal, Brailsford, 112
Brickett, Margarett F., 1
Bright, Arthur A., Jr., 74
Brissenden, Paul F., 14, 117
Broach, Howell H., 74
Brock, E. J., 99
Brody, David, 79
Bromfield, Louis, 79
Brooks, George W., 27
Brooks, Harold C., 111
Brooks, Robert R. R., 20, 79, 99
Brooks, Tom, 25
Brophy, John, 62
Brotherhood of Locomotive Firemen and Enginemen, 111
Brotherhood of Maintenance of Way Employees, 112
Brotherhood of Railroad Signalmen of America, 112
Brown, Bernard D., 91
Brown, Emily Clark, 24, 92
Brown, Giles T., 117
Brown, Leo C., S.J., 84
Brown, Rollo W., 62
Brown, W. R., 30
Browne, Henry J., 1, 8
Bruce, Robert V., 104
Bruckner, Molly Acreman, 43
Bruner, Dick, 124
Bryner, Edna, 59
Buchanan, Joseph R., 8
Budish, J. M., 56
Building Service Employees International Union, AFL, Local 32B, 128
"Building-Trades Bargaining Plan in Southern California," 70
Building Trades Employers' Association of the City of New York. Committee on Welfare Funds, 70
Bullard, Arthur (Albert Edwards, pseud.), 59
Burbank, David T., 35
Bureau of Information of the Eastern Railways, 104
Burn, James Dawson, 5
Burns, Matthew J., 86
Burns, Robert K., 91, 92, 124
Burns, William F., 104
Burns, William J., 13
Burt, Edward W., 84
Byington, M. F., 79

C

Cabe, J. Carl, 98
Cahn, Bill, 99
Caldwell, Janet Taylor, 79
Cale, Edgar B., 5
California, University of, Bureau of Governmental Research, 94
Calkins, Clinch, 20
Calkins, Fay, 22
Calkins, Robert D., 98
Calmer, Alan, 8
Cantwell, Robert, 86

DeLeon, Solon, 8
Dell, Floyd, 99
Delli Quadri, Carmen Leonard, 88
Denison, Thomas S., 105
Denker, David, 92
Dent, James K., 98
Derber, Milton, 20, 71, 75, 76
Destler, Chester McArthur, 8, 38
"Detroit Auto Worker," 51
Developments in White Collar Unionism, 124
DeVyver, Frank T., 36, 79
Dewey, John, 59
Dewsnup, Ernest R., 105
DiDonato, Pietro, 71
Di Roma, Edward, 1
Doerflinger, William M., 86, 117
Doherty, William C., 95
Dolnick, David, 46
Donahue, Gilbert E., 3
Dorfman, Joseph, 5
Douglas, Amanda M., 99
Douglas, Dorothy W., 5
Dowd, Douglas F., 124
Dowling, George T., 105
Downey, Ezekiel H., 39
Downs, Frederick T., 34
Dreier, Mary, 16
Dubin, Robert, 52
Dubinsky, D., 43
Dubofsky, Melvyn, 14
Dulles, Foster Rhea, 4
Duncan, David, 115
Dunlop, John T., 28, 46, 71
Dunn, Robert W., 17, 51, 99
Dunne, William F., 20, 99, 117
Dvorak, Eldon J., 126
Dyche, John A., 18
Dyer, Walter A., 5

E

Eaves, Lucile, 37
Ebert, Justus, 14, 99
Eckert, Leone W., 1
Eddy, Arthur J., 76, 113
Edelman, Murray, 43
Edmunds, Murrell, 99
Eklund, John M., 74
Eldridge, Seba, 18
Eliel, Paul, 86, 117
Eliot, C. E., 13
Elliott, Russell R., 63, 88
Ely, Richard T., 8
"Employment Conditions in the Longshore Industry," 117
"Employment in Social Welfare and Related Organizations," 128
Employment Relations Abstracts, 1950 —, 1
Engberg, George B., 39, 86
Engineering Societies Library, 126
Engler, Robert, 48
Engler, Rosalind, 48
Epstein, Albert, 22
Epstein, Melech, 14

Erickson, Charlotte, 8
Errant, James W., 95
Estey, Marten S., 127
Evangela, Sister Mary, 63
Evans, Chris, 63
Everett, Edward, 6
"Executive Order Governing Procedures of Departments and Agencies of New York State for Resolution of Employee Complaints," 95

F

Faber, Gustav, 115
Fact Finding Board, 79, 117
Fact Finding Board in re *General Motors Corporation and United Automobile Workers (CIO), January 10, 1946*, 51
Fagan, J. O., 105, 112
Fairley, Lincoln, 117
Fall, James, 117
Farnam, H. W., 117
Fast, Howard M., 8, 63, 99
Faulkender, Robert Edgar, 90
Faulkner, Harold U., 4
Faunce, William A., 51
Federal Council of the Churches of Christ in America, Commission on the Church and Social Service, 33, 63, 79; Department of Research and Education, 63, 111; Research Department, 80
Fein, Marvin M., 92
Feinsinger, Nathan P., 113
Feis, Herbert, 55
Feldman, Egal, 56
Fenton, Edwin, 14
Ferguson, John B., 38
Field, Ben, 36
"Fifty Years of Peace," 71
Fine, Nathan, 6, 15
Fine, Sidney, 9, 51, 52
Finer, Herman, 126
Finger, Eleanor, 43
Fisher, Thomas R., 52, 63, 80, 105
Fisher, Waldo E., 63, 126
Fisher, William, 128
Fitch, John A., 11, 80
Fite, Emerson D., 6
Fleming, R. W., 86
Fleming, Ralph D., 115
Folsom, J. C., 48
Foner, Philip S., 4, 6, 11, 84
Foote, Mary H., 89
Foran, Martin A., 105
Ford, Matthew, 75
Ford, Paul Leicester, 105
Fordyce, Wellington G., 74
Forsythe, Edwin James, 40
Foster, William Z., 18, 80
Fountain, Clayton W., 52
Four Years in the Underbrush, 18
Fowler, Charles B., 63
Fox, Mary Harrita, 15
France, Robert R., 127

Francis, Robert E., 117
Frankfurter, Felix, 13
Franklin, Charles L., 25
Freeman, Mary E. Wilkins, 36
Freund, Peter, 115
Friedman, Morris, 13
Fulton, Justin D., 111
Furuseth, Andrew, 118

G

Gaer, Joseph, 22
Gagliardo, Domenico, 18
Galenson, Walter, 20, 28, 52, 55, 56, 59, 63, 71, 75, 76, 80, 86, 88, 92, 97, 99, 105, 113, 118
Galster, Augusta E., 85
Galton, Frank W., 56
Gambatese, Joseph M., 30
Gambs, John, 14
Garland, Hamlin, 89
"The Garment Workers," 59
Garraty, John A., 80
Garside, Edward B., 39, 76
Gates, Francis, 1
Gazzam, Joseph F., 89
George, Henry, 11
Ghent, W. J., 11
Gibbons, James J., 95
Gibbons, William F., 63
Gilfillan, Lauren, 63
Gillingham, J. B., 113
Gilpatrick, Thomas V., 71
Ginger, Ray, 9, 15, 25, 63, 100, 105
Giovannitti, Len, 57
Givens, Charles G., 42
Gladden, Washington, 11
Glasser, Carrie, 64
Glazer, Sidney, 39
Glock, Margaret S., 86
Glocker, Theodore W., 32
Glück, Elsie, 64
Godine, Morton R., 95
Gold, Norman, 122
Goldberg, Arthur J., 29
Goldberg, Joseph P., 95, 118
Golden, Clinton S., 50
Goldfinger, Nathaniel, 22
Goldmark, Josephine, 12
Goldstein, Bernard, 126
Gomberg, William, 43
Gompers, Samuel, 9, 11, 18, 44
Goodrich, Carter L., 64
Goodstein, Anita Shafer, 86
Gorter, Wytze, 118
Gould, Helen M., 80
Gould, Jean, 56
Graham, Margaret (Grace Lois McDonald, pseud.), 64
Grant, Luke, 71
Grant, Robert, 9
Green, Archie, 64
Green, Marguerite, 13
Greenberg, Max, 128

Greene, Homer, 64
Greene, Josiah E., 48, 76, 80
Greene, Nathan, 13
Greenslade, Rush V., 64
Greenwood, David C., 126
Greer, Scott A., 25
Grey, Zane, 42, 48
Griffin, Richard W., 100
Groat, George C., 40, 118
Groat, Margaret Schaer, 124
Grob, Gerald N., 6, 9, 25
Grogan, William, 80
Grossman, Jonathan, 6, 80
Groves, Harold M., 88
Gsell, Donald, 2
Guest, Robert H., 52, 54
Gulick, Charles A., 46, 80
Gunton, George, 9
Gutman, Herbert G., 64, 80, 105

H

Haas, Francis J., 57
Haber, William, 71
Hadcock, Editha, 100
Hagboldt, Peter, 83
Hale, Edward E., 100
Hall, James T., Jr., 96
Hall, John A., 105
Hall, John Philip, 85
Hall, William S., 128
Halper, Albert, 32, 80, 128
Halverson, George, 88
Hamilton, Walton H., 64
Handley, William J., 44
Handlin, Oscar, 25
Hanna, Hilton E., 76
Hansen, W. Lee, 126
Hapgood, Hutchins, 11, 86
Harbison, Frederick H., 52, 80
Hard, William, 92
Harding, Alfred, 90
Hardman, J. B. S., 46, 57, 64
Hardwick, A. F., 35
Hardy, Jack, 57, 99
Hardy, Margaret, 44
Harriman, Job, 38
Harrington, Michael, 28, 75, 128
Harris, Abram L., 26
Harris, Cyril, 81, 86
Harris, Evelyn L. K., 42
Harris, Frank, 9
Harris, Herbert, 21, 52, 59, 64, 71, 91, 100, 105
Harris, Lee O., 105
Harrison, Charles Yale, 75, 118
Hart, Alan, 86
Hart, C. W. M., 52
Hart, Wilson R., 95
Harvey, G. B. M., 81
Harvey, O. L., 2, 95
Haskel, Harry, 59
Hass, Eric, 64, 113
Hatcher, Harlan H., 41

New York State, Factory Investigating Commission (Robert Wagner, chairman), 12, 40; Joint Legislative Committee on Housing (C. C. Lockwood, chairman), 72
New York State School of Industrial and Labor Relations, Cornell University, 120
"New York State Survey of Industry—Apparel," 58
"New York's Waterfront," 120
Nichols, Frances H., 66
Nolan, Loretto R., 96
Nolen, Russell M., 35
"No-Raid Agreement between UAW and IAM," 53, 88
Norgren, Paul H., 26
Norris, Charles G., 120
Norris, Frank, 108
Norris, Martin J., 121
Northrup, Herbert R., 26, 98, 108, 126
Norton, Nancy P., 101
Norton, Thomas L., 85
Norwood, E. P., 53
Nyman, Richmond C., 101

O

Oakes, Russell C., 74
Obermeier, M. J., 129
O'Brien, Howard V., 32, 77
O'Connor, Harvey, 55, 81
Odegard, Peter H., 19
Odencrantz, Louise C., 19
Odets, Clifford, 116
O'Donnell, L. A., 2
Ogg, Elizabeth, 121
Older, Fremont, 37
Olds, Marshall, 81
[Oliphant, Herman], 116
Oliver, Eli L., 103, 108
O'Malley, Michael, 66, 81
Oneal, James, 60
Opinion Research Corporation, 53
Orrell, Herbert M., 127
Orth, Samuel P., 4
Owen, Homer Leroy, 22
Ozanne, Robert W., 53, 75, 77, 89, 121

P

Pacific Maritime Association, 121
Page, Dorothy Myra, 101
Painter, Leonard, 111
Palmer, Dwight L., 121
Palmer, Frank L., 81
Palmer, Gladys L., 18, 101
Parker, Carleton H., 47
Parker, Glen L., 66
Parsons, Edgar A., 97
Partridge, Bellamy (Thomas Bailey, pseud.), 72
Paschell, William, 93
"The Passing of Marion Hodges," 75
Patkin, A. L., 14
Paul, Elliot H., 21

Paul, George S., 101
Pearlin, Leonard I., 90
Pearse, Robert F., 74
Peckworth, H. F., 127
Pell, Orlie, 125
Pelling, Henry M., 4, 10
Perkins, Alice J. G., 7
Perkins, Frances, 21
Perlman, Mark, 38, 47, 88
Perlman, Selig, 4, 6, 19, 23, 47, 58, 60, 66, 93
Perrigo, H. W., 66
Person, Carl E., 108
Pesotta Rose, 21, 53, 61
Pessen, Edward, 6
Peters, Paul, 122
Petersen, William J., 89
Petro, Sylvester, 24, 53
Pettingill, Stuart A., 75
Phelps, E. A. M., 121
Phelps, Orme W., 47
Phillips, Edward L., 101
Phleger, Herman, 121
Pidgeon, Mary E., 21
Pierson, Frank C., 53, 61, 66, 108
Pinkerton, Allan, 10, 108
Pinkowski, Edward, 66
Polakov, Walter N., 66
Pollack, Jerome, 53, 108
Pollard, John A., 10
Pollard, Spencer D., 53, 66
"Polluted Port," 121
Pomper, Gerald, 24
Poole, Ernest, 121
Pope, Jesse E., 58
Pope, Liston, 101
Porter, Arthur R., Jr., 93
Porter, Eugene O., 66
Potofsky, J. S., 58
Potwin, Marjorie A., 101
Pound, Roscoe, 28
Powderly, Terence V., 10
Powell, Leona M., 93
Presidential Railroad Commission, 108
Preston, John H., 38
Prestridge, Virginia, 2
Price, Wesley, 103
Princeton University, Industrial Relations Section, 127
Prosser, William H., 125
Public Opinion Index for Industry, 31
Pullman, George M., 108
Purcell, Theodore V., 77

R

Raddock, Maxwell, 72
Railroad Brotherhood Unity Movement, 108
Railway Labor Executives' Association, 108
Raimon, Robert L., 82, 103, 104
Randall, Edwin T., 7
Randall, Roger L., 77, 87
Rankin, Carl E., 101
Raper, Arthur M., 49
Rasco, John E., 113

Raskin, A. H., 24, 67, 75
Rasmussen, Wayne D., 49
Rastall, Benjamin M., 89
Raushenbush, Carl, 53
Raushenbush, H. S., 62
Rayack, Elton, 58
Rayback, Joseph G., 4, 7
Raymond, Allen, 121
Raymond, Margaret T., 93
"Recommendations on the Airlines-Flight Engineers Dispute," 104
Record, Jane Cassels, 121
Record, Wilson, 26
Reid, Ira De A., 49
Reuter, Frank T., 10
Reuther, Walter P., 53
Reynolds, Lloyd G., 2
Rezler, Julius, 29, 78
Rezneck, Samuel, 7
Rhodes, James Ford, 10
Rhodes, Lynne, 58
Rhyne, Charles S., 96
Rhyne, Jennings J., 101
Rice, Charles Owen, 53
Rice, Elmer, 125
Rice, Stuart Arthur, 19
Rich, J. C., 61
Richards, Henry E., 90
Richardson, Reed C., 111
Ricker, Ralph R., 41
Riegel, John W., 127
Rieger, Morris, 2
Rieve, Emil, 101
Riker, William H., 22
Robbins, Edwin C., 111
Robbins, Hayes, 49
Roberts, Benjamin C., 29
Roberts, Harold Selig, 38, 97
Roberts, Peter, 67
Robinson, Aileen W., 74
Robinson, Donald, 121
Robinson, Dwight E., 61
Robinson, Harriet H., 36, 101
Robinson, Harry P., 10
Robinson, Jesse S., 82
Robinson, Robert M., 114
Rochester, Anna, 67
Roe, Mary A. (C. M. Cornwall, pseud.), 67
Roe, Wellington, 22, 30
Rogin, Lawrence, 101
Rogin, Michael, 16
Rogoff, Abraham M., 14
Rogoff, Hillel, 14
Rollins, Alfred B., Jr., 12
Rollins, William, 101
Romer, Sam, 114
Roney, Frank, 37
Rood, Henry E., 67
Roosevelt, Theodore, 67, 89
Rose, Arnold, 114
Rose, Fred Duane, 2
Rose, William T., 72, 93
Rosen, George, 67
Rosen, Ned, 2

Rosenberg, Abraham, 61
Rosenthal, Robert J., 98
Ross, Clinton, 82
Ross, Irwin, 61
Ross, Malcolm H., 67
Ross, Michael, 44
Ross, Murray, 90
Rothbaum, Melvin, 55
Rovere, Richard H., 58
Rowe, Evan Keith, 53
Rowland, Donald, 26
Roy, Andrew, 67
Rubin, Jay, 129
Rudolph, Frederick, 14
Ruppenthal, Karl M., 104
Russ, George L., 129
Ryan, Edwin, 121
Ryan, Frederick Lynne, 35, 67, 72
Ryan, Paul W. (Mike Quin, pseud.), 121
Rygg, A. N., 121

S

Sabghir, Irving Howard, 49
Sakolski, A. M., 82
Sakr, Carmelita, 2
Salmons, Charles H., 109
Samuel, Howard D., 58
Sanderson and Porter, Engineers and Constructors, 121
Sandmeyer, Elmer C., 26
Saposs, David J., 16, 19, 21, 53, 75, 77, 82, 85, 87, 89, 90, 91, 96, 97, 116, 121, 125, 128, 129
Sartorius von Waltershausen, August Johann Georg, 7, 10
Savage, Marion Dutton, 19
Savage, Sarah, 101
Saxton, Alexander P., 26, 109
Scanlon, Joseph N., 55
Scarborough, Dorothy, 49
Scheinberg, Stephen J., 16
Scherer, Joseph, 129
Scheuch, Richard, 72
Schiff, Albert, 74
Schlegel, Marvin W., 67
Schlesinger, Arthur M., Jr., 7
Schlossberg, Joseph, 58
Schmidt, Emerson P., 116
Schneider, Betty V., 121
Schneider, D. M., 19
Schnepp, Gerald J., 114
Schreiner, Olive, 17
Schulberg, Budd, 121
Schwartz, Donald A., 53
Schwartz, Harry, 49
Schweppe, Emma, 96
Scott, Leroy, 72, 82
Scruggs, Otey M., 50
Seafarers International Union of North America, 121
Seaman, Bernard, 61
Seattle Union Record Publishing Co., Inc., 19, 35

Segal, Melvin J., 70
Seidman, Harold, 24, 72, 75, 77, 90, 114, 128, 129
Seidman, Joel, 22, 27, 30, 58, 67, 70, 72, 77, 82, 102, 112
Selekman, Ben M., 67, 82, 102
Selekman, Sylvia K., 19
Seligman, Daniel, 75
Seligson, Harry, 38
Seltzer, George, 82
"Settlement of Hawaiian Longshoremen's Strike," 121
"Seven Seamen," 122
Seybold, John W., 93
Seymour, Harold, 74
Shannon, David A., 109
Shannon, Fred A., 47
Shaughnessy, D. F., 2
Shaw, Frank L., 72
Shea, T. E., 127
Shefferman, Nathan, 24, 114
Sheldon, Charles M., 89, 102
Sheldon, Horace E., 72
Sheppard, H. L., 52
Sheppard, Muriel Earley, 67
Sheridan, Frank J., 14
Shields, E. L., 19
Shister, Joseph, 29
Shostak, Arthur B., 78
Shotwell, Louisa R., 50
Shugg, Roger Wallace, 33
Shultz, George P., 82, 85, 87
Siegel, Abraham, 121
Sigmund, Elwin W., 109
Silver, Henry D., 72
Simler, Norman J., 47
Simon, Charlie M., 37, 50
Simon, Hal, 26
Simon, S. Fanny, 4
Simons, Henry C., 47
Simpson, Alexander G., 67
Simpson, Dorothy, 96
Sinclair, Upton B., 32, 67, 77, 82
Skeels, Jack, 53
Skidmore, Hubert, 42, 72
Sklar, George, 122
Slichter, Sumner H., 19, 29, 98
Sligh, Charles R., Jr., 28
Slocum, John Howard, 129
Smith, Abbott E., 7
Smith, Elliott D., 101
Smith, Francis H., 122
Smith, John S., 12
Smith, M. Mead, 55
Smith, Russell A., 96
Smith, Thomas R., 102
Smith, William Dale, 82
Smitter, Wessel, 53
Snow, Sinclair, 44
Snowden, Yates, 41
Sobel, Irvin, 97
Sobotka, Stephen P., 72
Society for the Psychological Study of Social Issues, 54

Soffer, Benson, 47, 93
Solomon, Benjamin, 29, 125
Somers, Gerald G., 55, 67, 127
Sorokin, Pitirim A., 19
Soule, George, 56, 58
"Southern Campaign, 1946," 37
Spencer, Robert C., 80
Spencer, William H., 109
Spero, Sterling D., 26, 96
Spohn, William H., 98
Staley, Eugene, 38
Standard, William L., 122
Stanley, J. Perham, 54
Stanley, Marjorie Thines, 54
Starnes, George T., 36
Starr, Mark, 4
State University of Iowa, Bureau of Labor and Management, 2
Stavis, Barrie, 15, 89
Stead, William Thomas, 33
Stedman, J. C., 37
Stedman, Murray S., 7
Stedman, Susan W., 7
Steele, H. Ellsworth, 106
Steele, James, 54
'Steel Negotiation Documents,' 82
"Steelworkers Are Tough and Their Union Is the Best Organized in the C.I.O.," 82
"Steelworkers Want Wartime Justice," 82
Steffens, Lincoln, 12
Stegner, Wallace, 15
Stein, Bruno, 22, 115
Stein, Leon, 12, 59, 61
Steinbeck, John, 37, 50
Stevens, George A., 93
Stevens, Harry R., 7
Stevenson, George James, 111
Stewart, Ethelbert, 93
Stewart, R. C., 3
Stieber, Jack, 29, 54, 82
Stieglitz, Harold, 124
Stigler, George J., 129
Stimson, Grace Heilman, 33
Stockett, Joseph Noble, 109
Stockton, Frank T., 13, 83
Stolberg, Benjamin, 21, 61
Stone, Harry W., 36
Storrow, Charles S., 102
Stowell, Charles J., 58
Stowell, Myron R., 83
Strand, Kenneth T., 73
Stratton, S. S., 79
Straub, Adelbert G., Jr., 73, 114
Straus, Donald B., 55, 58, 83
Strauss, George, 73, 125, 127, 129
Strong, Earl D., 58
Stroud, Gene S., 3
Stuart, John, 65, 72, 91, 107, 120
Stuckey, Lorin, 39
Sturm, Herman M., 122
Sturmthal, Adolf, 44, 47
Stutz, Robert L., 96
Suffern, Arthur E., 67
Sufrin, Sidney C., 98

141

U.S. Congress. Joint Committee on Atomic Energy, 55, 97
U.S. Congress. Joint Committee on Labor-Management Relations, 54, 97
U.S. Congress. Senate. Committee on Education and Labor (1883), 10; Committee on Education and Labor (Robert M. LaFollette, Jr., chairman), 21; Committee on Government Operations, 115; Committee on Government Operations, Permanent Subcommittee on Investigations, 54, 91; Committee on Interstate and Foreign Commerce, 123; Committee on Interstate Commerce, 109; Committee on Labor and Public Welfare, 38; Committee on Labor and Public Welfare, Subcommittee on Labor and Labor-Management Relations, 30, 50, 70, 73, 83, 89, 97, 102, 109, 123, 125; Committee on the Judiciary, 89, 115, 123; Select Committee on Improper Activities in the Labor or Management Field, 24
U.S. Department of Labor, 17, 23, 84
U.S. Department of Labor, Bureau of Labor Statistics, 20, 21, 23, 30, 102, 109; Women's Bureau, 17
U.S. Eight-Hour Commission, 109
U.S. Emergency Board, 1943 (Carriers and Employees, Diesel-Electric Operators), 110
U.S. Emergency Board, 1943 (Carriers and Employees, Non-Operating), 110
U.S. Emergency Board, 1943 (Carriers and Employees, Operating), 110
U.S. Industrial Commission (1898), 12, 50, 61, 73, 76, 84, 85, 91, 94, 103, 116, 128, 129
U.S. Library of Congress, 3; Legislative Reference Service, 23
U.S. Maritime Administration, 123
U.S. National Archives, 3, 123
U.S. National Historical Publications Commission, 3
U.S. National Labor Relations Board, 23
U.S. National Mediation Board, 110
U.S. National Recovery Administration, 54
U.S. President's Commission on Migratory Labor, 50
U.S. President's Task Force on Employee-Management Relations in the Federal Service, 97
U.S. Strike Commission, 110
U.S. Work Projects Administration, Federal Writers Project, Oklahoma Writers' Program, 41
U.S. Works Progress Administration, Federal Writers' Project, New York City, 3
"United Steelworkers of America," 84
United Textile Workers of America, 103

V

Vandecarr, Annie B., 61
Van der Slice, Austin, 20, 45
Van de Water, John R., 54
Van Kleeck, Mary, 67, 68, 94
Van Valer, Ralph Walden, 39

Van Vorst, Marie, 103
Varg, Paul A., 110
Varney, H. L., 123
Velie, Lester, 29, 76
Venkataramani, M. S., 50
Von Rhau, Henry, 24, 33, 73
Vorse, Mary Heaton, 21, 84, 103
Votaw, Albert N., 115

W

Waldman, Louis, 123
Waldman, Seymour, 123
Walinsky, Ossip, 85
Walker, Charles R., 33, 54, 84, 115
Walker, Edith, 39
Walling, William E., 12
Walsh, J. R., 21
Walsh, William J., 68
Walter, Henriette R., 18
Walton, Perry, 103
Walton, Richard E., 127
Wander, Paul, 20
Ward, Elizabeth S. Phelps, 103
Ward, Estolv, 88
Ward, Frank B., 110
Ware, Norman J., 4, 7, 10, 68, 73, 78, 84, 85, 94
Waring, P. Alston, 50
Warman, Cy, 110
Warne, Colston E., 13, 23, 68
Warne, Frank J., 14, 20, 68
Warner, William L., 86
Warren, Samuel E., 26
Waterfront Commission of New York Harbor, 123
"Waterfront Mess," 123
Watillon, Léon, 10
Watkins, Gordon S., 20
Watkins, Harold M., 68
Watts, Claude S., 18
Weatherwax, Clara, 87
Weaver, Robert C., 27
Weber, Arnold R., 30, 54, 55, 76, 84, 87
Webster, Henry K., 88
Wechsler, James A., 54, 69
Weinberg, Edgar, 69
Weinberg, J., 116
Weiner, Abraham, 70
Weintraub, Hyman G., 124
Weisbord, Albert, 103
West, George P., 69
West, Herbert F., 69
Westin, Alan F., 84
Whalen, Robert G., 124
Wharton, A. O., 88
"What the AFL-CIO Merger Means," 30
Whitcomb, Robert, 73
White, Leonard D., 97
White, Victor, 84
Whitman, Alden, 7
Whitney, Alexander F., 113
Whitney, John R., 39
Whitney, Nathaniel R., 73

CORNELL STUDIES IN INDUSTRIAL
AND LABOR RELATIONS

Cornell Studies in Industrial and Labor Relations and International Reports are research monographs developed by faculty and staff at the New York State School of Industrial and Labor Relations.

I *Wartime Manpower Mobilization: A Study of World War II Experience in the Buffalo-Niagara Area,* by Leonard P. Adams. 184 pp. 50¢.

II *AFL Attitudes toward Production: 1900–1932,* by Jean Trepp McKelvey. 160 pp. $1.00.

III *Sources of Wage Information: Employer Associations,* by N. Arnold Tolles and Robert L. Raimon. 368 pp. $1.00.

IV *The Labor Injunction in New York City, 1935–1950,* by Jacob Seidenberg. 192 pp. $1.00.

V *Nonferrous Metals Industry Unionism, 1932–1954: A Story of Leadership Controversy,* by Vernon H. Jensen. 344 pp. $1.25.

VI *The Industrial Mobility of Labor as a Probability Process,* by Isadore Blumen, Marvin Kogan, and Philip J. McCarthy. 176 pp. $3.00.

VII *Empire in Wood: A History of the Carpenters' Union,* by Robert A. Christie. 376 pp. $2.25.

VIII *Workers and Industrial Change: A Case Study of Labor Mobility,* by Leonard P. Adams and Robert L. Aronson. 224 pp. $3.00.

IX *Hawthorne Revisited:* MANAGEMENT AND THE WORKER, *Its Critics, and Developments in Human Relations in Industry,* by Henry A. Landsberger. 132 pp. $1.75.

(Continued on page 146)

X *Conflict Within the AFL: A Study of Craft versus Industrial Unionism,* 1901–1938, by James O. Morris. 336 pp. $5.00.

XI *Union Democracy: Practice and Ideal—An Analysis of Four Large Local Unions,* by Alice H. Cook. 256 pp. $4.75.

XII *Procedures and Policies of the New York State Labor Relations Board,* by Kurt L. Hanslowe. 224 pp. $4.00.

CORNELL INTERNATIONAL INDUSTRIAL AND LABOR RELATIONS REPORTS

I *Labor Unions and National Politics in Italian Industrial Plants,* by Maurice F. Neufeld. 160 pp. $2.00.

II *American Labor and the International Labor Movement, 1940 to 1953,* by John P. Windmuller (out of print). 260 pp. $3.00.

III *Jobs and Workers in India,* by Oscar A. Ornati. 236 pp. $1.50.

IV *Contemporary Collective Bargaining in Seven Countries,* Adolf Sturmthal, editor (out of print). 392 pp. $4.50.

V *Italy: School for Awakening Countries,* by Maurice F. Neufeld. 600 pp. $9.00.

PUBLISHED BY

THE NEW YORK STATE SCHOOL OF INDUSTRIAL AND LABOR RELATIONS

A Contract College of the State University
Cornell University, Ithaca, New York